T0333276

ELLA HICKSON

Ella Hickson is an award-winning writer whose work has been performed throughout the UK and abroad. Her most recent play, *Oil*, opened at the Almeida Theatre in October 2017. In 2013–14 *Wendy & Peter Pan*, adapted from the book by J.M. Barrie, played to wide acclaim at the Royal Shakespeare Company. Other credits include *Riot Girls* (Radio 4), *Boys* (Nuffield Theatre Southampton/Headlong Theatre/HighTide Festival Theatre), *Decade* (Headlong Theatre/St Katharine Docks), *The Authorised Kate Bane* (Grid Iron/Traverse Theatre, Edinburgh), *Rightfully Mine* (Radio 4), *Precious Little Talent* (Trafalgar Studios/Tantrums Productions), *Hot Mess* (Arcola Tent/Tantrums Productions) and *Eight* (Trafalgar Studios/ Bedlam Theatre, Edinburgh). In 2011 Ella was the Pearson Writer-in-Residence at the Lyric Theatre Hammersmith and she was the recipient of the 2013 Catherine Johnson Award. She has twice been a MacDowell Fellow. She is developing new work for the National Theatre, the Old Vic and Manhattan Theatre Club. Her short film *Hold On Me* premiered at the 55th BFI London Film Festival. She is also developing various projects for TV and film.

ELLA HICKSON

Plays: One

Eight

Hot Mess

PMQ

Precious Little Talent

Gift

Boys

with an Introduction by the author

NICK HERN BOOKS

London

www.nickhernbooks.co.uk

A Nick Hern Book

Ella Hickson Plays: One first published in Great Britain as a paperback original in 2018 by Nick Hern Books Limited, The Glasshouse, 49a Goldhawk Road, London W12 8QP

Cover image: Original production of *Boys*, 2012, photograph by Bill Knight

Designed and typeset by Nick Hern Books, London
Printed in Great Britain by Mimeo Ltd, Huntingdon, Cambridgeshire PE29 6XX

ISBN 978 1 84842 753 2

Contents

For
Xander, Henry, Simon, Michael, Holly,
Alice, Solomon, Ishbel and Gwennie

Introduction

The plays collected here cover the first five years of my writing career, from 2008 to 2012. The period of life that they chronicle, the memories they contain, the people and productions that surrounded them, form a chapter of huge joy, excitement, promise and laughter. As beginnings to writing careers go, I have been extraordinarily lucky.

I wrote *Eight* in my bedroom, on Lauderdale Street, in my final year at Edinburgh University. I had just done my finals and was working for the Edinburgh International Film Festival. I was an intern, sorting out gala tickets and looking after A-list celebrities – I made sure Keira Knightley had space to dance, it was impressive stuff. In the evenings and weekends, setting myself the task of two per week, I wrote the eight stories that would go together to form the show. I had done one playwriting workshop with David Greig, who has since become my mentor and friend, so I had some sense of structure, protagonist, reversal, and so on. I also had a youth full of passions and interests to draw on. I'd spent my gap year in the South of France where I'd met a fascinating lady artist – hence Jude. I'd written an article for a local newspaper on Tracey Emin's recent exhibition and loved studying 'The Politics and Aesthetics of Contemporary Art' – hence André. I'd had a wonderful Home Counties childhood of tennis lessons, garden parties, beautiful Christmases and studying Betjeman. I'd had a university of big parties, dramatic love affairs, great friends and all the attendant tears and heartache. *Eight*, in one way or another, was a chronicle of life up to that point.

If the content was in some way retrospective, the fallout from *Eight* was all about the future. It was a blast. I'd cast eight brilliant friends from Edinburgh University Theatre Company – and we'd shaped and edited and staged the thing together with the help of Xander Macmillan, our technical wizard. First came the good reviews, then Joyce McMillan (to whom I pretty much owe my career) put it up for a *Scotsman* Fringe First, then Carol Tambor came to see it and offered us a transfer to New York for a month-long run on the Lower East Side. The ten of us, in our early twenties, stood arm in arm and sung Sinatra's 'New York, New York' on the final night of the Fringe. I don't think I've ever, since, been so presently aware of being in the very middle of the best of things.

New York was incredible. We shared apartments in Midtown, we performed each night at Performance Space 122, we'd drink in bars that some of us had to fake-ID our way into. It was impossibly exciting. Instead of just enjoying it, however, I could already feel the anxiety at turning this stroke of luck into something more concrete. The only way I knew how to deal with that panic was via hard work. I had to write another play. David Greig had told me to get one done in time for the next Fringe and it was already March.

I was going out with a wonderful, big-hearted optimist at the time. I felt scared of the future – he felt positive about it. We sat on a New York rooftop one night and shared our competing visions, we kissed in Grand Central Station, we – all of us – went to watch Obama inaugurated for the first time. The optimism was palpable. The adventure was dizzy-making. Miles's monologue, written a year earlier, had imagined a world where banks might fail... and then, less than a year later, they did. We were heading home into a world of recession.

Precious Little Talent dealt with this strange tension between optimism and fear. Again, the context for one show provided the material for the next, and I wrote the play in the bedroom of said optimistic boyfriend. He was living with three other flatmates; raucous boys that I loved, boys that I envied for their capacity for partying and living in the present whilst I sat, alone, typing and trying to teach myself to write dialogue and form. It was those boys, in that flat, that three years later would make it onto paper in *Boys*.

With some brilliant dramaturgical help from Katherine Mendelsohn at the Traverse, in 2009, *Precious Little Talent* did well at the Edinburgh Fringe, but didn't change my life in the way that *Eight* had; no prizes, no transfers. It couldn't have. I found it hard coming to terms, over those first five years, with the fact that you can't have a beginning like we had, twice. 2009 was the year to turn beginner's luck into hard graft. I produced and directed *Precious Little Talent* in Edinburgh, *Eight* at Trafalgar Studios in London and at The Ringling International Arts Festival in Florida, and wrote *Hot Mess* ready for the 2010 Fringe. I got an agent and was starting to get into TV and radio with BBC Scotland, as well as doing smaller scratch-night shows in London. As a career started to emerge, it became clear that the theatre industry wanted me as a writer.

By the time I directed *Hot Mess* in Edinburgh I knew that my chance at a secure career would mean moving to London, focusing on the writing and leaving the directing, producing, and working with a big gang of friends, behind. It felt like it was time to be a grown-up. That Fringe production of *Hot Mess* was the last of my own plays that I both directed and produced myself. I miss that time dreadfully and yet it was the gateway to a new world of practitioners that would teach me so much. Ellen McDougall directed a wonderful new production of the play, produced by the Arcola at Latitude Festival, the following year.

I wrote *PMQ* for *Coalition*, a night of political theatre curated by Nadia Latif at Theatre503, and it was directed by James Dacre, whom I subsequently asked to direct *Precious Little Talent* at Trafalgar Studios in 2011, which I produced. After opening night, I ran across town to do the Old Vic New Voices: 24 Hour Plays. I was so loath to leave Edinburgh and my old, safe life that, when I got into the Royal Court Young Writers' Programme, I commuted between London and Edinburgh for nearly a year, on the sleeper train. It was insane. I was living between my Edinburgh flat and my gran's spare bedroom and writing in cafés and restaurants. I can still remember the Baker Street Pizza Express where I wrote *PMQ* and my gran's upstairs study where I wrote *Boys* – a play about not wanting to give up on the best bits of youth.

I pushed myself incredibly hard, and was exhausted most of the time. I was very sure that hard work was the antidote to the uncertainty of the future. The problem was that the producing – the emails, phone calls and publicity pushing – responded well to high-octane efficiency. The writing, less so. If you push it, you panic and the writing stops. It's like a small horse, you have to be kind to it. I had no idea how to do that. I was a long way from any understanding of myself as an artist or what I was doing as art. I did, however – even then – get this strange tingling sense when I felt things were a bit good. It was usually in the monologues, a sense of flow, where my brain would get out of the way – a break in the panic clouds. Something was starting to get a bit sure of itself.

Eventually I gave in, broke my own heart, left Edinburgh and moved down to London and into my friend's flat on Southgate Road. There's a great David Foster Wallace quote: 'Everything I've ever let go has claw marks on it.' I left Edinburgh kicking and screaming.

What I'd lost in terms of team and kindred spirits by leaving the university years behind, I'd started to gain in a new community in London. Many of the people I'd met on *Coalition* are still friends now. That year I did a Radio 4 workshop that resulted in my first radio play, *Rightfully Mine*, but also, and much more importantly, my long-standing friendship with Nick Payne. Simon Stephens came to see *Hot Mess* at the Fringe, he set up my attachment at the Lyric Hammersmith and gave me a theatrical home when I came to London. Simon also asked Nick, Ben, Alice Birch and me to teach at Rose Bruford College, creating the world's best supper club that is still going strong. Those early offers of belonging were crucial.

Robert Icke and Rupert Goold took a collection of young writers away for the week with Headlong Theatre to create *Decade*. Rupert, Rob and Headlong became a new gang that I was very proud to be part of. It was there that I learnt about theatre as provocation and met another good friend, Adam Brace. Rupert, more than anyone, taught me to say the unsayable (Brace runs a close second) – which was totally formative to the work I've written since, and which led to my writing *Gift*. It was written straight out – I hardly changed a word. Whatever that thing was that I had been starting to get sure of, was getting stronger. It seemed to work in monologue, when I could work from instinct. The second I tried to hammer it into form or structure, my mind got in the way and I stumbled and things became unclear.

Boys was the big attempt at trying to conquer conventional dramatic form. Three acts, six characters, a full-length play. It was written on the Royal Court Young Writers' Programme and, whilst the Court didn't produce it, it became my calling card for meetings with other theatre companies. Headlong became the home for *Boys*. My first meeting was with Ben Power, then at Headlong, who I sold on some idea about a play set on an oil rig, which would arrive in a different form, at a different theatre, six years later. Rob had picked *Precious Little Talent* out of a pile of scripts and asked if I had anything new, I sent him *Boys*. He would go on to direct it for Headlong at HighTide and Soho Theatre. It was a collaboration and production that cemented my sense of myself as a writer as something distinct from directing or producing. I came to see direction as transformation rather than facilitation. It was a letting-go of total control that liberated my writing. The writing became the central concern and has remained an uncompromising pursuit ever since. When *Boys* played at Soho Theatre in June 2012, I realised I was a professional writer. It also led me to Rachel Taylor, my agent, expert note-giver and constant ally, in a career that is ever-shifting.

Boys was the gateway to bigger commissions, bigger plays and new stages. It led me into a very happy time with the Royal Shakespeare Company on my adaptation *Wendy & Peter Pan*, developing two new plays with the National Theatre, and the six-year challenge of writing *Oil*, which, whilst exhausting, gave me some of my best work, most valued collaborators and a discovery of what I was capable of – in terms of grit, rigour and interrogation of form.

I have continued to struggle with the solitude of being a writer, and still – in the loneliest moments – am desperate to direct, run a venue, or just run hard away from myself/my computer towards the belonging of a gang and the pragmatism of making things happen in the world rather than the central, daily conversation being with yourself, inside your own mind. What I am always grateful for, however, are the people that my profession has brought my way: incredible collaborators, friends and artists with whom I have had the most exciting conversations of my life.

The particular preoccupation of writing, the constant nagging pursuit of the next project is an obsession and a privilege that, when I started, I had no idea would make my life's work. I think now, if I'm honest, as hard as I try to run from it, it's got me. I am a writer, and there's probably no escaping it, and maybe I don't want to. As one play is finished the next starts forming in my mind, a new sense of something impossible that is asking, in vain, for a solution. The task gets more demanding every time. When I love it, which is often, there's nothing better on earth. There's maybe something liberating about realising it's not really a choice. And as for gang? We might all be working in different buildings and often on our own, but writers and theatre-makers are an incredible community that I look forward to spending the next decade being part of.

Ella Hickson
April 2018

EIGHT

Introduction

I created the characters of *Eight* in the hope of showing the effects, when taken to their extremes, of growing up in a world in which the central value system is based on an ethic of commercial, aesthetic and sexual excess. I, like my characters, am a twenty-something and have grown up in a world of plenty, unscathed by war or recession, a world defined by consumerist boom.

As far as I could see, the effect of such affluence was neither contentment nor discontent. It was, instead, wholesale apathy. In creating the characters of *Eight* I asked a group of twenty-somethings what they believed in – the almost unanimous answer was 'not very much'.

Eight, then, when it was written, aimed to show a generation that had lost the faculty of faith. These eight characters are societal refugees – who are struggling to muster belief in themselves or the world around them. The result is either apathy or, perhaps perversely, fundamentalism. Faith is a human impulse; if there is no outlet for it in mainstream society it can become warped and misguided.

A year has passed since I wrote this play and much has changed. What was then a whisper of recession is now an undeniable reality. The students I was writing for and about had little idea about what the job market would look like by the time they tried to enter it the following September.

The next few years for recent graduates are going to be extremely tough – the *Guardian* recently announced that up to 40,000 of this year's graduates will still be struggling to find work this September. Apathy is no longer going to be an option.

Whilst times will be hard – and I realise this may be easy to say when the worst is yet to come – I feel a little struggle may be no bad thing. For it's only when times get really tough that you work out what really matters – and maybe, by then, we'll be ready to believe in it.

Premise

One of the central characteristics of the commercial world that *Eight* explores is 'choice culture'. From channel-surfing to Catch-Up TV and *X-Factor* voting – we are a choosy bunch, we get what we want when we want it. *Eight* reflects this in its set-up.

When I directed the first production of the play, I offered the audience short character descriptions of all eight characters before the play began. I then asked them to vote for the four characters whom they wanted to see. As the audience entered the auditorium, all eight characters were lined up across the front of the stage – but only the four characters with the highest number of votes would perform. The other four characters would remain onstage, reminding the audience that in each choice we make we are also choosing to leave something behind.

Such a process is not essential for a performance of *Eight* and directors, of course, should remain in control of the line-up and order of play if they should so wish.

Eight was first performed at Bedlam Theatre, Edinburgh, during the Edinburgh Festival Fringe, on 2 August 2008, with the following cast:

DANNY	Henry Peters
JUDE	Simon Ginty
ANDRÉ	Michael Whitham
BOBBY	Holly McLay
MONA	Alice Bonifacio
MILES	Solomon Mousley
MILLIE	Ishbel McFarlane
ASTRID	Gwendolen von Einsiedel
Director	Ella Hickson
Stage Construction	David Larking
Technical Director	Xander Macmillan

The production transferred to Performance Space 122, New York, as part of the COIL Festival, on 6 January 2009, and Trafalgar Studios, London, on 6 July 2009.

Characters

DANNY, *twenty-two*
JUDE, *eighteen*
ANDRÉ, *twenty-eight*
BOBBY, *twenty-two*
MONA, *eighteen*
MILES, *twenty-seven*
MILLIE, *thirty*
ASTRID, *twenty-four*

(BUTTONS, *mid-thirties*)

DANNY

Danny is a well-built man in his early twenties. He sits on a black box in the centre of the stage with a corpse's head lain across his knee, he is feeding water to the corpse. He is wearing jeans, a black wife-beater and black boots. Danny is twenty-two years old but he appears much younger; his learnt manner is one of faux aggression; however, he fails to disguise an underlying vulnerability. Danny is a little slow but essentially sweet.

Danny, hushed, talks to the corpse.

Here you go, little one – head up, 'ave some water, come on, your lips are all crackin', come on. Look, I can't be doin' everyfing for you, it's 'ard enough sneakin' in for nights, that fat bastard porter is gunna see me one a these days and I'll get fuckin' nailed. Now come on, darlin'.

You're a nightmare, int you? I used to be the same. Mum always said I was a pain in the neck, always bawling when she was tryin' to get stuff done.

Danny walks forward and begins to address the audience.

Mum used to work for one of them poncey magazines; it's why we had to move up north, to Preston; it's newest city in England, you know? I was dead excited, shouldn't have been... borin' as fuck here. Mum's job was to make sure all the people on the front cover of the magazine looked right. I used to watch her, it was like magic, she'd give 'em big old smiles and scrape off all their fat, anything not perfect she'd jus' rub out, make it disappear. When she was done all them people looked beautiful, like, like – dolls. The problem was it made me sort a sad to look at all the ugly people after that; all them people who look fat or spotty or just sort a strange, when Mum made it seem real easy to look just right.

At school, Hutton Grammar, I was never bright so sports were always my thing, and I was always big, like my dad has been. They used to call him Monster Cox, which I always thought was cos he was built like a tank but it turned out it was cos he had a massive dick. He died in the Falklands, he was a Sapper, part a the Royal Engineers, had a bit more up top than me. (*Laughs – self-deprecating.*) Mum always seemed a bit afraid after Dad had gone, she seemed sort a smaller, she didn't look 'right'. I guess that was why I wanted to get big, like Dad had been, to make things better – protect her, like.

I was sort of keen on goin' down the gym after school, cos it helped wiv rugby, and girls and that, so Mum, for my eighteenth birthday, bought me my first tub a protein shake, CNP Professional. At first it was just a hobby. I'd do, say, two hours after school, not much, like, reps of twelve – squats, crunches, lunges, flat-bench press, barbell curls – just the usual stuff. But it started feelin' really good.

I was feeling better and lookin' better, I can't remember which one came first – they sort of seemed like the same fing after a while. So I upped my hours. And yeah, there was pain but I could ignore it – I was focused like crazy; I felt I could do anything. I was like one a Mum's pictures, getting tighter and bigger and more and more perfect.

And soon it came. I could feel it. Sitting at the back of the classroom – I could feel my traps straining to get out a my school shirt, and all the girls were lookin' too, they could see that I was different, they could see the strength, the fearlessness – my body was proof of the size a my balls. I didn't need to be a hero, it was enough just to look like one.

But, but after a while people stopped lookin', and it didn't feel so good, it didn't feel right. I was still getting a bit bigger but the change wasn't as, as powerful as it was at the start so I started thinking all the same things again like why I didn't have a girlfriend, what the fuck was I going to do with my life and what Mum was going to do all on her own if I went 'n, 'n… It was like down the gym I'd felt perfect, unstoppable, and then suddenly nothing was perfect any more.

My dad always said, 'The more you sweat in training, the less you bleed in war.' (*Trying to be brave*.) So I signed up, 4th Battalion, Duke a Lancaster's Regiment, trainin' every Tuesday down Kimberley Barracks. We were the new boys; they called us Lancs in 4th Battalion, the babies. Hauled in one day 'n pretty much shipped out the next – direct service to Basra, unsure whether you had a single or return, that's what all the lads said. We didn't have a fucking clue what we were doing, but I wasn't bothered, I was there to fight – end of. I was pretty popular too; apparently it's quite comforting to have your arse covered by a lad built like a brick shithouse.

His vulnerability dissolves a little – his face hardens, suddenly he seems older, tougher.

'Bout halfway through my tour, the day came, the older squaddies had always said it; one thing'll happen, one day and you'll never be the same. Mine came, 24th June 2007, it was my twenty-second birthday. We're creepin' into some sleepy suburb, the Warrior tanks were following us up. Tension was up, the drivers were spiked, chewin' coffee granules 'til they dribbled black – but all was quiet – we were just having a nose about – (*Stops, stares at the audience*.) – I'm out front. (*Snaps head round*.) Suddenly, in bowls a fuckin' Yank Humvee – (*Danny jumps on top of the box*.) – they're chargin' through, all shouting 'GET SOME', pelting out bullets like it's a fuckin' fairground ride… my lot hit the deck thinking Jonny Jihad's out to play – (*He jumps down and hauls the corpse up in front of him as if it were a rubble barricade*.) – I'm squatting, low behind some rubble, waiting for the storm to pass when 'Booooom!'… There's smoke, I can hear screams but muffled, like, and… I'm down. (*He falls to the floor, begins to drag himself back up onto the box, panting, frightened*.) There's pain… in my left leg, those tosser yanks had woken a mean fuckin' beast, there were rag'ed Fundie Jundies runnin' fuckin' everywhere – I looked down and the whole of my left leg, hip to toe, skinless.

He is now back on top of the box, he stares down at his leg – he pauses, quiet, shivering.

It was like the bullets stopped, like there was silence. I stared.
My leg was red and bloody, not a patch a skin on the thing – I
could see all the muscles, workin', t... t... twitchin', all the
ligaments – I couldn't even feel the pain. I touched it, it was
soft and warm and huge, it was the most beautiful thing I had
ever seen.

Then, suddenly the pain and the smell, the stink of burnin' flesh
– I screamed – Aaaaaaaaah!

There was no way I was seeing service after that. Burns all over
me leg, they took the skin from my arse and patched it together,
scrape bits off, add bits on. It fuckin' fascinated me and as it
healed, I, I missed it. It was like, seeing that, seeing how
perfectly constructed I was beneath it all, I guess it was Dad's
influence, the engineer in me – but I... I swear I'd never seen
anything work so well. It was like suddenly all Mum's front
covers, all those perfect men and women, they were nothing
now, even getting ripped wasn't the same, the buzz is
underneath the skin, that's where everything was right.

So I started workin' here. I'm a stripper... of bodies... dead
ones. They ask me to peel back the skin, but careful like cos
they use it for people with burns, like me. Then I slough off all
the fat so they're ready when the medical students come in...
(*He turns to the corpse.*) Shh, I know, it's horrid, don't worry
little one. (*He puts his hands over her ears and hugs her to him,
whispering.*) Medical students use 'em for their anatomy
classes, it's not fair to talk 'bout it in front of them, though.
(*Takes hands off.*) I work during the day, but then I hide whilst
the porters swap shifts – when everyfing is dark, I creep out, it's
awful quiet and somehow calm, like – and they're all lying
there and I can just be with them, sitting a while.

I give 'em nicknames like all the squaddies used to do, like Dad
was Monster Cox and I was Danny Boy, so over here we have
Holey Joe, not because he's religious or anything but on
account of the hole they left when they cut his pacemaker out,
apparently they make the crematoriums explode and no one
needs that at a funeral, eh? Then there's Bruiser, through there,
cos he's a little banged up, I don't know why, something must a

happened to him before he came in. He's like a father to me; he just listens and listens for hours.

And then here, here she is, this is Mouse, my little mouse, cos she's so small and fragile but so perfect-looking, I look after her real well, I never let her get cold or leave her on her own for too long, she gets lonely, like Mum did.

What it is, is that when someone is willing to sit with you, all exposed and vulnerable like they are, it makes you want to share, makes you tell 'em things you'd never tell anyone else. Cos they don't mind if you're big or strong or if people like ya, they'll listen anyway. And you listen right back... listen... hard... to that silence... beneath all the noise... and you can hear 'em... breathing, and quietly now... real quiet like, their hearts start to beat.

He climbs in next to the corpse on the box, places his head on her chest to hear her heart beat then lies down next to her and pulls her arm over him and drifts off to sleep.

Blackout.

JUDE

Jude is eighteen years old, dressed in school trousers, shirt and a tie. A large black block, centre stage, acts as a bed and a dinner table – navigated around in the opening sections.

This time last summer, Dad sent me to the South of France. The day I left, he stood on the front step and saluted my departure, like some bloody sergeant major, pair of baggy corduroys, copy of the *Guardian* wedged under his arm.

'Off you go, my son,' he yelled. 'You will walk away a boy and return a man!'

Except I could barely hear him cos he had Haydn's 'Farewell' Symphony booming out of every window. (*Moves to sit on block.*) When I stepped off the plane, the first thing I felt was the heat – it smacked me in the face, the stairs burned my feet through my shoes; I strained to see the city in the distance, but I couldn't see a thing, I was shitting myself.

Taxi dropped me off at Boulevard Victor Hugo. Now, my dad would have been in his element. I could hear his voice in my head: 'Did you know, Jude, that without Victor Hugo, I strongly doubt we would've ever had Dickens.' Really, Dad, that's fascinating. I felt for the sandwiches he'd put in the bottom of my bag, but I'd eaten them on the plane.

He starts moving behind the block, down a 'street'.

Twenty-three, twenty-four – fuck a duck... It was huge. Wrought-iron gates squeaked open, I carried my suitcase up to this big green door; the paint was all cracking off it in the heat. There were old-fashioned shutters and yellow walls. It looked like all the Riviera photos that Dad had showed me before I left, all those stories about – (*Sits, imitates Dad, talking down to imaginary Jude.*) – 'Fitzgerald, Picasso and Hemingway, when genius was valued, Jude, and the women, oh, the women,

beautiful muses with wild eyes and...' Oh, what did he say?...
Oh yeah, 'reckless abandon', as if he was a hundred years old
and he had been there himself – sad act.

I breathed in. I knocked. I was shown to my room by a crazy
and crooked-looking woman with fag breath who kept scowling
as my bag slammed against the stairs; 'Pardon,' I whispered
weakly, with this pathetic smile like I'd just peed myself.
(*Smiles.*) She growled – (*In a growly French accent.*) –
'Madame Clara will return later, little boy, for the dinner,'
alright. (*Sits on the side of his bed and looks around agog.*) As
much as I wanted to be back in Poynton, my French room
was... pretty fucking cool. The walls were covered in black-
and-white photos that looked like scenes from old movies and
that. There was a hat stand, here, in the corner – (*Imitates
popping his hat up onto it.*) – next to the bookshelf... busting
with crusty old novels, all in French, then my window... floor
to ceiling, old shutters that proper creaked and a balcony, little
radio, huge old mirror – it was brilliant.

*He flicks on the radio – Laura Fygi's Le Continental – he
continues absentmindedly whilst dancing a bit and unpacking.*

Three months here might not be so bad, there was sun and sea
and there were bound to be women – (*He thinks.*) – in bikinis. I
was an independent man, my own room – I could be a Riviera
gent; look sharp, become fluent... in the language of looove...
eat well, get to know the place, maybe make friends with a...
baker. (*Jumps on block.*)

'Bonjour, Jude!'

'Bonjour, Pierre!'

'Say, Jude, where is that young lady I saw you with, eeh, she is
very good-looking, no?

'Eh, Pierre, she some needs some rest... from all the lovin'.'

I'm bloody hungry. What's that smell? It's like peppers or
something... this could actually be bloody brilliant... God, it's
hot, I need to get out of this stuff, I'm sweating *comme un
cochon – (Finds himself funny, starts taking off his shirt and*

shorts as he's dancing.) – and cologne, I'm definitely the kind of man that likes… colooogne – (*Imitates spraying.*) – mmm, the smell of that food…

He does a final twist, pretending to spray the perfume in his pants… He suddenly stops and the music cuts.

'Hello… um, um… p… pardon… Madame, Bon-bo-bonjour.'

His eyes hit floor, the same weak, 'peeing smile' continues, painfully embarrassed, humble…

(*To front.*) She was standing there, in the doorway; half woman – half silhouette. I glanced up, red nails and long, chocolate hair – blurry through the cigarette smoke.

(*Looks at his feet.*) I want to die, I want to die… I want to be wearing trousers.

Pause. One quick second glance.

Her cleavage, crinkly, brown – like a Sunday roast. (*Looks down at his crotch.*) Oh God, no, don't you dare, don't you dare make this any fucking worse –

He edges his hands over his… Looks up, smiles. He puts on a very strong accent, changes pose to imitate her.

'It's Jude, no?' she says… perfectly…

(*Gulps.*) 'Yes, oui, yes.' (*Clears throat in an overly manly way.*)

'Dinner is ready – in the kitchen, downstairs, you should – err – dress for dinner.'

'Yup, yes… yes, I should… I should, I will – thank you, pardon.'

Whilst re-dressing, he pulls trousers up from ankles, moves over to the kitchen, pulls out a chair – and nods recognition to imagined dinner guests.

The table was full of wine and strangers. Funny-sounding French and hands grabbing at massive bowls of food: salami and anchovies, little blobby tomatoes and fat balls of mozzarella, all swimming in thick oil, it smelled of basil and olives. I took one olive – just the one. Clara looked down from the head of the table at me, '*C'est tout, Jude? Tch tch...*' (*Wags his finger.*) The two other lads, sitting opposite me, laughed. Jimmy on the left – a painfully stupid American who was absolutely, totally, incredibly excited about everything... always, and couldn't speak a fucking word of French – made me look pretty good. Then on the right we had Fabian, the quatri-lingual Bavarian; this scrotum-bursting, yak-haired, man-beast who kept having to pop off to play contact sports and plough wenches... twat.

It was a circus, controlled by the heavenly hostess, the red-lipped ringmaster. Not a piece of food passed her lips, she just quietly supped on red wine, and watched, smiling, as we gorged ourselves.

He moves over from the chair to the bed.

For the next three months, between language school in the morning and getting drunk in the evenings with Dipstick and Goliath, I spent my days sneaking glimpses of Clara. Her gold St Christopher twinkling in her cleavage over breakfast; wrinkled fingers dolloping handfuls of breast into expensive French lace. I had inhaled the heavy scent of woman. Perfection did exist, Dad had been right to have his idols. Clara Moretti, my Madonna.

Dad, in his absence, had finally come into his own. I had all this, this... urgh inside me, I couldn't sit still, I couldn't concentrate, there weren't enough wanking hours in the day. The only thing that made it any better was that little library Dad had packed me. I devoured every book, cover to cover. She became my aged Lady Chatterley, my jaded Juliet, my latter-day Anna Karenina, but I was just Quasimodo – looking longingly from afar, catching glimpses of her perfection whilst I remained this skinny, pasty and increasingly terrified teenager. It killed me; the more time I spent with her, the worse it was. I read books to her, I helped her cook, I watched her paint and all whilst she looked at me with sad and sympathetic eyes. She'd let me sit on the end of her bed when she got ready in the evenings – I'd fix the clasps on jewellery that glinted in the eyes of other men.

She wore her age differently with me, like it was heavy to carry, as if her skin was like an old friend that wouldn't let her forget a thing, not for a second.

As it got late, Mediterranean men would arrive in dark cars and wrap her in their heavy coats and they'd take her away from me; for those men, her age became like armour – I fucking hated those men for making her that way.

He takes his shirt off and lies on the bed.

At night, I could hear her fuck those Mediterranean monkeys, grunting and squealing as I lay, staring at the ceiling, sweaty and sleepless.

One night, Clara got a phone call at about ten. It was pouring with rain, the wind was furious, slapping the shutters back and forth against the walls. I could barely hear the conversation over the noise, but she was going out, to Monaco, for the night. I tried to sleep, I couldn't. It was so hot and humid, I paced my room, I smoked a bit. I was, I was… I had to walk, to breathe. I found myself outside her door. I pushed it open. The inner sanctum, without her in it; it was quiet, airy, the storm couldn't touch it.

He enters 'Clara's room' and sits on the bed.

Her white bed, the wooden floor, the tiny crystal bottles and trinkets sat gracefully and quietly, they were delicate, sophisticated, they aimed to tempt… one by one, the perfect crystal shattering, clouds of musk and powder flew up in my face. (*He chokes and backs away.*) Her lingerie, where *I* knew it was. Those perfect puckered legs wrapping around some fat Italian. (*He starts pulling at the stockings.*) Whore's stockings, black silk, all over her pure skin; expensive bras, made by a million hands, grubby little Parisian hands on her perfect body, holding her up and in… and – (*Runs back to her dressing table, mimics making-up.*) – pots of paint, the black soot in her eyes and the blood red on her lips, to paint the idol, as if she could get any more beautiful! Dad hadn't said it was like this! The lovers in his books – they were heroes, the passion of battle, he said – the honour of devotion, love makes a man but look at me

– (*He sobs a little.*) – I'm fucking pathetic. I'm nothing…
because she's everything.

*He slides to the floor, sobbing, head in hands – he's young,
vulnerable – quietly now, much more sombre.*

And then she came back, she found me – in amongst her
underwear. She stood above me, backlit by the street lamps on
the road, her coat was wet, she said, she had to get dry – and her
dress fell around her ankles, aging flesh creased and beautiful
around her waist and down her thighs. She came towards me,
lifted my face to hers and kissed me, hard; she asked me to hold
her, to undress her – I did. And she was there, naked, all of her,
to touch, to be had – she was above me, around me; she told me
I was beautiful, angelic – she was human now. Her flesh
between my hands, the weight of her, her perfume faded, there
was just the smell of skin – her eyes pleading, the wet of her
lips, her hands on me, I had her.

*He wakes next to her, we see disgust in his face – the idol has
fallen.*

When I woke, the rain had stopped; the morning sun lay across
her wooden floor and it crept into the creases around her eyes.
She looked her age; too old to smell of wine and cigarettes, too
old to have mascara down her face, too old for her lipstick to be
smudged across the face of a seventeen-year-old boy.

*Pause. He wipes his hand across his face, gets up and gets
dressed back into school uniform. He stares out at the audience,
something has been lost.*

Blackout.

ANDRÉ

André, originally Andrew, is a twenty-eight-year-old gallery owner. He enters his gallery, clearly shaken, takes a moment to catch his breath and positions himself on a high stool.

I have to say, this wasn't the ending that I had in mind. I'm not sure what I did have in mind. Probably a whisper of a 'happy ever after', you know, wearing matching cardies, sharing digestives, but I hadn't thought I'd been stupid enough to pin anything on it actually happening. It's easy for the Cinderellas and Sleeping Beauties of this world, but we're a little low on route planners for Prince Charming and... Prince Charming. Serious lack of 'fairy' tales.

This certainly isn't one, is it? I think we can all agree that coming into work half an hour late on a Monday morning and finding your boyfriend hanging from the rafters by a Hermès scarf, well... it's not exactly 'happy ever after', is it?

That bloody scarf; I've always maintained that a high price means high quality but who knew Hermès could take a man's weight? And let's be clear, he was no skinny little fag, he was a big fat chunky. He was never going to wear it; I don't know what I was playing at giving it to him. He wasn't the scarf type, you see, Hermès or otherwise – never had been. I spent my teenage years trying my very hardest to look like Cyndi Lauper. Him? No, going with a button fly over a zip was his idea of outrageous.

Where's that sodding ambulance? He can't just be, up there, like that. I guess the rush isn't on once they know resuscitation heroics are out. More or less a removal job now – heavy load, lads, mind your backs. His big, purple face is dribbling all over an Emin print. Why he chose the bloody stockroom? It's not like he was being shy, putting a Hermès noose round your neck, it's not quite the same as popping a few pills and drifting off, is it? He might as well have done it in the front fucking window, nice bit of performance art... No, he wanted to save this one just for me, one-man show.

I bet I'm not insured for suicidal dribble either – that's 5k down the shitter.

They're bound to judge, aren't they, snoopy little paramedics? One art gallery, two queers, one corpse, that's never going to look good, is it? They'll look for syringes and... hamsters and expect some paid-by-the-hour twelve-year-old to pop out with a dummy in his gob. I wish we'd ever been that bloody exciting. He used to get a hard-on doing the tax return... seriously... it was the stationery, he said, the smell of fresh paper, straight-lines, colour-coding, gave him a buzz. He kept this place shipshape. It's our empire; Captain Admin and Sergeant Schmooze. It's all you need in the art world: a number-cruncher and someone that can talk bollocks at a million miles an hour, that's me.

He was never in it for the art. We caught the wave of the YBAs, you see, all that Hirst and Emin nonsense in the early nineties, when you could piss in a pot of formaldehyde and make a million, as long as you did it loud enough and in front of enough people. Dingy Hoxton warehouses and precocious teenagers sticking two fingers up at the establishment; like it had never been done before, like this time it might all crumble at the sight of their shit-for-brains art and polysyllabic waffle.

And all of them led by the grand high witch of overpriced nonsense... Miss Tracey Emin!

He turns and talks to Tracey Emin as if she is there.

'Now, Tracey dear, what you've done here with this little "bed" piece, is just not do your washing for a long while and what's happened is you've come off looking like a bit of a grubby slut, so come along, pumpkin, pop yourself in the shower and we'll get this tidied up.'

He really hated that Tracey Emin, and it took a lot for him to hate anyone; he said she looked selfish. I mentioned that might be because we were standing in front of a ten-foot photo of her scooping money into her lady garden. He said not, he said she had selfish eyes; that she was making tragedy a commodity and that was unforgivable.

You'd bloody love this, wouldn't you, Tracey darling... 'World's most boring man recovers old birthday present from flamboyant boyfriend and hangs himself with it' – wonder how she'd flog it? Something simple, get right to the core of it, probably some of those embroidered stick-men things – five grand a piece, for a game of Hangman.

He hated it, the drama, the hype – he tried not to, he read everything there was to read, he really felt that if people were paying all that money then there must be something in it that he couldn't see. Bless him. He always tried to see the good in things, invariably it wasn't there. See, it was never his world, it was mine.

I loved it, the parties, the glam, the feeling that you were getting away with it, free booze, free food, free drugs – people knowing your name. Recognition, it's short on the ground, you get it where you can. But he never needed it, not like me. I'd be raving my tits off in DayGlo and he'd have a pint and go home early, boring sod, didn't like the noise.

It was the same at the openings, print fairs, biennales – he'd lurk, he'd actually look at the art, whilst I schmoozed, made us contacts, did deals, showed my face, it's who you know not what you know, always has been, always will be. He never understood that, he felt that things should succeed on their own merit. Tch, tch... Not any more, love.

He never used his gayness either, and gayness is pretty serious ammunition in the art world. It's an indisputable qualification; gay men do aesthetics like black men can sprint, it's just fact. But he just didn't have very much gay in him. (*He raises his eyebrows.*) What I mean is, he was the least gay gay I'd ever met – well, excepting this recent episode, which, if he doesn't mind me saying so, is somewhat queeny. He drank Stella, hated gyms, never wore a pair of matching socks in his life, practically heterosexual. It was his niche: 'Totally normal bloke that happens to fuck men, please keep off the grass' – no cottaging, no arty wankers, no underage sex – go back to the nineties or see my seedy boyfriend if interested in any of the above. I was the yin to his yang, the Vivienne Westwood to his Marks & Spencer's, the St Tropez to his Bognor bloody Regis, and he needed me, I made him sure of who he was, by constantly reminding him of what he'd never be, what he'd never want to be. He was safe and sound on his patch, the only straight gay in the village.

Then all of a sudden, about two years ago, out of nowhere, he's overrun, in come the queers that aren't queer, they're getting married, they're wearing wellies and walking black Labs, they've got people carriers and kids instead of drug habits. The back alley had become memory lane and the sodomite became suburbanite. The poof had evaporated. These days being subversive is more of a hobby than a necessity. Even the names have changed – poof, queer, fairy, fudge-packer – they're not whispered or spat at you any more, they're hair products, club names, magazine titles, turn on the telly before work and watch Lorraine Kelly rubbing Poof in her hair.

So it all stopped, all changed, nothing left to hide or defend, why do it in the dark when it's all over bloody GMTV?

He hated it, how was he meant to tell himself apart? All that acceptance, you've never seen a man so lost – he had nowhere to go; he'd been sucked in, invaded, by normal.

Finally, Emin's getting old, that's where I got back from this morning, before… before this. I was at the National Gallery, twenty-year retrospectives start showing the wrinkles, love. Get a little bit of distance on it and it looks even more like bollocks than it did in the first place. If only he could've seen that. If he could've stepped outside of it all for long enough, got out of this place, got away from me, he would've seen that this isn't it, that this world of overpriced nonsense wouldn't win. I guess he couldn't see how it could be any other way; the faithlessness got to him, ate away from the inside.

I could see it happening, I watched him quietly shatter beneath it all. Sitting on the couch, eating himself into oblivion, there's more macaroni cheese in that corpse than I can bear to think about. But I didn't do anything. I told myself he knew, that deep down he could see, this world that I had brought him into, this shallow, shameless world of men with millions pandering to the tantrums of teenagers like Emin, of queers desperately trying to stay queer, I thought he could see it for what it was, see me for what I was, a joke.

But no, he thought we wanted more, he thought that if naked and dirty wasn't enough then it was time for paraplegic or post-op and he didn't want to see it, he didn't want to see me scrabbling around in the dirt for the last bits of different that were left, the not yet exploited; it was me; it was the fact I was still doing it, that's what he couldn't bear – if we could have both laughed at it from the sidelines, fine – but he thought I hadn't seen, he thought all of this, was me.

But what if I'd stepped down, if I'd stopped pretending... I couldn't carry him, I tried to get him down, lift him from the knees, I did, I had him in my arms, I took his weight for a second but he was too heavy. So I had to let go, let the Hermès take the strain. I stood there, watched his bloated, purple head loll forward – there was the shock factor, first time I'd felt it in a decade. And so perhaps this was his parting gift? To remind me of what it was like when people... stared, the thrill of shocking – how it had been when we were something to look at.

So this is it, the final fling for the queers at the fringes, the underground fairies... a little souvenir of when difference existed. And he thought this was what I wanted, what I missed? I would have given up the drama the day I met him, in all his beige glory. I've been bored of pushing the sodding envelope for half a decade, I just never thought to tell him, I thought he knew I was playing make-believe – but he didn't, I never told him that he, he was home.

Blackout.

BOBBY

Bobby is a twenty-two-year-old mother of two – wearing a red Adidas tracksuit. She is seated on a table. We imagine her kids, Kyle and Chloë, four and six, at her feet in front of the telly. She's reading down to them with enthusiasm. Bobby has a strong, working-class Edinburgh accent, she mimics an upper-middle-class English accent when impersonating Mrs Beeton.

(*Reading*.) ''Twas the night afore Christmas, an' aw through the hoose, no' a creature was stirrin', no' even a moose – '

Chloë, will you shut up and listen!

'The stockin's were hung by the chimney wi' care, in the hope that St Nicholas soon wud be there.'

I know we dinnae hae a chimney, Chloë… but we do have a lovely plasma-screen telly. We can hang our stockings b'that, right? – Yes, Santa will know where to find 'em – They have so got televisions in the North Pole… How else d'ye think Santa got so fat if he wasnae watchin' telly aw the time, eh? Now enough, you two, bed, now scram.

As (*imaginary*) *Chloë leaves, smaller Kyle turns around to Bobby.*

Kyle, darling, what's wrong, wee man? Off you go with your sister.

She pulls him up onto her knee, wipes his tears.

Big boy like you's no' scared of Santa, is he? What is it? (*Listens to him.*) Oh darlin', I dae ken if yir dad's gonna be here in the mornin'. Who knows, eh? But what I do know is that he loves you very, very much and he's sent me the biggest, bestest present in the world for you to open in the mornin'. But he wrote me a wee note to say that you werenae to get it unless you were in bed by twelve… there's that grin, go on – awa' you go, oot like a light – ye've got ten minutes afore I'm coming to check!

Bobby moves to behind a small table where she is packing stockings. She addresses the audience from here on in.

He's got them the biggest, bestest present in the world? What cack. That selfish cunt costs me double every fuckin' year, just makin' sure they dinnae realise what a pathetic shite he is. I'm too skint. I got caught by work, back in November; fiddling gift vouchers oot on the scheme. I was nicking the odd bundle, and sellin' 'em on for half the price, everyone's happy – 'cept Mr Tescos, o' course, he wasnae too pleased. Smug bitch in management caught me, gave me the push, three fuckin' weeks before Christmas. Is she havin' a laugh?

'Sorry, bairns, Christmas is cancelled this year!' Tch, as if.

I'd started thinking up some pretty scary ideas for makin' cash when I seen this advert in the local newsagent: 'Housewife seeks home help to aid in Christmas preparations.' Ten quid an hour, eight hours a week – brilliant. What the fuck kinda Christmas takes two people three weeks to prepare for, I dinnae ken, but I needed the cash.

This house, right – (*Whistles*.) – fuckin' mental! It was oot Corstorphine way, proper big-square number, fuck-off front door, little path, four windaes. It was like the pictures Kyle brings hame frae school. Actually, I dae ken why he's no' drawing concrete blocks wi' wee orange windaes? Mind you, he's still drawin' me an' his dad holdin' hands – so he's clearly an optimist.

The woman I was workin' for, her name was Mrs Beeton – she was really old and sweet, always makin' me cups of tea wi' these wee ginger biscuits. She had this big old family comin' up from London for Christmas, so she had to make puddings and cakes and pies but she was old, she got really tired, dead quick. I was sort o' glad I could gie her a hand. I thought it was a bit rough none o' her lot stayed tae help oot. They'd just come, stuff their faces and fuck off. She'd say, 'That's what mothers were for' – guess she's right. I don't think any of ma lot'll stick about once they're old enough to go… why would they?

She pulls her jumper in tight and heads over to the window.

It's getting cold. (*Looks out.*) Aw, would ye look at that? It's snowing – aw please stay till mornin', they'll love that.

There was this one afternoon at Mrs Beeton's, she called it 'Stir-up Sunday'. She'd come in frae walking the dogs. I was daen the ironin' in the kitchen, listening to *The Archers* – her choice, no' mine. I've got no patience wi' a bunch a twats that were getting fuckin' radgey over a duck. When oot o' her cupboards, no sort o' ceremony aboot it, Mrs Beeton starts pullin' bags an' bags o' currants, an' sultanas an' nuts and cherries an' all of it swimmin' in eggs. It was like Jamie Oliver's Christmas special but wi' a bit o class.

'Silent Night' slowly begins to play.

An' in her big old kitchen, fu' of heavy plates and heavy cutlery, and heavy old chairs and tables, wi' big orange lights an' wee little candles and her in her red apron, and her hair all pinned up, elegant-like. And she was playing these Christmas songs. Noo, we're no' talking Wham or Mariah Carey, or none o' that shite, this was a choir, and it was dead beautiful. And I watched her chuck aw this stuff in. She kent exactly what she was daen, like she'd been daen it for years, like it was some sort o' ritual.

Music down.

She asked me to grate an orange fir her. I felt stupit for gettin' sort o' excited, like a kid. Int that pathetic? Here I was, daen this old dear's ironing and peeling a fucking orange an' I could hardly contain masel. Life's no' that bad that some old dear's skiv work was going to make ma day; but it did... it really did. It was the smells. Oor Christmas, at hame, when I was a kid and Ma was aboot, it looked awright but it ne'er smelt a much, part frae Mum's fags and a wee wiff o' Iceland turkey. But the smell o' Mrs Beeton's kitchen! My God, I asked her what it was.

'Cloves, mostly,' she said. 'Cinnamon, your well-pithed orange of course, Bobby, a bit of brandy, nutmeg... sugar and spice and all things nice.' She laughed, she found hersel' quite funny quite a lot. She was sweet, though, there was nae agro to her, just sort of calm and quiet an' – just solid, ken?

As I was standing there aw misty-eyed, looking at her, wishin' I could take her hame and give her to ma kids for Christmas:

'Here you go, bairns, happy Christmas, have a better mum!'

She turns to me and says:

'Have you made your wish, Bobby?'

'Wish? Wish what?'

'Wish while you stir, dear. Oh, you have to wish, that's the whole point of it.'

'Oh right... Silly me, eh, forgot aboot ma wish, didn't I?'

Slower, softer, begins to cry.

So, I started makin' this wish about Christmas and my kids and... that... that... maybe it would be nice if we... maybe for once... could... (*To the audience, apologising for tears.*) – Sorry. I'm sorry. Like a stupit bloody kid maself I started cryin', and Mrs Beeton looked embarrassed, which is fair enough, what with her cleaner blubbing into her Christmas cake. She says:

'What on earth is the matter, dear?'

Through sniffles – getting progressively violent, building to a crescendo that is uncomfortably aggressive:

'I... I don't know,' I said to her. 'But it's just that it's Christmas and your hoose, it looks like Christmas and it feels safe and my flat disnae look like Christmas and it's never felt safe, no' for one single, fucking day and I don't know how to fix that, but I want to fix it, cos it's no' fair that my kids can't have what you have! Why can't they have a Christmas like this, eh? Wi' aw them smells, and carols, and the big old tree aw covered in twinkling shite an' everything that feels rock fucking solid. What did you do, Mrs Beeton, that I never did, eh? Did you work harder? Cos I work fuckin' hard and I cannae make it like this. Or did you just have some good luck? Or, or maybe you just got given it aw an' you didnae dae a fuckin' thing!'

She'd backed her way into the armchair in the corner when I'd been shoutin'. She looked scairt, just a wee old lady, a wee old lady wi' me aw up in her face. There was silence, felt like hours o' it. And then slowly, I just sort of gave up.

Mrs Beeton pulled herself up oot the chair, and looked doon at me, this pathetic greetin' mess. I thought she was gonnae shout, or throw me oot but she just wiped her hands doon her apron, and said:

'Come along, Bobby; pull yourself together, these cakes won't make themselves.'

She drove me to the bus stop that night, she got out the car, an' handed me my things and said she'd see me the next day. No' even a whisper o' what had happened. As I was walking away, she caught my hand:

'If you must cry, Bobby, do it quietly, where they can't see you. Children are like animals – they can smell the fear on you. Plenty of people will show them real life. You, Bobby, you must give them magic. Birthdays, Christmas… it just has to be better than real, that's all.'

She hugged me. It felt like Mum, wrappin' me up in a towel, oot o' the bath when I was wee, aw warm and red and bubbly.

So this is it, I'm gonnae give them the best Christmas they've ever had. An' when they've got kids o' their ain they'll say, 'Aw, do it like Nan does, go on, do it like Nan does.' An' I'll hide wee treats for the bairns, and I'll make the biggest, bestest puddin's you've ever seen, and do you know what? You know what? It's going to smell great, fuckin' great. Just you wait, it's gonnae be magic.

Blackout.

MONA

Mona is a small, dark-haired girl in her late teens, with a mild pregnancy bump that is not seen immediately. Her hair is loose around her face; she has the innocence of youth and yet acts with disquieting intensity. The stage is set with a central block and one chair placed at its side.

She stands, quietly humming a child's nursery rhyme and climbs into the centre of the block.

This is the house that my mother built. This is the house that lets the outside in and keeps the inside out. There are no rules, no 'don't' or 'can't', no time to get up, no time to be home; just in and out, always in and out and everything always open. This is because when I was six, Mum discovered what Dad had done, what closed doors were really for – she called a builder man and told him to take all the doors away, every last one. The house became a big, toothless mouth, with gaping gaps where all the doors had been. Soon Mum found strangers to fill up all those gummy gaps. She filled the house right up with people, like grains of multicoloured sand; in they'd pour and out they'd run, rivers of funny-looking faces and brightly coloured clothes.

Mother has a hundred gods; she makes idols of them all – money, sex, beauty – she had the strongest, wildest laugh, as if nothing will ever matter ever again. She is the spoilt kind, the hair, the nails, the men, she takes what she wants. Nothing matters. She is, what you call... young.

Freedom, she said, that was my blessing. She said that I was part of the luckiest generation ever because girls like me had knowledge, and knowledge is freedom. My mother made sure that I knew all the truths before the world even began to speak to me. She made sure that I saw everything that there was to be seen.

But there was just one thing that was mine. (*She clambers to fetch the box, excited.*) A small box that I kept beneath my bed, for all the thoughts that hadn't been hers first; I'd whisper my secrets onto tiny pieces of paper and roll them into little balls, I'd blow them into the hole in the top of the box – (*Blow.*) – and plug my hand over it – (*Slap.*) – in case they ever grew legs and escaped. But they did escape, right out through the gaps where all the doors had been. Mother found my box and took it to her friends – they tipped out all my secrets, the tiny paper balls scurried across the table top searching for somewhere to hide, but there wasn't anywhere. Those Bohemians, with their red-wine mouths, laughed all my secrets right out loud. All the dark I'd ever had, all the dark that was mine, they pushed up into the light.

Mummy said that I was 'darling' and 'funny' and 'delicious' and 'odd' and that I was very silly for having secrets.

I ran away that day I...

Blackout. Someone approaches her, a young man with a hoody pulled over his head. He sits on the ground with his back to the block; she lies down, looking over him.

That was where I found you. You were slouched against a tombstone in the dark backyard of St Barnabus. You were strong and silent as if you were a thousand secrets stitched together into skin. I remember your body, bullish and defiant, even in the twilight. You picked me up, curly like a comma.

Music begins to play softly in the background. The boy rises and walks offstage.

I slept that night between the bright crimson walls of the room you gave me, the smell of incense up from the dim cloister below. There in the eaves, safe and sound – where I heard sermons in my sleep – (*She smiles rapturously.*) – there were doors, locks, keys, commandments – remember me, honour me, respect me, thou shalt not, thou shalt not – it was like sherbet on my tongue. You showed me the freedom found behind locked doors, the freedom of silence, never seen and barely tasted. Things there were firm and forbidden and I was found.

She pulls herself forward, writhing almost, sexual.

So there, in St Barnabas, I made a brand new box of secrets, I piped them in and plugged them shut, a new colony of thoughts... of you, and you never came to find them and you never poured them out.

On that last Sunday before they found me, you told me to wait for you, beneath the back arch, where all those concrete saints stared down at me in the cold. You stood a little way off, in a pool of street light. As you came closer, the width of your shoulders cast shadows across my face. I was humbled by your presence. You smiled down at me and asked if I was ready. You took my hand, I felt the scars on your palm press into my skin; those man-made life-lines that had made the gypsy scream, the fear in her funny black eyes, she'd never seen the likes of you. No one had.

The boy from before appears, hoody still up and approaches her. He travels with her back up onto the top of the block and sits beside her.

So I let you take me back to St Barnabas. It was colder now as the sun lowered behind scratchy black trees. I stared up at you, in awe, I listened to you and your silence; there was strength in your secrecy and yet you, the king of men, seemed a little vulnerable.

Mona removes the boy's top – we see a black crucifix tattooed onto his back. She climbs around him.

I clung to your back like a child; I ran my fingers down that black tattoo, across your shoulders and down your spine. You hadn't said a word when that little needle had thudded into your back, not a sound. And you were silent still but your breath was heavy, like a beast that knew his slaughter date was near.

The boy swings Mona over, onto her back and looms over her, the implication is sexually aggressive.

You roused and came above me, with eyes as black as death – dredging me – and then, unlocked me, like a door that had never been opened, by a master that knew the sanctity of what had remained hidden. To you and for you, I gave up my secrets, you didn't take from me, I gave you what was sacred.

The sun shattered into darkness and all was black. The beast in you was calm. I felt you slump against me, as you exhaled I felt your life in me, I was sacrosanct. I felt you heavy in my arms. You had chosen me to bear your weight, to stain, as your black blood ran inky over my clean, white palms.

They found me lying on the cold stone, with the sun just up – eyes wide open, where you had left me. Mother and her multicoloured strangers brought me back to this doorless house where she and they and all the world cried and held me tight. They called you a million names; they found a thousand words for evil, a thousand new ways for telling this, the story of you.

They took me back to St Barnabus and found my box and tipped out all my secrets, all my thoughts of you, the tiny paper balls scurried across the table top searching for somewhere to hide, but there wasn't anywhere. Those Bohemians, with their red-wine mouths, read my secrets but they stayed silent now. No one laughed – I was no longer funny, delicious and odd.

You see, they fear the faith you've given me. They fear that I believe in you. And this, this is your testament, this is salvation. If only they would listen. But no, even this, they are taking from me now; they will take what is dark and push it up into the light. To them I am the dirty teenage child of a Bohemian. They think this is the price you pay for too much freedom. This is not a price to pay, the price has been paid, this is the only hope of redemption now. They will take this child from me and smite it because they no longer have the lungs for faith.

I have been returned to this boundless house, where laughing women break down doors and take what is not theirs; women, that steal childhoods from their children, so that they can wear a youth that is not their own. There is always a price to be paid for what we take; to open doors that should be shut, to take what is not freely given – it is not choice, it is not freedom, it is violation; you are gluttonous thieves, all of you. When you take, something must be lost, something breaks and someone somewhere is left wanting. Don't let them take this from me, it is what he has given me to give the world, it is all I have, it is all you have.

Blackout.

MILES

Miles is an American man in his mid-twenties. He is dressed in a sharp suit and is attractive due to a corporate aesthetic. He should carry himself with ultimate bodily and vocal composure. The cracks in this composure should be perfectly synchronised with the glimpses of weakness in his performative façade.

Voiceover: 'This is the final call for all passengers to board flight BA293 to Washington. This is the final call, can all passengers proceed to Gate 13.'

Pause.

July 7th 2005, ten-second snapshot: a goofy young Asian guy is in front of me buying a Mars Bar, I'm in a drugstore, King's Cross Station, London. He turns to me, he's short ten pence, I give it to him. (*He mimes.*)

'Take it easy.'

It's early morning. I'm in a suit, I look down, I have slick shoes on. I walk out to the front of the station; it's summer, it's bright. I see the big white letters scroll across the top and I board a number 30 bus to Hackney Wick.

This is all that I have of that afternoon; snapshots, shards, flickers, facts.

Here's the facts: My name is Miles Cooper, born in Washington DC, 1982. I've won everything I've ever touched. At twenty-four I was the most successful broker Merrill Lynch had ever seen. I was the glory boy of the trading floor, making more money than I knew what to do with. My father was planning my biography before I was out of my teens; he always used to say to me, 'Miles, fifteen to fifty, make sure there's not a blank page – you're going to hit the top and keep on going, boy.' In April 2005 the DC office decided my skill was good enough to export, so I was going to London.

He sits, stares front – sinister.

Tick tick tick… boom.

I had lent Hasib Mir Hussain ten pence to buy a Mars Bar ten minutes before he boarded a bus to Hackney Wick and pressed detonate. He killed himself and thirteen other people that day. I, the one American on board, got out alive. I figure that would have pissed him off, right? Maybe he didn't catch the accent or maybe he was grateful for his final Mars Bar so he gave me some space.

I incurred some memory loss. Things broke up a little, fractured – so to speak. Everything from before the accident had a hard time holding together.

University College Hospital informed my family of my injuries and told them I would return stateside as soon as I was able. Merrill Lynch covered the cost, and I was booked to fly back to Dulles Airport, Washington DC, BA first class, August 2nd 2005.

My mother and my pregnant wife were waiting; they were excited to be having me home.

I think about Hasib Mir Hussain a lot. They printed his photo in the newspaper a week after the accident. I carry it in my pocket. He looked young, kinda dopey, he was lost. I remember his face when he asked me for the ten pence, he smiled at me. He didn't look like a murderer; he looked like a kid that was happy to have ten pence. He bit into that chocolate bar like a kid that knew it was the last chocolate bar he was ever going to taste. I'm glad I lent him that money. I owe him.

The night my flight left, I stayed in Heathrow Airport in a coffee shop; I just sat and watched the world walk past me. Everyone hiding behind newspapers or with music in their ears, eyes down and solitary but always acting like somebody was watching, performing, in their own tiny little music videos. I watched all those people, like a million little Charlies all hunting for the golden ticket, all desperate to believe that the chocolate factory still exists.

And then the sun rose, and I walked. I walked out of the departure lounge, out of Heathrow Airport, I walked onto a train, I walked out of Paddington Station, I walked through the city of London. That was the day I walked away.

He shifts from being dazed and controlled into a kind of commercial fever, choosing, spending, buying.

Eventually I walked into a tailor's. The guy asks me what kind of suit I wanted. I had no idea, I say, 'A suit like this one,' I say. I got three suits like this one. I walked into Starbucks, the guy asks what kind of coffee, I say, 'Coffee, just coffee.' 'Yeah but what kind?' he asks. 'I don't care,' I say, 'Just coffee.' I ordered a cab, I ordered a hotel room, 'Which room sir?'; I don't know, I don't care, it doesn't matter.

For the first six months following the explosion in Tavistock Square, I woke every day at 6 a.m., I ran for two hours, I showered, I dressed, I read the newspaper front to back and I was ready for my day. During those six months I stayed in fifteen different hotels, I fucked over two hundred women, consumed one hundred and sixty-seven grams of cocaine, and drank nearly two thousand units of alcohol. By December 31st 2006, I was nearly dead. During Christmas week the world had not afforded me any human interaction.

Early in the New Year, I started getting low on funds. I returned to Merrill Lynch and explained to them that the accident had led to my absence and necessitated my resignation. As I had hoped, I received a handsome golden handshake. I was speaking to my manager, Billy Driscoll. Fifteen floors up on King Edward Street:

'They want you home, Miles.'

'Sir.'

'I have a responsibility to tell them where you are.'

'Sir.'

'You know they think you are dead, Miles?'

Pause.

'Yes, sir.'

He didn't ring them. I don't know why. Maybe he thought they were better off without me, it would've been the first thing Billy Driscoll and I had ever agreed on. So I was dead. It was a year and a half since my accident and I'd finally died, I could stop running. If I was dead, I was free. Free of the suit, free of the wedding band, free of... free of fatherhood – I could do what the fuck I wanted – guilt-free.

After all you can't blame a guy for dying.

He punches the air, he's triumphant, crazed, he is possessed by the power of his freedom.

I felt like the elect! Like I'd been given a second bite of the cherry. I spent three months feeling and acting like a superhero. With Hasib Mir Hussain, Merrill Lynch and death as my benefactors, I was loaded and liberated. I looked right, I talked right – I fucked right – I was the American all-star once again, but this time without any of the weight. I'd cheated the system. I fucked a lot, I drank a lot, I spent, a lot. Paris, Milan, Berlin, Tokyo – I ate the best food, drunk the best wine, stayed in the best hotels and people fucking loved me for it. They chose to be around me – men marvelled at me and women wanted me. Now, they couldn't have me because there was nothing to have but they didn't know that. To them, my inaccessibility was a mark of quality. They couldn't get what they wanted and women will always love you for that. It was so easy – onto yachts, into penthouses, into pussy – easy as fucking pie.

A break in pace.

And did I feel guilty? Did I feel guilty for the life I was leading – no. The actions of Hasib Mir Hussain on July 7th 2005 had made one thing very clear to me – that my existence was incidental. I had stayed alive because it had taken some time to get the change for my fare out of my pocket, because I had chosen to sit at the front and not the back of a bus; I had stayed alive because, having paid for his chocolate bar, I thought Hasib Mir Hussain might have wanted to make conversation and, frankly, I wasn't in the mood. I had stayed alive because I was

an anti-social fuck. I was alive by chance and chance alone.
Now, ask if I feel guilty – you show me the point of right and
wrong when the difference between dead and alive is that tiny.
What? You think I should be scared of not going to heaven? His
or mine? Huh?

And the payback? The justice for walking away? For having
spent my daughter's first birthday fucking a hooker called
Lissi? For being that kind of man? There is none. If you agree
to walk and you keep on walking – if you stay dead – it just
disappears – conscience, guilt, bullshit – as long as you don't
look back, easy as fucking pie.

But eventually you'll wonder, you'll wonder when it happened,
on which day it became impossible for you to pick up a phone,
on which day it was you could no longer walk through the door
and take back what you gave away – you'll wonder when it
became irreparable. And when you wonder you'll wonder
yourself into the realisation that your escape has trapped you,
and you'd kill for someone to give you an out, for someone to
do something that justifies your behaviour.

As I said, I think about Hasib Mir Hussain a lot – I owe him.

*Voiceover: 'This is the final call for passenger Cooper to board
flight BA293 to Washington. This is the final call, can passenger
Cooper go straight to Gate 13.'*

Last week the Missing Persons Bureau received a call – Miles
Cooper was staying in the Dorchester Hotel, London. The bomb
blasts of July 7th 2005 had caused him retrograde and
temporary antereograde memory loss – he called it global
amnesia. Three years on and his memory had returned – he
could remember snapshots, shards, flickers, facts.

Here's the facts. My name is Miles Cooper, born in Washington
DC, 1982. I've won everything I've ever touched. My father
used to say to me, 'Miles, fifteen to fifty, make sure there's not a
blank page – you're going to hit the top and keep on going,
boy.' On July 7th 2005 I had lent Hasib Mir Hussain ten pence
to buy a chocolate bar, ten minutes before he boarded the bus to
Hackney Wick and pressed detonate. I can now remember that I

am a husband and a father, but unfortunately nothing else of the last three years – blank pages, so to speak. Today is my little girl's third birthday. I am flying home. My family will be happy to see me – easy as fucking pie.

Blackout.

MILLIE

Millie is an apparently well-to-do lady, in her early thirties, dressed in tennis whites and wielding a tennis racket. She is mid-mime, straddling an imaginary middle-aged man, flailing wildly…

She recites the first verse of John Betjeman's 'A Subaltern's Love Song'.

She smiles a motherly smile down at her 'tennis' partner and dismounts.

There we go, Robert, all done. Gosh, I always forget how much the old tetrameter really sets a pace, I'm puffed! (*Brushes herself down.*) Well, you better be getting back to your wife then – parents' evening tonight, isn't it? Well… luck to Amber and don't be beastly to her –

She turns and accidentally sees him in some sort of state of undress, and turns prudishly back to face forward, stumbling over her words.

– Oh, sorry, don't be beastly to her, I'm sure she's just creative rather than academic, we can't all go to – oh, you're done, excellent! If you could pop the cheque on the table by the door as usual and I'll see you Tuesday. Bye now! Bye bye.

She waves, smiling, until he leaves.

Robert Kendrick, lovely chap, massive fan of Betjeman, hats and slacks and fifties sensibilities. He hasn't dealt with the end of it all one little bit. Still longs for the soft twilight of a Surrey evening, cricket on warm afternoons, cardigans, and Pimm's. He's quite the old romantic, actually – (*Gets a cup of tea.*) – demands I recite Betjeman every time we 'have a cup of tea'. Robert shares Betjeman's passion for the robust lady – 'The strongly adorable tennis-girl's hand' – I try my best but I'm no Sharapova. It's so difficult keeping the scansion straight with all that flailing, and when he demands I climax on those bloody dactyls, well, it's a tricky business, I can tell you. But Betjemen it is, he can't get enough of it. It's so hard for him, he despairs of his eldest, Amber, she's doing some sort of Gender Politics nonsense. He can't understand all that. No, Robert's education is more of the classical genre: Homer, Virgil, Plato – (*Pronounced with a hard 'g' and 'plah-toh' respectively.*) – who I always get mixed up with Pilates, but they're totally different. That's where we started, actually, with the classics. Then we tiptoed on up, through Donne, where we 'sucked on country pleasures', then a little raunchy Rochester, got very quickly bored by all those mild-mannered Victorians and ended up at Betjeman – blissfully short and comprehensible, really cuts down on a lot of bedtime reading. Very few people appreciate the kind of dedication that my line of business requires.

She looks at her watch.

Oop, listen to me gabble, only ten minutes 'til Thomas arrives, better start preparing those potatoes! It's Saturday morning, you see, busiest time of the week for me. It's ever since that *Saturday Morning Kitchen* lot set up, it's been tantamount to an invasion, suddenly Delia was off and that Antony Worrell Thompson was on. The results for my boys have been disastrous. Delia, Pru Leith, even good old Mrs Beeton in her day, they were role models, kept us girls on the straight and narrow – family values. But all these new Antony Worrell Thompson types have got wives across the country salivating over their slowly rising soufflés. You know what it is? It's all that feminism guff, it's led to such injustice. Along comes Nigella and – oop, televisions off, wives suddenly not interested. The minute their lovely hubbies want to indulge in a little gastro-porn of their own, it's unacceptable, disgusting even: 'Ooh, look at her, Jane,' they say. 'She's so gluttonous, so greedy, feeding her big fat face, oh look.'

Take my next client, Thomas Bishop, perfect example. He came to me last week and as he was having the little post-coital cry that he likes, do you know what he said to me, he said, 'Millie... do you know what?'

I said, 'No, Thomas… what?'

He said, 'I watched my wife orgasm last night, Millie.'

'Why, Thomas,' I said, 'Surely that's a good thing…?'

'To a Marks & Spencer's advert, Millie,' he said 'To a Marks & bloody Spencer's advert, just as all this cream cheese was oozing out of a burger… she squealed. I've never heard her make that noise before. And they're right, you know, Millie, this is not just food… this is adultery.'

Sad, isn't it? Watching it all fall apart like that. So I offer my services, I look after these lovely husbands, I take in the waifs and strays. I say, come one, come all. Come Rogers and Roberts, come Harrys and Humphreys, come to Millie Faucett-Reid's, she'll wipe your furrowed brow, press your shirt, serve a Sunday roast and offer a good, old-fashioned bonk, all within the hour. A traditional service at traditional prices.

Anyway, due to Thomas's new found 'gastronomic insecurity', his demands have become somewhat specific. Initially we thought we could combat the problem with a little role-play. If I became the food, he could triumph over me. Only, all we could find was a carrot outfit, and he had to sort of topple me into the bed, and penetration was a nightmare, so that ended quick-smart. Besides, he decided that to triumph over the food was not enough; if his wife lusted after grub, he must become said nosh. And there we had it, the breakthrough, he became the banger and I… let's just say I've had mashed potato in some very funny places.

Ooh, my tea! (*Runs back over to abandoned teacup.*) You see, absolutely everything is on the move for these men. Corduroys and a quiet country pub simply don't cut it any more. Women are being spoiled. They want new-age, new money, metrosexuality. My boys don't understand all that. Lovely Thomas wouldn't know a piece of pak choi if it boshed him in the face. No, my loafer-wearing warriors weren't made for yoga and tofu; they are men, soldiers, child soldiers, trained to make money and climb ruthlessly through what was once the glittering hierarchy of the British class system.

And then it came, the blackest of Wednesdays, the economic crash of '92. I was sixteen at the time, new to the profession, somewhat of a debutante, trained by my mother, but I could see what was happening, I could taste the terrible change in the air. I remember gasps and cries from my mother's bedroom, the tears of great men soaked her pillow that year. But as the economy crashed, FTSE falling... left, right and centre... my mother's takings soared. In they came, the soulless sound of a thousand wing-tipped brogues crossing the threshold. The day we pulled out of the ERM, my mother held the Right Honourable Sir John Major whilst he sobbed. He cried 3.4 billion tears that night. And that wasn't the worst of it: a thirteen-per-cent fall in the Conservative majority. Who can stand after that, I ask you? What man can hold his head high knowing that... Labour has got its grubby hands on power? They were done for, my Rogers and Roberts, my Harrys and Humphreys, finished. Oh, and it didn't take their wives long to philander: personal trainers, plumbers, mug-ugly football types – these were the men with money now, while my educated angels of the eighties, my proud boys, broken, faithless, unemployed.

So I came to my position with a passion for reinvigoration. Here, my boys could feel history, legitimacy and institution. My family have been in the industry of marital supplements for over five hundred years, we count Nell Gwyn amongst our own. And we're not going to stop now, no sir. 'We will not falter,' there, see, above the door, so they know, no matter what price is offered –

She stands to attention using the only salute she really knows, the Brownie salute.

I will never bed a Beckham
Nor bonk a barra boy,
The Faucett-Reids
Will mount their steeds
But never, ever the hoi-palloi!

She mimes spitting.

And I've been challenged on it too. Susie booked me a client last October, she does all my admin, I find it such a fiddle. Anyway, she let him past on account of his title, a title which, if you ask me, proves that even our dear old Queen can have an off day. I was all dressed up in my crimson corset, I usually find the aristocracy like a bit of bodice-ripping. So leg up, crop out, ready to receive my thoroughbred, when who should walk in the door but that bloody Alan Sugar! Oof – I was incensed! That four-foot-high, Furby-faced, epitome of everything that is wrong with this country. Predictably vulgar, he simply dropped his trousers and demanded a little 'how's your father'. Well, I firmly told him and his tic-tac to leave the building quick-smart.

She has already worked herself up and she tries to rein in this passion initially in the following lines, but it slowly builds until she cracks, revealing herself.

You see, we can't be doing with this… infiltration, this weakening. So much that is so beautiful will be lost. Everything, everything with meaning is under attack. My boys were once the best of British and now they're laughable – these are the chaps that made Britain great. Soon there won't be a Labrador or a welly in sight, then who'll be sorry, eh? I know I will. Let's keep our gentlemen, gentlemen, eh? Give them supper at eight, meat and two veg, let them play cricket at the weekend, I'd give anything to keep that alive, almost anything to be one of those wives.

She stumbles on the last word, repeating it, catching herself out, revealing too much. During the final line she composes herself, building up the mask again.

Come on, Millie, you silly old stick. Thomas'll be here soon. Better get those potatoes on the boil.

Blackout.

ASTRID

*Astrid is in her early twenties. She is slim and attractive, the
kind of girl that seems comfortable in her own skin. Tonight,
however, she is a little drunk. She is returning from a night out
and is dressed accordingly. There is a bed in the centre of the
stage – the audience can see a man sleeping in it. She slowly
climbs into bed next to the man – desperately trying not to wake
him. She lies there, restless for several seconds, then
sits up.*

People talk about guilt as if it's an instinct. That the second you
do something wrong, you feel guilty. I don't; what I'm feeling
is power. You always join the story at the bit where they're
sorry, when they're desperately begging for forgiveness; but
there's something before that, there's now. In the space after the
act and before the consequences, when you've got away with it;
when you're walking out of an unknown door, back down
unknown streets and it's still thumping in you – dawn's
breaking, dew's settling and you're skipping back home, flying
on the thrill of it, you can taste it. Even back here, the quiet
click of the door, the tiptoe in – the alcohol's wearing off too
quickly, I want it back – our bed and all the stuff that makes up
life, our life – and – I don't feel like a traitor; I can lie here
whilst another man's saliva dries off my lips and I can
remember another man's face bearing over me – and I enjoy it, I
enjoy that all this seems new again.

His alarm's going off in ten minutes. He'll roll over and grunt,
curl himself round me like a monkey with its bloody mum. Just
like every morning. He won't notice that anything's different –
he won't see that I have mascara down my face or that my hair
is wet, because I've been running in the rain to get back before
he wakes up, he won't notice that I haven't been here, that I'm
drunk, no – for him, I became invisible a long time ago.

She jumps up onto the bed and starts to inspect him, creeping around him as if he's an anthropological specimen.

That's not even snoring, is it? Listen? It's definitely more aggravating than breathing, but it doesn't quite have the conviction of a snore. Nope... just a slow dribble of air, as if it was engineered to be as aggravating as humanly possible; sort of like a tiny pony having a tantrum.

He sniffles slightly.

Oop – oh, that's nice, isn't it, a little wind from the baby. Having been with someone else, it's like I've left the room for the first time in years, and come back in and realised... this is the man that I once thought I might marry.

The man spreads himself across the whole bed; she jumps up and out of the way to avoid him.

Ah, and here we have – the spread. (*Mimics a wildlife programme presenter.*) Allowing air to all orifices at once, in vain hopes of ventilation, the male of the species spreads himself, much like a starfish, allowing little or no room for the female of the species to co-exist with him in the domestic habitat. It's as if she wasn't even there.

She shakes her head dismissively and climbs down.

It won't even occur to him that I could have done what I have. There could be all three of us in this bed and I still don't think it would cross his mind. That much trust... yesterday it made us strong, this morning it makes him weak.

Look at him. The sleep of the innocent, or ignorant... either way, it's bliss. For once I have him in my hands, ten minutes' time, he wakes up, and I make the call – I tell him or I don't tell him.

Let's say I tell him...

The sleeping man rouses and plays out the following scene in silence as she reacts.

He'll stare and gulp, breaths – big heavy breaths – then the anger will rise, he'll stand and it'll seem like something might break in him. (*He grabs her and roughly throws her onto a seat, she remains placid.*) And I will just sit, in silence – I'll squeeze my eyes shut and try not to hear him, because he might say some things that are true, about what kind of person this makes me, and I won't want to hear that. I don't want to see what I've done in his face.

The man puts his hand, softly now, under her chin and pulls her face round.

Then he'll make me look at him, and I'll remember how he can be soft – and he'll try to make me understand, to make me feel what he is feeling, realise how much I've ruined, but I won't. I won't feel what he will feel because I haven't had anything taken from me; what we've lost, I gave it away – but he, he's had it stolen from him.

The man gets back into bed.

But really, really what he'll feel, is a sense of thievery, and everything that I thought was soft and feeling will have been his ego speaking. He'll want to know, who the other man was, how big his dick was, if he was better in bed – this baffles me as a question. I mean, it's bold, isn't it, that, that 'Was he better than me?' I feel I want to offer some kind of recap, show him some clips of the last six months and then give him the chance to rethink the question. Here's the top three; him burping vindaloo on me as he ejaculated, the synchronisation was incredible, then there was me asking him to stop so I could remove his toenail clippings from beneath me because they were digging into my back, and finally the seven-pint impotence, Yeats had it spot on, it's like trying to stuff a muscle into a slot machine. And yet he'll still ask, 'Was he better than I am?' and if I respond honestly – 'Yes, Ben, he was much better in bed than you – it's barely even a contest…' then I'll be lying.

Break. She sits.

I've done the same – I've asked that question. I do remember how it feels – I remember being the unwitting victim. (*Softly approaches his sleeping head, says it to him:*) Sleeping quietly and faithfully, and then it's said or you just know – and then you're angry or more, desperate, to stop the moment when you accept your insignificance; when you realise that you were not enough. So you try to defend it, 'Was she better than I was? Hmm, bigger tits, eh?' and you realise you wouldn't be asking if the answer wasn't yes. And then? Then the visuals – you imagine him with her, the room, her cheap knickers on the floor, you like to think they're cheap – they're probably not, they are probably more expensive, more see-through, more size-eight than yours have ever been – and then you see his hands on her, his face in the moment that you are entirely forgotten. You wonder whether during the hour that he's fucking her, if you even crossed his mind – and you know you didn't.

She turns back to the sleeping man.

And you wonder whether during the past year and a half you even crossed his mind and you know you didn't.

But he – he was never entirely forgotten – no, no – I didn't forget him for a second. He was in every pant, and gasp, in every drink that got me drunk enough, drunk enough to want to see what it might take to make me visible. Such deliberate infidelity; it won't have been enough. Stay or go, tell him or don't tell him; to him it won't really make the slightest difference. Once you're invisible there's no way left to win, no buttons left to push. You see, the first one to stop loving has it – get left in the game and you're fucked.

She goes as if to leave the room, hesitates at the door and returns and climbs back into bed with the sleeping man.

Blackout.

Buttons was the first of these monologues to be written. It was performed by Henry Peters at a scratch night called *Candlewasters* at Bedlam Theatre, Edinburgh, early in 2008.

Buttons was left out of the final line-up of *Eight* because his syndrome was too niche to appeal to the wide demographic at the Fringe – he was a little too weird. I am, however, incredibly fond and proud of this monologue; this ninth man, is, after all, where it all began.

BUTTONS

'Buttons' is a well-built, tensile-looking man in his mid-thirties, grunting his way through press-ups on the floor of a prison cell. The room contains a grubby campbed, a dilapidated toilet, a desk and a chair. He will reach the end of a ten-year jail sentence tomorrow morning. He knows the small space well, it fits him and he owns it. There is a sense of latent sexual and physical power about the man.

I often dream I'm a Victorian gent, suited and booted; top hat 'n all. Head high, nose in the air, I'd 'ave those funny little white things that fit just over the top a your shoes and with the nimblest of fingers I'd apply myself to the tiny spines of buttons running up the sides of the clean, white material. Buttons... them buttons, black, black buttons... patent, shining, glinting into the beady little eyes of all them Victorian guttersnipes that'd snatch at my feet as I swaggered past. I'd be dead good at swaggering too, elite swaggerations, Captain Swagger, hung like a horse; the kind a genitalia that makes a swagger a practical necessity rather than an aesthetic choice. Me 'ands stuffed into those unfeasibly small, velvety little pockets, feet

clacking, teeth glinting – and I'd be off to frequent a
wenchsome establishment.

The wench, *my* wench, would be called... let me think, she'd be
called – Ruby Tease. She'd love me... proper, unquenchable,
salivating, lusty-type love, snatching at me, needing me all the
time. Her feet would stay strapped tight into gripping, turgid
little leather hooves of shoes, studded with those filthy little
golden buttons, globular and glintin' – and – and – I'd rip 'em
off, hold her fast and do her every which way. All those lovely
Victorian ruffles scrunching in fistfuls... and she'd never stop
smiling – cos she'd love me, proper love, cuddles-afterward
love. She'd never make me pay; she'd just grin in a thank-you-
very-much sort a way and I'd just walk away; free into my
freedom, paying nothing and taking everything – magic, pure,
human magic.

But then, when it's late and dark and I'm sitting here, deep
into year three of this eight-by-ten grey igloo of an existence,
and I'm so bored of staring at my own knob that I start to play,
say, that game of... 'If my knob got trapped under a rock
whilst out climbing in the Rockies, as I may well be of a day,
and my only chance of survival was to lop the fucker off...
how would I go about such a thing...?' I'm skirting through
thoughts of penknives and razor-teethed racoons when all of a
sudden, Ruby returns to my thoughts, only this time she ain't
playing nice.

In this little ponderment, she's ripped the shiny black buttons
right off a my shoes and they're glinting between her teeth...
she's awfully angry, see. Her salivating, lusty-type love has
turned to the incendiary kind, the kind that busts out a things,
breaks doors, strains seams, scratches cheeks and draws blood,
and I'm scared – I envision my Ruby's spitting fury and I know
from the fire in her eyes that I have become the only man that
matters to her – and so in my little Victorian, stuck-cock,
dreamworld, I do the only thing I can do, the only thing that's
kind; I smite her pretty little head against a wall, dash her
brains. And all of a sudden-like, in my little cell-bound fantasy,
my knob is free; I am free, out from under that colossal boulder.

But I ain't got no buttons on my shoes, I always went with
Adidas Superstars – half-shell, not whole, greater flexibility for
the all-star ducker and diver, see, but in 'ere they don't let you
have the laces so I had to resort to the Stan Smith Velcro
variety. I told 'em, I could just as easily top myself with Velcro,
but they quite sensibly asked for a demonstration and truth be
told, I came off lookin' a little silly.

I did get my way with the work-shirt situation though. When
you enter the unit they issue you a costume of T-shirts, shirts
and trousers – all having been inhabited by previous ne'er-do-
wells, trusting, I suppose, that criminality ain't contagious. For
transport into the unit they asked me to put on this work shirt,
buttons straight up the front, the fiddly see-through-little-
fuckers sort. I flipped my fucking lid – 'No way!' – I screamed
and I kept screamin' 'til they brought the psych in. He had a
kind old doctor face; said I was unusual but he'd seen it before,
referred to my case notes. Sparky little number, he was; saw I
wasn't lyin' soon enough, and I got to wear them beautiful
button-free roundnecks for the rest of my stay at Her Majesty's
pleasure.

I'm no freak, there are loadsa people out there with the same
problem. You read stuff about folk getting nosebleeds when
they touch 'em, or making their mates wear roundnecks on
nights out cos the idea of a full-button shirt makes 'em vomit. I
went to this group-therapy thing once just when it started; I
was sixteen, I think. Mum made me go cos the lawyers had
claimed my button phobia was at the root of my apparently
aggressive disposition. I told the court it was a big bad 'four-
holer' cut free of the granny's cardie that made me belt her
round the head, nothing to do with her recently replenished
pension book... But I must admit, in hindsight, it was probably
a combination of the two.

This therapy shit was mental, it was sort of group hypnotism
stuff, 'cept no one really got hypnotised, they were all just there
with their massive made-up button phobias trying to get away
from wives or parole officers. There was this one guy, Tobias;
some joker sent to button therapy by his wife, he'd convinced

her that he was so scared of the little buttony-munchkins that he had to stick 'em up his arse when he found one. Apparently that was the only place they couldn't get at him. But it was clear as day that his button therapy was more of 'I like it up the bum and I've got a wife' therapy, kinky fucker.

It angered me, you know, that the Tobiases of this world were just out for thrifty kinks and were using my very serious and troublesome disorder as some sort of excuse. I was for ever getting in scrapes because of it. Buttons just seem to sit on the sidelines of my life and just jump in, in all their terrifying discoid splendour, at moments when all I'd needed was a clear head. Just like with that granny, the free-falling freedom of three centimetres of circular plastic and suddenly I'm clockin' her round the noggin and stealing her bag.

Similar thing happened with a young Brazilian lady called Cildo, the very sound of which... as you can imagine... made me want to do the horridest things to her. Admittedly I was asking for trouble as she was part of my buttony-nutters therapy group. She invited me back to hers for a little after-hours therapy, all sweet and unassuming-like, I wasn't to know, really, was I. There I was, all de-boxered, standing to attention, gazing up at a ready-to-roll Cildo, when swift as a feckin' whippet, my new phobic friend opens the drawer of her bedside table, pops on a pair of latex and apparently button-resistant gloves, and starts pelting me, ten to the dozen, with all shapes and sizes of 'em, screaming, 'Dirty, nasty, wrong button-lover... dirty, nasty, wrong button-lover.' She'd been through a good ten repetitions and I had fucking awful bruising by the time I managed to re-boxer and get the fuck out of there. Nutjob, I tell ya, button nutjob.

You see, with behaviour like that, and with my heightened sense of anxiety due to my Johnson sitting there all vulnerable and eager, it's little wonder that I threw something back; admittedly it didn't have to be a bottle, and no I didn't have to smash it first, but it was close at hand and I was very angry. The buttons made me do it, I swear to you... they freak the shit out of me and they were *everywhere*. I needed to make her stop... and once she had, once she'd gone very, very quiet and all her thick, dark Brazilian hair just lay about her quiet head... then I was calm, and sorry, really calm and really sorry. You see, it's all sort of explicable, sort of understandable with just a little hindsight and a comprehension of the mitigating circumstances... factor in a few buttons here and there, and suddenly I ain't so evil after all.

Tomorrow morning, having done my time in here for the granny and that bottle I stabbed into that filthy little buttony Cildo, I am walking free. I'll pop on my metaphorical top hat and velvety waistcoat, and stick my dirty little hands in the teeny little metaphorical pockets and clack my dapper shoes that glint their dazzling black leather, into the eyes of all the pokey grubbers at my feet. I will strut to see my Ruby Tease and clench fistfuls of her Victorian ruffles whilst I gruntingly exhale the pleasures of my freedom; and I hope I won't be back, stuck back in here with my cock under that rock again; cooped up and riled, tensile and angry... but I don't know. All depends, doesn't it? Buttons or no buttons, it's all about them buttons, I'm telling you – mitigating circumstances, psych said so – see, I ain't so evil.

Blackout.

HOT MESS

'Love is a fashion these days… we know how to make light of love and how to keep our hearts at bay. I thought of myself as a civilised woman and I discovered that I was a savage.'

Jeanette Winterson, The Passion

'I love you can only ever be taken to mean "for now" – my words were time-bound promises, a truth too disturbing for most relationships to fully take on board.'

Alain de Botton, Essays on Love

'The intensity of life with somebody and the sense of it passing has its own pathos and poignancy. There was a sense of futility about it all disappearing into the void and I just wanted to pin something down that would defy time, so it wouldn't all just go off into thin air.'

Frank Auerbach, note for 'Head of E.O.W' IV.

Author's Note

Hot Mess was written in response to a series of interviews and conversations that I had with girls in their late teens and early twenties in the spring of 2010. These interviews revealed a high number of girls that claimed to enjoy and indeed demand sex with no emotional investment. It occurred to me that today's society has a paradoxical relationship with 'connection'. We are more connected than ever and yet each connection means less. *Hot Mess* questions the inherent significance of sexual practice; have we successfully socialised ourselves so that we can enjoy the act of sex separately from its emotional implications? *Hot Mess* focuses on the dialectic between those that love and those that fuck – and proposes that if casualness becomes the norm then love must be marginalised. I am fascinated by what happens to people if they are forced into those margins; I believe that this is where fundamentalism grows. If we make freaks of those that are still capable of connection, those that still believe that things can endure, then what will those people be driven to?

Production Note

Hot Mess was originally written to be performed in a nightclub, in the round. The only props used were those that would otherwise be found in this setting; glasses, straws, bottles, etc. No additional lighting or sound equipment was installed. The technical manager, the impossibly skilled Xander Macmillan, ran all the lights and sound from the DJ booth. The members of the audience could see him and each other at all times.

Music was, obviously, incredibly important to the premise of the show. We worked with the contrast between contemporary club hits and the acoustic music played by Twitch. Gwendolen Chatfield, the original Twitch, reworked club hits into acoustic pieces in order to develop this idea. We also used 'One Thousand Miles', an original piece written by Gwendolen.

The audience were seated in the round, circling the dance floor. They had their hands stamped on entry, by Polo and Jacks, one stamp saying 'HOT' the other 'MESS'. Coats were taken, money was paid – from start to finish *Hot Mess* aimed to replicate the nightclub experience.

It is, however, also possible to stage the show in a traditional theatre space. The scenes in *Hot Mess* are written as units with the intention of emphasising the fact that the story can be told in many different ways. The text, as it stands, is representative of the first staging, and all the stage directions have been included to conjure this. Subsequent directors are, of course, encouraged to start afresh.

Acknowledgements

I would like to thank Michael Whitham, Gwendolen von Einsiedel, Kerri Hall, Solomon Mousley, Ellie Chalmers and Xander Macmillan without whom this play would not have made it to the stage. I thank them for their contributions to the script and the staging and for a fun summer. It was a pleasure and a privilege to work with such a talented team and such good friends.

I would like to thank Ben Harrison, Katherine Mendelsohn and Simon Stephens for their help and tutelage whilst the script was being written.

Finally, I would like to thank Jessie Buchanan and Izzy Quilter for being impossibly tolerant, for drinking more tea and listening to more moaning than anyone should ever have to.

Hot Mess was first performed at the Hawke & Hunter Below
Stairs Nightclub, Edinburgh, on 6 August 2010, as part of the
Edinburgh Festival Fringe, with the following cast:

TWITCH	Gwendolen Chatfield
POLO	Michael Whitham
JACKS	Kerri Hall
BILLY	Solomon Mousley

Director	Ella Hickson
Technical Manager	Xander Macmillan
Producer	Eleanor Chalmers for Tantrums Ltd

Characters

TWITCH, *twenty-five, gamine – Polo's twin sister*
POLO, *twenty-five, cool and caustic – Twitch's twin brother*
JACKS, *twenty-six, well-tanned and big-breasted*
BILLY, *twenty-four, American, good-looking*

Preset

The audience are made to queue outside of the club. On entry they pay or hand in prepaid tickets, and have their hands stamped by JACKS *and* POLO. *A VIP cordon is removed by a bouncer and they are allowed into the club. The DJ plays a short set, contemporary club hits. The audience are free to buy drinks from the bar and seat themselves.*

'She Said' by Plan B plays from the DJ booth. TWITCH *enters playing acoustic guitar, she sings an acoustic version of 'She Said'. Slowly the club version sinks away, so that only* TWITCH *can be heard.* TWITCH *sings two choruses, on the second time she reaches 'stop this crazy talk',* POLO *enters, stares at her, smiles.* TWITCH *stops playing. Removes her guitar and places it at the side. The club lights turn totally blue; we can hear the sound of the sea. The twins are telling us a story.*

One

POLO. The island is small; five miles by two, no more.

TWITCH. It sits tucked into the Solent. There is one way on and one way off.

POLO. When you come across the bridge you've got two choices:

TWITCH. Left for Northeny – the big houses, the posh bit –

POLO. Or straight on –

TWITCH. You head on the main road into the heart of the island, Mill Ryhthe, Sinah Warren, Mengham, the salon, The Hut. Take West Lane and you end up in West Town which, I suppose, makes sense and beyond all that –

POLO. Well, it's an island.

Beat.

TWITCH. There's the sea.

POLO. It comes in from every angle.

TWITCH. It keeps us calm, it holds us tight, it tucks us in.

People that live by the sea –

POLO. Walkers, talkers…

TWITCH. I used to sleep with the boat radio by my bed at night and tune it in to the coastguard. Right through the night, stories swam in from the sea, right into my ears. The great adventures of –

POLO. Mayday mayday, we've found a –

TWITCH. Lifeboat men trying to save boys that thought they were bigger than the waves.

POLO. Mayday – we've found a – off the coast of –

TWITCH. The sea. It keeps us calm, it holds us tight, it tucks us in.

POLO. She used to say –

TWITCH. That the island would sink with all those stories.

POLO. Like the one they'd always told –

TWITCH. About Polo and me.

POLO *and* TWITCH *approach the DJ booth. They pick up a glass each;* TWITCH *a tumbler,* POLO *a martini glass. Both are half full with water. The water stands for the heart throughout the scene. They chink the glasses, the lights change, the sound of the sea stops. A new state. They take a step forward, smile warmly at the audience. Glasses in hands, narration begins again.*

POLO. They didn't know that they were in for a duo.

TWITCH. When they pulled him out, feet first, he bawled himself deathly 'til they cut the cord, 'til they wiped the mess and muck off him. From the second he was free: snip, wipe and wash him down – he simmered, he calmed, he sparkled – it was like the boy could only breathe when he was squeaky-clean.

POLO. They'd only banked on one; they said they'd only seen one.

TWITCH. They said I'd been hiding.

POLO. So they only got my grinner on the screen.

TWITCH. Polo was striking a pose for the ultrasound.

POLO. Sepia; even skin tone. Dream.

TWITCH. Two babies laid on scales.

POLO. A blip in the bureaucracy – there were two and they'd only planned on one.

TWITCH. Polo's clean by now so he's stopped crying.

POLO. But Twitch is still covered in –

POLO *struggles to say it – he looks at the water in his glass with disgust.*

TWITCH. – all that mess and muck. The red and the brown and the slime and the –

POLO. I'm silent and spotless.

TWITCH. I'm bawling and bloodied.

POLO. But there were two.

TWITCH. And nobody had told the heart department.

POLO. Nope.

TWITCH. Twins.

POLO. But only one heart had followed after.

POLO *pours all the water from his glass into* TWITCH's *glass.*

TWITCH. It was the surgeon's decision: one tiny beating fluttering thing.

TWITCH *delves her hand into the water, flutters her fingers about, the water flies everywhere.*

POLO. The surgeon, heart in hand, between his finger and his thumb, the little thing, flapping there – straining to break into one chest or another; big call.

POLO *cleanly balances the martini glass between his finger and thumb.*

TWITCH. He didn't know what to do, the case was unprecedented.

POLO. Two of us there – gasping for breath –

They gasp.

– in the clean, cold white of the delivery room.

TWITCH. One was red and bawling.

POLO. The other white and silent. And the heart –

TWITCH. 'The' did you hear? 'The heart'. Not his. Not Polo's.

TWITCH *looks longingly at the full glass of water.*

Mine.

TWITCH *gulps the water greedily, it spills, it dribbles down her chin.* POLO, *meanwhile, slowly rotates his empty martini glass, a final drip falls onto the floor.*

POLO. Twitch's. She was cup-full, brimming.

POLO *turns to look at* TWITCH, *her hand over her mouth, guilty.*

TWITCH. And Polo?

POLO. Likes a fine line, a good crease and clean nails.

TWITCH. Polo Calvino was not looking to be loved.

POLO. And Twitch, his kid sister –

TWITCH. Came a thousand seconds after –

POLO. And she could do nothing but – l– (*He stumbles.*)

TWITCH. Love.

POLO *exits.* TWITCH *kneels and plays with the water she has spilt.*

Two

TWITCH *is kneeling, spreading the spilt water into a heart shape. 'Sunny' by Bobby Hebb plays, we are on the beach. We can hear the sound of the sea, lights are soft, sunny.* BILLY *enters, the music fades.* POLO *watches.*

BILLY *walks over to* TWITCH *to try to talk to her, chickens out; walks past her.* TWITCH *sees,* TWITCH *smiles, turns to him.*

TWITCH. Hi.

BILLY. Hi.

Beat.

You're always here.

TWITCH. Um – yes, I suppose.

BILLY. You should come and hang out on the beach. The water's really warm.

TWITCH. Um – no, I –

BILLY. Oh, okay – that's fine – it doesn't matter – I –

TWITCH. I like the shade.

BILLY. What are you working on?

TWITCH. Sorry?

TWITCH *steps forward, covering the heart she has drawn on the floor.*

BILLY. I saw you earlier – it looked like you were drawing.

TWITCH. No.

BILLY. Sure?

TWITCH. Yeah.

BILLY. Cos you've got pen all over your finger.

TWITCH. No I haven't.

BILLY. Yes, you have.

BILLY takes her finger and shows her that it's inky. He licks his finger and rubs the ink off.

TWITCH. Oh, I was annotating my book; I star things, if I like them, underline, or –

BILLY. Right.

Still holding her finger – it's awkward for a moment. BILLY shakes her finger.

I'm Billy, by the way.

TWITCH. I'm Twitch.

BILLY. Would you like your finger back?

TWITCH. Not really.

POLO stands – Scene Three starts.

Three

Memory One.

TWITCH and BILLY become puppets enacting POLO's narration, expressionless. BILLY plays the part of all the boys mentioned in the memory scenes.

POLO. It was troublesome from the get-go. Kicked off in kindergarten, first sign of trouble – Jimmy Trinkoff, six years old, had soiled himself and it was no fault of his own.

BILLY *as* JIMMY. Mrs Cook! Mrs Cook! I made a puddle.

POLO. He'd been taught to put his hand up if he needed to go.

BILLY *as* JIMMY. Not my fault.

POLO. Twitch had taken a shine to little Jimmy; he'd held her hand in story-time. But then he'd told her he had to go, it was time to be off, time for the little boys' room.

BILLY *and* TWITCH *put their hands up at the same time; they are stuck.*

Superglue. She'd stuck herself to him, palm to palm; took the nurse two hours to get them apart.

BILLY *and* TWITCH *stand, wrestle their hands apart.*

There was so much of it that she'd ended up having to rip little Jimmy's skin. The nurse shouted at Twitch, told her she'd done a terrible thing, told her there would be a scar, that it would be there for the rest of Jimmy's life. Wherever he went, he'd always remember our Twitch. The tears stopped, suddenly, and where the tears had been a smile spread across her pretty face.

POLO, TWITCH *and* BILLY *exit.*

Four

JACKS *enters. We are in her bedroom. She uses the audience as a mirror, adjusts her cleavage, etc. Lady Gaga plays throughout the scene, 'Poker Face' and then 'Paparazzi'.*

POLO *enters unseen.* JACKS *turns, delighted, hugs him.*

JACKS. Pooooolooooooooooooo!

POLO. Kiss me – I'm old.

They hug.

They air-kiss and wipe the corners of their mouths.

JACKS. Happy bloody birthday, arse-face.

POLO. Thanks, bitch-tits.

JACKS. It's good to see you.

POLO. You got any drink?

JACKS *pulls out the front of her pants.*

JACKS. Look at this!

POLO. Uh, Jacks – my eyes just curdled!

JACKS. It's meant to be a Playboy Bunny but the ears don't look like ears, they look like – fingers, fingers flicking a freaking V – which means anyone going down there is going to think I've got a –

POLO. Hostile fanny.

JACKS. Exactly.

POLO. Is anyone here yet?

JACKS. Uh? Me.

POLO. Should have got them to trim a welcome mat in there.

JACKS. Funny.

POLO. Park-and-ride sign?

JACKS. Worst thing is it looks like I've made a fucking effort now.

POLO. A pubic rabbit wouldn't have looked like effort?

JACKS. No, it's a logo, isn't it.

POLO. And two fingers says 'I care'?

JACKS. God, it's good to see you. You look different.

POLO. I've aged, horribly. I'm a hag.

JACKS. No you're not.

POLO. I know, I've got the skin of a twelve-year-old boy… in a jar under my bed. Where is she?

JACKS. You're horrible! How's London?

POLO. Fine.

Beat.

JACKS. And?

POLO. And what?

JACKS. God, Polo, turn twenty-five and you turn into a total fucking buzz-kill, eh?

POLO. I've been ringing her all day but I haven't heard a thing.

JACKS. Fuck Uncle Fester. She'll turn up – she always does. Tonight it's you and me – the power team, reunited. We're like LiLo and that lezzer, Paris and Nicole, Cheryl and –

POLO. Laurel and Hardly.

JACKS. – Dannii.

POLO. Susan Boyle and her cat Pebbles.

JACKS. It's your fucking birthday!

POLO. Halfway to fifty. Where is she? You'd think she'd want to be on time.

JACKS. Oh God, it's so fucking good to see you!

POLO. Come on then, Jacqueline! Get some bloody crotch-swatches out. It's not a celebration unless half the island can see your ovaries!

JACKS. Waaaa! Guess what?

POLO. What?

JACKS. Caroline Granger, Meg Watson, Sophie Cooper.

POLO. Dream team. Not.

JACKS. Married.

POLO. Fuck me. Who the hell married Meg Watson and that mole?

JACKS. Nick Hastings. They've got a kid.

POLO. God, that's got to be one fucking ugly baby.

JACKS. It got the mole 'n' all. Meg brings it into the salon to get the little hairs removed, makes me want to puke.

POLO. Vomit stations.

JACKS. It's been a bit horrible, Polo.

POLO. I bet, I hate all the lying that's involved with an ugly baby and then they want you to touch it and put your face really close to it and it's all too –

JACKS. No. It's all been a bit horrible; without you.

POLO. Chica.

JACKS. Everyone's sold out, it's like the island's got smaller. The only thing there's any more of is rust.

Beat.

POLO. Which I see you've been bathing in?

JACKS. What?

POLO. You look like a Dorito.

JACKS. What? No I don't. I've just caught the sun.

POLO. You've caught something! It looks like you've been using HP for hand cream.

JACKS. Fuck off, dough-boy.

POLO. Pumpkin.

JACKS. Fish-flesh.

POLO. Basketball.

JACKS. Polar bear.

POLO. Tangerine.

JACKS. Ice queen.

POLO. Wotsit.

JACKS. Prawn cracker.

POLO. Yoke.

JACKS (*slow*). Yogurt-body. Coconut, marshmallow, Michelin Man.

POLO (*with aggression*). Neon cunting whore!

Silence descends for several seconds.

Come on! It's fucking party time!

JACKS. We'll do it like we used to. We'll get shit-faced, we'll drink 'til we can't stand and dance, dance 'til everything spins –

POLO. And they'll all be watching.

JACKS. Every set of eyes in the place – dragging on us –

POLO. Like tide round a –

JACKS. Buoy.

POLO. A good-looking boy!

JACKS. A perfect-looking boy!

POLO. Eyes like cameras.

JACKS. Each blink like a paparazzi snap.

POLO (*repeats as an echo*). 'Papa – papa – papa –'

JACKS. 'That's Polo and Jacks.'

POLO (*repeats as an echo*). 'That's Polo and Jacks.'

JACKS. 'Fuck me – she's hot!'

POLO. 'Fuck me – he's dreamy.'

JACKS. 'If only I could nail a girl like that.' Clawing at my pants they'll be – biting at the bit.

POLO. Your bits.

JACKS. You'll pick me a good one.

POLO. Tall, not too tall, well-built, charming not clever. Looks good, seems good, sounds good.

JACKS. Just enough to make me want to –

POLO. But not too much, can't have you falling.

JACKS. I'm no limp dick.

POLO. Course not.

JACKS. I snare him.

POLO. You fuck him – toilet, beach, bed, who cares, don't ask for his name.

JACKS. I won't give him mine if he asks.

POLO. You're done.

JACKS. I cum.

POLO. You leave.

JACKS. You laugh. I walk away feeling –

POLO. Powerful.

JACKS. Untouchable.

POLO. He –

JACKS. He?

POLO. Sees us high-five.

They high-five.

JACKS. He frowns.

POLO. Not sure he understands.

JACKS. Not sure he wants to understand.

POLO. Little boy blows out his chest and tries to stand like a man.

JACKS. You laugh!

POLO. You laugh! He looks like he might cry.

JACKS. We gave him one for womankind!

POLO. And so and so and so we drink until we go blind!

They laugh.

Beat.

JACKS. Polo?

POLO. Hm?

JACKS. New dresses didn't feel like new dresses when you weren't here.

Beat.

POLO. Have you got anything to drink?

JACKS. Downstairs, but don't go – we'll go later, when the taxi arrives.

POLO. I'm parched.

POLO goes to leave. JACKS flinches and grabs him.

JACKS. No.

POLO. Why?

JACKS. Don't.

POLO. I'm just going to say hi.

JACKS. Stay here. Please.

POLO. Why?

JACKS. She'll be washing up.

POLO. So?

JACKS. Stay!

POLO. Jacks?

JACKS. We're having fun!

POLO. Jacks. Get a grip – I'll be back in two minutes.

JACKS. She splashes around in the water because it covers the sound of her sniffing, but she forgets to wipe her face before she turns around, so she'll turn and grin at you, but she'll have red eyes and black tracks of mascara down her cheeks.

Beat.

Dad's gone.

POLO. Right.

Beat.

JACKS. Mum's a fucking buzz-kill these days.

POLO. When?

JACKS. About a year ago – just after you left.

POLO. And she's still blubbing?

JACKS. Yeah.

POLO. Fucking hell.

JACKS. Dad's pumping chicks left, right and centre – he's got it made. I just don't know what Mum thinks she's winning by not getting over it.

Beat.

POLO. Fairy-soft hands?

JACKS. Maybe.

POLO. Nobody likes a party pooper.

Beat.

JACKS. I can't bear to look at her before a night out. It makes me feel a bit sick.

POLO. Have you rung her?

JACKS. Who?

POLO. Twitch. She's nearly an hour late, we should ring her.

JACKS. Right.

POLO. I'm going downstairs to get a drink.

POLO *exits.* JACKS *stands a moment, exits.*

Five

TWITCH *grabs* BILLY *and drags him on stage. We can hear the sound of the sea. 'Sunny' by Bobby Hebb plays, lights are soft, we are on the beach.* TWITCH *talks to the audience unless otherwise indicated.* BILLY *is unaware of the audience throughout the scene.* POLO *watches.*

TWITCH. He has green eyes. When he gets out of the sea –

TWITCH *pours a glass of water over* BILLY*'s head; she rubs it through his hair. He shakes it off and dries himself on her T-shirt.*

I look at him and the water has stuck his eyelashes together in clumps. As they dry, the salt crystallises on the ends. It looks like he has tens of tiny magic wands where his eyelashes should be. Alacazam.

TWITCH *runs away from* BILLY*; he catches her, tucks her head under his arm.*

He's big enough that I fit into the crook of his arm. I rest my head on his chest – (*Does so.*) in one ear I can hear his heart and in the other, I can hear the sound of the sea.

The sound of the sea fades. They are in TWITCH*'s bedroom.* BILLY *pulls* TWITCH *down onto the floor; she rests on his chest and tries to speak to him. He's tired, he tries to sleep.*

(*To* BILLY.) When I was small –

BILLY. Hm?

TWITCH (*to* BILLY). I'd leave the window open when I went to sleep; I'd close my eyes and listen – I'd imagine that the waves were tucking me in.

BILLY. You're such a geek.

TWITCH (*to* BILLY). Oi. (*Beat.*) Don't you think afternoon sun is a special kind of sun?

BILLY. What?

TWITCH (*to* BILLY). The way it looks like lemonade on the duvet.

BILLY *tries to make* TWITCH *hush; he smothers her in a hug. She laughs, wriggles out and away from him, he curls, he sleeps.*

He sleeps, curled, comma-shaped – it looks like a comfortable alien has landed. I imagine that this might be the beginning of our story.

TWITCH *picks up her guitar and begins to play an acoustic version of 'Sex on Fire' by Kings of Leon. She sings initially to the sleeping* BILLY *and then to the audience; she builds complicity with them, she's mischievous, fun.*

TWITCH *stops singing, puts her guitar down. In hushes she begins to talk again.* BILLY *sleeps.*

Imagine ten years' time, kitchen table, friends. He catches my thigh as I walk from the door, holds me to him and laughs. (*Does an impression of* BILLY, *older.*) 'How did we meet? Ink, finger – you know. Long story.' His palm rises casually up my bum cheek onto my waist, friends look jealous. I smile – you should be. (*Back as* BILLY.) 'We didn't think it was going anywhere – God no, it was a fling, a flirtation, a sojourn, but there was nothing we could do; it was – unavoidable, necessary. We just fell.'

TWITCH *climbs back into bed alongside* BILLY. BILLY *rouses.*

BILLY. What you thinking?

TWITCH (*to* BILLY). Nothing.

BILLY *jumps up and straddles her.*

BILLY. You have an awesomely flat stomach. It's like the – Sahara.

TWITCH (*to* BILLY). That's quite hilly.

BILLY. Holland.

TWITCH (*to* BILLY). I guess. (*To audience.*) He looks up at me from my stomach. (*To* BILLY.) Hi chum.

BILLY. Hey dude.

TWITCH. He looks like a toddler. He's pretending his finger is stuck in my belly button.

BILLY (*speaks into an imaginary walkie-talkie*). Tsch, tsch… Billy to base camp! Tsch… Billy to base camp! I've fallen down a pretty killer ravine here, guys!

TWITCH. I look at his face. I like his face. I kiss his face.

They kiss.

BILLY. Base camp, base camp we've discovered – a –

TWITCH. A…?

BILLY. A…

BILLY *pushes himself up, thumps his chest – he pretends to be a gorilla. He nearly falls on* TWITCH, *she laughs.*

TWITCH (*to* BILLY). If we're going to have sex you're going to have to stop pretending to be King Kong.

BILLY. Bear Grylls?

TWITCH (*to* BILLY). Nope.

BILLY. Indiana Jones?

TWITCH (*to* BILLY). Definitely not!

BILLY. Attenborough?

TWITCH (*to* BILLY). Hmm?

BILLY. Oh really?

They laugh, they quiet.

I like you.

TWITCH. I like you too.

They kiss.

Six

Memory Two.

We snap into memory lighting. POLO *stands.* BILLY *and* TWITCH *become puppets.*

POLO. Twitch is thirteen, Mrs Black's art class. There'd been rumours of her being a prodigy.

TWITCH *mimes painting.*

Mrs Black was impossibly excited about the unveiling of Twitch's long-awaited pastoral scenes. The Powells were our next-door neighbours. Two kids; Sarah – a snotty thing – Nick, Twitch's age.

BILLY *as* NICK *presents himself.*

Good-looking boy. There'd been some kissing I believe.

BILLY *as* NICK *and* TWITCH *stand apart and snog the air, tongues out.*

Mrs Black ordered the unveiling –

TWITCH *unveils the painting.* BILLY *as* NICK *looks horrified.*

– and Mum was nearly sick on her suedes. Thirteen-year-old Nick Powell sees fifteen finely drawn images of his own face, inter-spliced with photos taken from his next-door neighbour's top window. She'd caught him every which way, flexing, picking, fiddling, sleeping: it was all there, one big visual quilt of surveillance. In all the fuss Nick splits and Twitch slips. Her pen finds itself lodged in the deep tissue of Nick Powell's forearm. A small blue dot; hard as they tried to wash it off, they couldn't shift it. A tattoo, you might say.

TWITCH *and* POLO *exit.* BILLY *stands frozen until activated by* JACKS' *entry.*

Seven

BILLY *stands.* JACKS *enters, ready for a night out. We are back in* JACKS' *house, Lady Gaga plays.*

JACKS. Where the fuck have you been, Captain bloody America?

BILLY. I'm sorry, I got held up.

JACKS. Polo wants to go.

BILLY. So glory boy's arrived then?

JACKS. We were meant to leave half a bloody hour ago, the queue's going to be huge by the time we get there.

BILLY. What's with the name?

JACKS. What?

BILLY. 'Polo' – it's a weird fucking name?

JACKS. Hold up, Watson. Isn't your sister called yogurt?

BILLY. Yogi.

JACKS. Bet she can't bear it.

> JACKS *laughs at her own joke.* BILLY *grimaces.*

> Born with a hole in the middle.

BILLY. What?

JACKS. Hole in his heart. They say they used a bit of Twitch to patch him up – but I'm pretty sure they just whopped the beater right out of him.

BILLY. Shut up.

JACKS. Seriously, the boy's a tin man.

BILLY. You can't live without a heart.

JACKS. Polo can.

BILLY. He sounds like a really nice guy.

JACKS. He's the best of men.

BILLY. You mind if I have a shower?

JACKS. You haven't got time.

BILLY. I'll be really quick.

JACKS. No, Billy – I want you to meet Polo. Come on.

BILLY. Um, Jacks?

JACKS. Come on.

BILLY. I, uh – you know, you know that I'm not – we're not – I'm not your boyfriend.

JACKS. No! (*Laughs, loudly, sees that* BILLY *is earnest and becomes serious.*) No, no Billy, I know.

BILLY. Right, just because… you know, we had been… sleeping together and I didn't want you to…

JACKS. What? Order a table for two at Pizza Hut?

BILLY. Get hurt.

JACKS. Billy, trust that I would let you know if you were my boyfriend.

Beat.

BILLY. Right, sure.

JACKS. Just hurry the fuck up, alright?

BILLY. Yep, yes I will. Sorry I –

BILLY *turns to go.*

JACKS. Billy?

BILLY. Yeah?

JACKS. Don't make me out to be a limp dick, alright?

BILLY. No.

JACKS. It was jokes.

BILLY. Good jokes.

JACKS. Side-splitters. Now, hurry the fuck up, we're late!

JACKS *and* BILLY *faux-box for several punches, smile;* JACKS *exits –* BILLY *watches her go, a little uncomfortably, then turns. He is startled by* POLO, *who has been standing, watching.*

BILLY. Oh hey, mate – I'm Billy.

BILLY *offers his hand.*

POLO *ignores his hand.*

POLO. Polo.

BILLY. Yeah… I know. Jacks is your biggest fan. She hasn't stopped talking about you for weeks.

POLO. She didn't mention you.

BILLY. Right – well – I'm Billy and… I'm just going to grab a shower.

POLO. Are you living here?

BILLY. Just for the summer. Our parents are friends.

POLO. You're American?

BILLY. Yes.

POLO. Are you coming with us?

BILLY. I think so – Jacks said it was – uh, apologies, dude; I should have said, uh – happy birthday, man.

POLO. We're quite late.

BILLY. Sure, I'll be real quick. Twitch is on her way so we can head straight out when I'm done.

POLO. What?

BILLY. I'll be real quick –

POLO. Twitch?

BILLY. Hm?

POLO. You said Twitch?

BILLY. I bumped into her on my way – she said she was –

POLO. 'Bumped'?

BILLY. On the road.

POLO. Which road?

BILLY. The road.

POLO. Which road?

BILLY. I don't remember the name.

POLO. The island's very small.

BILLY. Sure – but –

POLO. Five miles by two – no more.

BILLY. All the same, I don't remember the name of the road.

Long pause.

Anyway – I should grab that shower.

POLO. She won't be long.

BILLY. No, I'm sure she won't. It was a pleasure –

POLO. Hm.

POLO *watches* BILLY *go.*

Eight

POLO *stands from Scene Seven,* TWITCH *enters unseen. They speak slowly; their mode is unnerving. We are still in* JACKS' *house, the hallway now; Lady Gaga has thinned to silence.*

TWITCH. Hello, Polo.

POLO. Sproggit.

Long pause.

Where have you been?

TWITCH. Where have you been?

POLO. You're late.

TWITCH. You're late.

POLO. Jacks said seven.

TWITCH. You're a year late.

Beat.

Have you missed me?

POLO. Twitch?

TWITCH. Thank you for calling.

POLO. I always asked Mum and Dad –

TWITCH. How I was? It's not quite the same though, is it, Angel-face?

POLO. No.

TWITCH. Well then.

POLO. Please don't be angry.

TWITCH. Why not?

POLO. I'm not used to it. You've never been –

TWITCH. You never left before.

POLO. I never came back before.

TWITCH. Because you never left before.

POLO. But now I'm back.

TWITCH. Why did you go?

Beat.

POLO. Dad said you're doing photography.

TWITCH. Yes.

POLO. What you snapping?

TWITCH. Things.

POLO. Twitch?

TWITCH. Pictures.

POLO. Fine.

TWITCH. I'm angry.

POLO. I can tell.

TWITCH. Tideline.

POLO. Seaweed?

TWITCH. It's rising.

POLO. Greenpeace, hippy shit?

TWITCH. Our kids won't play on the same sand we played on.

POLO. Sand moves anyway.

TWITCH. The island's disappearing.

POLO. Right. Will you kiss me?

POLO *steps forward.* TWITCH *steps back.*

TWITCH. Right?

POLO. To say hello. It's been for ever.

POLO steps forward. TWITCH steps back.

TWITCH. Just – 'right'? Don't you find that – unbearable? That our memories are tied to things that will be under the water by the time our children are born.

POLO. Yours.

TWITCH. No; ours, our memories, Polo, where we grew up.

POLO. Yours. Your children.

Long pause.

TWITCH. Happy birthday, Polo.

POLO. Not 'til midnight.

TWITCH. Twenty-five.

POLO. Quarter century.

TWITCH. We're getting older. I sometimes thought we might not.

POLO. Yes.

TWITCH. But we are.

POLO. We should go, can't be late. We'll be on our way to fifty before we start drinking.

TWITCH. Polo?

POLO. What?

Long pause.

TWITCH. There's a boy –

POLO says nothing. TWITCH moves closer. Close enough to touch him, she raises her hand to almost touch his cheek.

Polo – there's a –

POLO (*jolts his head away, they do not touch*). Come on!

POLO leaves. TWITCH is left standing for several seconds. TWITCH exits.

Nine

We are back on the beach. It is night now. We can hear the sound of the sea, the revellers walk in a line towards the club. POLO leads. POLO and TWITCH talk to the audience, BILLY and JACKS remain in the scene.

POLO. I wanted to get to The Hut by walking along the seafront, along the line of the tide, I just wanted to put my feet on the last bits of sand that were dry before the waves came in.

BILLY. Isn't it weird –?

TWITCH. What?

BILLY. Isn't it weird –

TWITCH. What?

BILLY. Isn't it weird –

TWITCH. What?

BILLY. Isn't it weird when it's dark and still hot – you can taste the salt in the air.

TWITCH puts her finger in the air and then into BILLY's mouth. He sucks it. JACKS appears, bringing up the rear.

JACKS. Polo!

The four characters take up static positions at intervals across the stage.

TWITCH. We're walking in a line, Polo up front; strangely quiet. Jacks keeps screaming –

JACKS. Polo! Tell us a joke – I want to hear a joke, Polo!

TWITCH. He doesn't say a word. Behind him, Billy, I stare at the space on the back of his head where I laid my hand this afternoon, whilst he slept.

JACKS. Polo – tell us a joke!

POLO. Billy pulls out a little plastic packet from his back pocket and passes it down the line. The taste is so familiar it might as well be milk and fucking cookies.

The four take pills from their pockets and swallow them down.

TWITCH. The tide is rising.

POLO. Nipping at your heels.

TWITCH. The sky is sweating stars. I look at Billy and the moon is making his face shine white, he looks beautiful.

POLO. Two moons – one in the sky, bright white – the other, its twin, is reflected in the water – you can barely see him.

TWITCH. I've always had this idea that when the tide rises around an island it means that there is less land to stand on –

JACKS. Polo! Tell us a bloody joke!

TWITCH. Which means that with each wave people must be moving closer together.

TWITCH *and* BILLY *kiss.* POLO *looks on.*

POLO. I'm not sure I can breathe.

Ten

'She Said' by Plan B plays. DJ emerges from behind his decks and becomes a nightclub attendant. JACKS, *at the back of the queue, rushes forward, pushing* BILLY, POLO *and* TWITCH. JACKS *turns and berates the imaginary queue barger behind her. The four characters pay the attendant, get their hands stamped, and give him their coats. He returns behind the decks. The four characters enter the club. They dance, they drink, they look at the audience as if they are also on the dance floor.* POLO *does not take his eyes off* TWITCH. TWITCH *watches* BILLY.

TWITCH. I keep pretending to wipe my nose with the cuff of my shirt; he used it today to dry his hair after we came out of the sea. The smell of him, skin, salt, sweat; I trace an exact line from where he is standing to where I am. Yes, that man, there, with the chequered shirt, by the bar – yes, him, making the bar girl laugh – 'Yes he is rather isn't he? Thank you – I know.'

I wonder if any other two people in this bar have had sex today. I like that I know, I can still feel, in my knickers – I look at the way he smiles and talks with other people and only I know what the underside of his penis looks like. It makes me smile. My secret, my man, I want to belong to him, to be his; be my boy for a thousand years.

POLO *clicks, snap into memory state.* TWITCH *and* BILLY *freeze.*

Eleven

Memory Three

TWITCH *and* BILLY *become puppets once again. They stand opposite each other;* BILLY *has a beer bottle in his hand.*

POLO. Peter Harris, sixteen years old, behind the bike shed of the Island Academy. It was the day before the school disco. I'd spent two weeks looking for the right dress for her, the right shoes, the right hairband.

We'd even gone to the trouble of organising a little choreography for the most probable hits of school disco 2002. 'It's getting hot in here'; chicken neck, chicken neck, beep, beep, chicken neck, chicken neck, beep.

But the day before the big night, little Pedro wanted a trial run; first boy to find his hand in our Twitch's knickers.

Pretended not to know her the next night, wouldn't even talk to her, said he couldn't remember her name. Who forgets a name like Twitch? Electrical mishap –

POLO *clicks. Blackout.*

– speakers wired funny they said, no one was quite sure what had happened. Little Peter was standing too close to the sound system – it certainly was getting hot in there –

Electric blue lights flash, back to blackout.

– two hundred and thirty volts, saw our Petey flying through the air – quite the spectacle, turned his hair into the short and curlies that he'd so enjoyed exploring the day before. And try as they might, they just couldn't make it straight again.

POLO, BILLY *and* TWITCH *stay frozen until* JACKS *arrives.*

Twelve

'Hot in Herre' by Nelly plays. JACKS *enters, we are back in the club. '(I've Had) The Time of My Life' by Bill Medley and Jennifer Warnes begins to play.*

JACKS. Polo! Let's do the lift!

BILLY, POLO *and* TWITCH *snap round, horrified.*

POLO. Jacks – no!

JACKS *jumps into the air.* BILLY *appears, seemingly from nowhere, and catches her.*

BILLY. Jacks, no! That is not a good idea!

JACKS. We used to do this all the time.

TWITCH. We were quite a lot smaller then –

JACKS (*wriggles free from* BILLY). Don't call me fat!

TWITCH. Stop shouting. I wasn't calling you fat.

JACKS. It's fine!

BILLY. Guys – people are kind of –

TWITCH. People are looking.

JACKS. It's fine!

POLO. I can't do it.

JACKS. It's like riding a bike.

POLO. I have literally no upper-body strength any more.

BILLY. Of course you do.

POLO. I don't.

BILLY. You must have.

JACKS. It has to be you, Polo, like old times! Okay – I'm coming –

POLO. Jacks – no! This is a bad idea.

JACKS. It's fine – it will be fine. You'll remember how –

POLO. No, Jacks! We're different, you're not Baby any more, I'm not Johnny any more.

BILLY. You were Johnny?

POLO. Yes.

TWITCH. He's actually dead now.

POLO. Why can't you imagine me as Johnny?

BILLY. I don't know.

JACKS. Say the line, Polo – Polo, say the line –

POLO. Bigot.

TWITCH. Polo?

POLO. What?

JACKS. Come on!

BILLY. Swayze is like a stallion.

TWITCH. Was. He's dead.

BILLY. He was a stallion.

POLO. What's your point, monkey boy?

JACKS. Polo, say the line and I'll run!

BILLY. You must, like, wank? That's forearm strength.

TWITCH. Billy, leave him.

POLO. I'm fine.

BILLY. He doesn't wank?

JACKS. Polo!

POLO. You can speak to me, you can ask me – I can hear you.

BILLY. You don't wank?

TWITCH. Billy – stop it.

POLO (*turns sharply away*). Jacks! Come on!

JACKS. I'm ready!

BILLY. You don't wank? He doesn't wank?

TWITCH. Billy, stop it. Jacks, stop!

JACKS. Shut your trap, Uncle Fester – I'm coming – say the line –

BILLY. You know that's fucked up?

TWITCH. Billy! Jacks!

JACKS. I'm coming!

BILLY. Dude? You don't wank?

JACKS. I'm coming! Polo!

BILLY. What the fuck are you?

POLO (*screams uncomfortably loud*). Nobody puts Baby in the corner!

JACKS starts screaming and running towards POLO, POLO stands with his arms out, ready to catch her. The music rises to a crescendo, at the point of flight – blackout.

Thirteen

Lights up. JACKS and POLO freeze. JACKS is sprawled, face down on the floor of the club, her head stuck under the DJ booth. POLO stands, hands over his mouth. BILLY and TWITCH sit on the bar/sea wall. We are on the beach.

TWITCH. Oh my God.

BILLY. That was hilarious.

TWITCH. Don't – don't laugh –

BILLY. Man, she just fucking face-planted in the middle of the bar.

TWITCH. Polo just stood there.

BILLY. He saw these huge tits coming towards him and he just couldn't move.

TWITCH. He just stood there.

BILLY. Tit-ma-tised!

Lights down on BILLY *and* TWITCH.

Fourteen

Snap back to the dance floor. Lights up on POLO *and* JACKS, JACKS *starts moaning in pain,* POLO *begins to shift about anxiously.*

JACKS. Polo, I think I'm stuck.

POLO. Get up!

JACKS gets up slowly, faces the crowd, is mortified and tries to retreat back to the floor.

Come on; just act natural!

JACKS. Everybody's looking.

JACKS and POLO *smile weakly, dance weakly.*

Natural? I just wiped out in the middle of the –

POLO. Where's Twitch gone?

Looks manically across the crowd.

JACKS. Polo, everybody's staring at me.

POLO. Where is she?

JACKS. Polo, everybody's staring.

POLO. Jacks?

JACKS. Polo.

POLO (*grabs her with both hands*). Twitch?

JACKS. I think she fucked off to fuck Billy.

> JACKS *totally absorbed by the eyes that are on her – starts to wave, wink. She sees the audience, sees that they are looking at her.*

POLO. Where?

JACKS. Looked like they were headed to the beach.

POLO. What?

JACKS. Sandy number, organ grinder. Now – look –

POLO. Right.

JACKS. Look; look, at them looking. Everybody is staring.

> POLO *looks up, around the club.* POLO *sees the audience.*

POLO. You're right.

> *Lights drop on* POLO *and* JACKS. *Lights come up on the audience.*

It must be because you're so hot, Jacks.

> *They walk slowly towards the audience, maintaining eye contact – they walk back again.*

JACKS. They can't stop looking. (*Beat.*) Look at him.

POLO. Where?

JACKS. Having to sit on his fucking hands.

POLO (*laughs*). Practically fucking dribbling.

JACKS (*to the selected audience member*). You like it? You want to touch it?

POLO. Go over to him. Give him a real show.

JACKS. You reckon?

POLO. Teach him a lesson.

JACKS. Look at him, he literally can't look away.

POLO. Touch him.

JACKS. Shut up!

POLO. Touch him!

> JACKS *touches the audience member.* JACKS *and* POLO *squeal with laughter –*

JACKS. He's gone red – he's gone bright fucking –

POLO. Over there?

JACKS. Which one?

> POLO *points to another member of the audience.*

POLO. There.

JACKS. Ha.

POLO. He's trying to look away – doesn't know where to look.

JACKS. Got to keep his eyes on this, can't help himself, can you, big boy?

POLO. Dance for him.

JACKS. I'm dancing.

POLO. Make him fucking squirm. Make him beg – he wants to watch, give him something to fucking look at!

> JACKS *goes right over, dances provocatively.* JACKS *and* POLO *squeal with laugher.*

> Him – over there, geek chic with the glasses.

JACKS. His eyes drag –

POLO. Like tide –

JACKS. On –

POLO. You.

They laugh sardonically.

Take something off.

JACKS. You reckon?

POLO. Look at them, it's pathetic – little bit of human fucking flesh and they can't keep their eyes off.

JACKS. Looky looky.

POLO. Licky licky.

JACKS. Can't stop staring!

POLO. Take something off.

JACKS. You want to see – you want a show?

POLO. You want to see a real show?

POLO rips off JACKS' jacket.

JACKS. He's shitting himself!

POLO. Careful the wife doesn't spot that trouser tent, sir.

JACKS. Come on, booooys!!

POLO. They're going wild for it!

JACKS. Like little fucking puppies. This is so funny!

POLO. They're shouting your name, Jacks – give them what they want!

JACKS tentatively goes to take her top off, POLO eggs her on. JACKS, excited by POLO, pulls her top off, leaving her bra on.

JACKS *(squeals)*. That was so funny! I can't believe I just did that!

POLO. Jacks, people are coming in off the beach!

POLO stands behind JACKS and angles her towards male members of the audience. From hereon in he shouts right into her ear.

JACKS. What are they saying? What's a 'tizau'?

POLO. 'Get your tits out!'

JACKS (*reels with laughter, screaming*). Everybody wants me!

POLO. Get your tits out!

JACKS. They're all taking pictures!

POLO. You're a celeb, Jacks!

> POLO *pushes* JACKS *forward aggressively towards the audience.*

JACKS. Polo! Take a picture of them taking pictures of me!

POLO. You're so fucking fierce!

JACKS. They can't get enough!

POLO. Get your tits out!

JACKS (*screams*). I feel invincible!

POLO (*screams*). Get your fucking tits out!

> JACKS *takes her top off. Blackout.* JACKS *exits.*

Fifteen

POLO *stands centre stage, the blackout remains.*

POLO. I was sitting in a café and a woman got out one of her breasts and pushed her thick nipple into her baby's mouth and I retched. (*Beat.*) You're gorgeous, you're fabulous, you're amazing – PS, if I had to actually look at what's between your legs I'd – (*Beat.*) When a pregnant woman passes me in the street I have to look away.

> POLO *retreats.*

Sixteen

Lights pull back up on BILLY *and* TWITCH, *still seated on the bar/sea wall. We hear sounds of the sea. We are on the beach.* BILLY *jumps down off the bar/sea wall and helps* TWITCH *down. They walk across the dance floor as if it were a beach.* POLO *looks on.*

BILLY. Polo really doesn't wank or – ?

TWITCH. No.

BILLY. That's fucked up, man.

TWITCH. I don't know.

BILLY. What?

TWITCH. It makes sense to me sometimes.

BILLY. Why?

TWITCH. It might be easier.

BILLY. I'd fucking explode.

TWITCH. Really?

BILLY. Well, you know –

Long pause, they wander.

TWITCH. Billy, how many people have you slept with?

BILLY. Hm?

TWITCH. Roughly?

BILLY. Oh, I don't know –

TWITCH. Roughly?

BILLY. Fucking look at that moon, man, it's incredible, it's so big and –

TWITCH. Billy?

BILLY. Hm?

TWITCH. How many?

BILLY. How many what?

TWITCH. Tell me.

BILLY. You?

TWITCH. Two. You're the second.

BILLY. Oh.

TWITCH. What?

BILLY. Nothing, I just. I don't know, that's not very many. Are your family like… religious or… unattractive? That was a joke. I was joking.

TWITCH. Neither.

BILLY. Right.

TWITCH. I'm just aware of my – I've learnt –

BILLY. What?

TWITCH. I don't have much of a capacity for casual sex.

Beat.

BILLY. Right.

TWITCH. It's natural.

BILLY. Hm?

TWITCH. Jacks, Jacks always calls me Uncle Fester because Uncle Fester's a freak, you know, from the –

BILLY. *The Addams Family.*

TWITCH. Yeah, them.

BILLY. A freak?

TWITCH. But since I started having sex.

BILLY. Just that once before –

TWITCH. You.

BILLY. Mm-hm.

TWITCH. I've read loads.

BILLY. Read?

TWITCH. Did you ever get told the story about teeth at school?

BILLY. Teeth?

TWITCH. About how you should imagine that your teeth had no enamel. (*Speaks with mouth open, imitating.*) Imagine that the roots were thirty-two tiny fishing lines, totally exposed, sensitive to the slightest touch –

BILLY. Ouch.

TWITCH. Then you gulp a big glass of water.

BILLY. Man, stop, it's horrible.

TWITCH. And all the fishing rods are waving in the –

BILLY. Stop it!

TWITCH. The enamel was trust or marriage or –

BILLY. Say again?

TWITCH. Armour.

BILLY. Armour?

TWITCH. You shouldn't go eating apples without enamel on your teeth.

BILLY. You lost me.

TWITCH. I get very – attached. I have trouble… letting go.

BILLY. Oh.

TWITCH. What I'm saying is, that it's Jacks that should be called Uncle Fester.

BILLY. Why?

TWITCH. For her it's all so –

BILLY. What?

TWITCH. I don't know… it doesn't… Do you fancy her? I mean, would you ever – ?

BILLY. Twitch – I – um –

TWITCH. I find it – incredible how she can sleep with people and it doesn't mean a thing.

Beat.

BILLY. I think that's pretty normal, or it's, it's you know, just being – adult.

TWITCH. Do you think you can choose?

BILLY. What?

TWITCH. What kind of heart you have?

BILLY. Yes.

Beat.

TWITCH. You know there's a hormone called oxytocin and it triggers the feeling of attachment. During sex, women produce around ten times more of it than men.

BILLY. Right.

TWITCH. And for the men, testosterone suppresses the oxytocin, so they are wired to be less attached. When men ejaculate they release prolactin instead, it makes them less risk-averse – they want to skydive and women want to cuddle.

BILLY. You know your stuff.

TWITCH. I've read.

BILLY. Clearly.

TWITCH. We're wired to want you to stay.

BILLY. But not all girls –

TWITCH. I think they're working against their wiring.

BILLY. Right.

TWITCH. I'm normal.

BILLY. Good to know.

TWITCH. Normal.

BILLY. You said.

TWITCH. Just saying.

BILLY. I'm not sure it needs repeating.

TWITCH. I'm sorry. It's just when I said the 'two people' thing –

BILLY. You don't need to justify –

TWITCH. I did. You looked scared.

BILLY. I wasn't scared – I just –

TWITCH. How many people have you – ?

BILLY. It's not the same –

TWITCH. I don't mind.

BILLY. I mean, I'd put my dick places I wouldn't put my fingers.

Beat.

TWITCH. Right.

BILLY. Not that – that doesn't mean –

TWITCH. It's fine.

BILLY. I like you.

TWITCH. I like you too.

BILLY *smiles.*

I wish there was a word in between.

BILLY. In between – ?

TWITCH. Like and –

Beat.

There's a gap.

BILLY. 'There's a gap'?

TWITCH. The gap. They say that's what really what makes people fall in – that there's a gap between men and women. A space in between what they mean – like a – and it can't quite be crossed because their languages build different bridges and the bridges never quite meet – and that, that – sex is like this thing between the bridges, like a dictionary, like translation, and when people fall – it means that they've jumped off their bridges.

BILLY. I don't get it.

TWITCH. I think that's the point.

BILLY. What?

TWITCH. You're not meant to get it, because I said it.

BILLY. What's the point in the story if I don't get it?

TWITCH. The point of the story is that you don't get it.

BILLY. I'm not sure I understand.

TWITCH. Exactly.

BILLY. Really?

TWITCH. Yes.

BILLY. Yes.

TWITCH. Right.

BILLY. Right. Okay.

Beat.

TWITCH. Billy, I love you.

Beat.

BILLY. Twitch, I'm leaving.

Lights fade out. BILLY *and* TWITCH *sit. We can only hear the sound of the sea.*

Seventeen

BILLY *and* TWITCH *sit silently on the beach.* JACKS *enters and stands nearby.* POLO *looks on.*

JACKS. I –

TWITCH. Sea.

JACKS. Him, across the bar.

TWITCH. We sit in silence.

JACKS. Never seem him before. He's hot. He –

TWITCH. Waves.

JACKS. His eyes drag on me like –

TWITCH. Tide.

JACKS. The club is thumping.

TWITCH. The water is calm.

JACKS. He comes over –

TWITCH. He's quiet. I can tell he feels the weight of my words, the responsibility sits like stones. Two silent silhouettes on the –

JACKS. Hi. Hi. Drink. You want to? Alright – are you – ?

TWITCH. Shore.

JACKS. Alright then.

TWITCH. It's funny how my love feels so heavy to him when his muscles are so much bigger than mine.

JACKS. He drags me – his eyes –

TWITCH. The tide is coming in. We sit on the last bit of –

JACKS. Land, on me. They stick to me. He wants what I've got and it feels like power.

TWITCH. I feel totally powerless.

JACKS. He pushes me into the cubicle. He locks the door behind him. The toilet lid is cold against the back of my thighs.

TWITCH. Kiss me.

JACKS. Fuck me.

TWITCH. I am close enough to see the tiny blacks of his pupils. My fingertips map his face in the dark.

JACKS. The neon light flickers over his head – it looks like camera snaps for the –

TWITCH. Stars. The sky is sweating stars.

JACKS. It's hot. It's so fucking hot.

TWITCH. The only thing I can hear is the sea. His big man hands falter over my waistband.

JACKS. He pushes himself between my thighs and I tell him to slow down. Apply myself to his belt buckle. He slows, he waits, bated fucking breath for me to give him what he wants. (*Laugh.*) Spoilt boy is hungry, I make him wait.

TWITCH. He lays me down and the pebbles dig into my back. He looks at me – Twitch, remember, please remember – strap yourself down, hold yourself back – never cut the kite string, never take your feet off the pedals, never let go of the balloon.

JACKS. There is a mirror, on the ceiling. I watch me. There's this tiny bit of flat brown skin, hairless, shining, where my neon knickers meet my thigh. I look hot. I feel invincible.

TWITCH. He's above me and I feel like I exist entirely in the two inches of clear space between his face and mine.

JACKS. I give him the green light. (*Laughs.*) It looks like a movie, my brown legs are wrapped around his white arse.

TWITCH. This will be the last time, that this will be the last time. I –

JACKS. – can hardly –

TWITCH. – breathe –

JACKS. – with the thrill of fucking someone –

TWITCH. –with the horror of sleeping with someone –

JACKS. – when you know –

TWITCH. – when you know –

JACKS. – that you will never see them again.

TWITCH. – that you will never see them again. (*Beat.*) I know he is going. I know he is going.

> TWITCH *and* JACKS *freeze. Snap to memory light.*

Eighteen

Memory Four.

POLO *walks into the scene as set in Scene Seventeen.*

POLO. Nathan Harvey, university. No place for someone with a heart like Twitch's. There was no fresher fresher; she was a certified first-timer. Nathan, poor schmuck, had no idea what he was unlocking. He didn't just fuck her either; he told her that he loved her. What was a twenty-year-old boy doing with a word like that on his lips? Two months later – on her knees, eye against the keyhole, start to finish, Twitch watched Nathan pump some bendy cheerleading skank.

> BILLY *moves his hands in front of his crotch as if having sex.*

> TWITCH *kneels, makes a keyhole from her hand and presses her eye against it.*

She got a shiner from how hard she'd pushed her eye against the keyhole.

> TWITCH *pushes her face against her hand painfully hard.*

Lovely Nathan ran himself a bath after, wash down, cool off, scrub up. I've always been told that you should test it with your toe but Nathan was one for jumping straight in. The sole of his right foot: scalded, scarred, third-degree. Freak accident, should have tested it with his toe, no one knows how it happened – but Nathan Harvey never walked the same again.

POLO *exits.* BILLY *exits.*

TWITCH *and* JACKS *remain on stage.*

Nineteen

We snap back into the set-up for Scene Seventeen.

TWITCH *stands, suddenly – she gasps.*

TWITCH. In one moment of wild idiocy I allow myself to forget what I know, I jump and whilst I'm falling I imagine a world where there need not be an end to everything.

JACKS. He comes. He's done. He zips himself up. He asks for my number.

TWITCH. And it feels like love.

JACKS *steps out towards* TWITCH. *They stop talking to the audience and begin talking to each other.*

JACKS. No. I say no. He calls – we fuck – we date – even if we fall? (*Laughs.*) Best-case scenario is you end up staring at the same cock for fifty years knowing that the man you wake up next to definitely doesn't think about you when he wanks.

TWITCH. When am I allowed to begin believing in for –

JACKS. Never being new or exciting ever again.

TWITCH. I imagine a world where there need not be an end to everything.

JACKS. I wasn't the first, I won't be the last.

TWITCH. I once heard that each lover is like a fingerprint –
totally unique.

JACKS. I think of all the girls he has fucked before me and all
the girls he'll fuck after me.

TWITCH. Like a fingerprint.

JACKS. I think of all the girls he has fucked before me and all
the girls he'll fuck after me

TWITCH. I want to be indelible.

JACKS. I think of all the girls he has fucked before me and all
the girls he'll fuck after me and it makes me feel free.

TWITCH. I don't want to be forgotten.

TWITCH *goes to get her guitar, lights rise and we slip into
Scene Twenty.*

Twenty

TWITCH *stands centre stage – she begins to play 'One
Thousand Miles', an original song by Gwendolen Chatfield.*
POLO *looks on.*

TWITCH.
What was there is no more
So alive when I called
Please give me time
One thousand miles across the seas I'll ride
We'll waltz on glass
Hand in hand this moment it's our last
It's our last, it's our last, it's our last…

POLO *enters.* TWITCH *continues to play the melody but
ceases to sing. She stares at* POLO *whilst he addresses the
audience.*

POLO. What was I meant to do? She was my sister, my twin,
my tally-man. I didn't tell a soul. Silent sibling. Each time

she fell – I would know what was coming – she dredged herself, turned herself inside out, she just couldn't shoulder it and with each boy it got worse. There was only so much I could stomach. So I left.

POLO *turns away from* TWITCH, *she sings, angry now, at* POLO*'s back.* POLO, *pained, does not turn around.*

TWITCH.
    Cityscape bright lights
    Empty room lonely nights
    There's a voice in my head
    Pulls my hair shares my bed
    Please give me time
    One thousand miles across the seas I'll ride
    We'll waltz on glass
    Hand in hand this moment it's our last
    It's our last, it's our last, it's our last…

POLO *retreats.* TWITCH *turns to* BILLY *who sits, frozen. She sings with romantic glee.*

    Never spoke at the start
    Instead of words we used hearts
    And our eyes and fingertips
    And our hands and our lips
    Please give me time
    One thousand miles across the seas I'll ride
    We'll waltz on glass
    Hand in hand this moment it's our last
    It's our last, it's our last, it's our last…

POLO. Twitch?

TWITCH *continues to play, louder now, trying to drown* POLO *out.*

Twitch!

TWITCH *continues to play, louder still.*

Twitch!

TWITCH *stops suddenly.*

Twenty-One

TWITCH, *having removed her guitar, stands opposite her brother. They stand in silence for some time. They are between the beach and the club.*

TWITCH. I want to go for a swim with Billy.

POLO. It's gone midnight.

Beat.

TWITCH. He's leaving, Polo.

POLO. Yes.

TWITCH. You should be dancing, it's our birthday. You should be dancing.

POLO. Twitch, he's leaving.

TWITCH. I'm going to take him swimming, it will be amazing – at night, when it's warm and the sand's between your toes and it's all black –

POLO. Twitch.

TWITCH. I love him.

POLO. Don't.

Beat.

TWITCH. I don't think I can bear it.

POLO. I don't suppose you can.

TWITCH. If he forgets me, I'll disappear.

POLO. He won't.

TWITCH. They always do.

POLO. No. They don't, they never –

TWITCH. He will, of course he will, he has to, I just... I want to pin it down to make it stick.

POLO. Twitch – I –

TWITCH. Please make him stay.

Long pause.

POLO *and* TWITCH *exit.*

Twenty-Two

Back in the club. 'In for the Kill' by La Roux plays, the base is turned up much higher than the melody, it throbs through the floor. POLO *stands at the bar; he sees something in the middle distance, he's transfixed by it.* JACKS *enters.*

JACKS. Polo! Polo!

POLO (*quietly*). Yes.

JACKS. There you fucking are – where d'you get to? You missed it, his face, Polo – he looked like he was going pee himself. 'Can I have your number?' 'No.' Aw, it was brilliant! You want a drink – I want a drink – I'll get drinks –

POLO. Jacks?

JACKS. One second.

POLO. Jacks?

JACKS. What?

POLO. Look.

JACKS. What?

POLO. There.

JACKS. Where?

POLO. In the corner – by the toilets.

JACKS. I can't see anything; it's too dark – what is it?

JACKS *makes to go and investigate.*

POLO (*stops her*). Don't.

JACKS. What the fuck is it?

POLO. She's giving him head.

JACKS (*lurches forwards to look*). Aww – that is cheeky, man! Not even in the – how can you see that? I can't see anything – it's too dark – you're making it up, Polo.

POLO. I'm not.

JACKS. Drinks, let's get drinks –

POLO. Jacks?

JACKS. Stop looking, Polo.

POLO. Jacks?

JACKS. Polo, it's pervy, alright, stop looking.

POLO. I can't quite see her but he's –

JACKS. Polo?

POLO. You can see his hair, it's silver.

JACKS. Fuck off!

JACKS *looks*.

Very long pause. JACKS *steps slowly back, she looks away.*

POLO. I'm sorry – I –

Beat.

JACKS. Fuck.

Beat.

POLO. They've stopped.

JACKS. Polo?

POLO. She's getting up. I can't see her face, it's too dark –

JACKS. Don't.

POLO. I think one of her knees is bleeding.

JACKS *tries to drag him round.*

Your dad's smiling… She doesn't look like she's one for washing up.

JACKS. Stop it.

POLO. He's got it made.

JACKS. Polo?

POLO. I'm going to find Twitch.

POLO *exits*. JACKS *slowly looks up*.

JACKS. There's a trickle of blood running right the way down the front of her leg. Dad's licking the corner of a napkin, bends down and wipes her knee. She must have been kneeling on some glass or something. Never seen her before, not from the island, one of those wonky hairdo's – they do 'em at the salons in Pompey – I was meant to go on a course but they never sent – m–

Long pause. JACKS *looks up, cautiously*.

She's walking like everyone's looking but not a single head turns. Her flesh is swinging from her arms, you can see the veins in her legs, the lines round her eyes, the folds on her neck – no one fucking looks – it's like she's invisible.

Beat.

Mum always says you can't afford to have bare legs after thirty. Mum says he'll still be hers, whatever happens. Doesn't matter how long it is or who he's with – says she'll always be his wife and he'll always be her husband. She says there's honour in it. She's a mug, my mum.

JACKS *exits. The music continues. It gets louder, the base gets stronger*.

Twenty-Three

The beach. POLO *enters, he walks slowly, almost dazed.* POLO *traces the tide line as he walks.*

POLO. When I was away I would go walking at night, through the city. The neon stung the dark and you couldn't see a star if you tried. You see, everyone wanted Polo at their party, everyone.

Always the last to leave – barely able to stand, I would just walk; I would walk and walk, no idea where I was going. Past strip clubs, and stag parties and twinks being touched by greying men, past drunks and dykes and whores and poofs and little girls in gutters with their skirts up round their armpits. It seemed like the whole world was walking home alone. And nobody was surprised to see me there.

POLO *stands, he stares, the music continues.*

Twenty-Four

TWITCH *bursts onto the stage. She is dragging* BILLY, *hard, he is laughing but having to strain to slow her down.* POLO *remains on stage,* BILLY *and* TWITCH *cannot see him.* POLO *watches. We hear the sound of the sea.*

TWITCH. Let's go swimming!

BILLY. What?

TWITCH. The sea – it's beautiful. Two moons – you can see the reflection so clearly. We should swim out and touch the moon!

BILLY. You're mad. It's freezing!

TWITCH. It's fine – come on!

BILLY. Twitch!

TWITCH. Come on – take your clothes off!

BILLY. I've only just put them back on.

TWITCH. At night, like this – you wave your arm through the water, all the algae lights up, it's phosphorescent, it glows. It's magic.

BILLY. Twitch.

TWITCH. Please.

BILLY. You're crazy.

TWITCH. Please, it's my birthday.

BILLY. Don't try that – you little –

TWITCH (*backs towards the sea*). Please, it will be a brilliant birthday memory.

BILLY (*follows, seduced*). You –

    TWITCH *and* BILLY *kiss*. POLO *watches*, BILLY *and* TWITCH *do not see him*. TWITCH *drags* BILLY *into the sea*.

Twenty-Five

'In for the Kill' by La Roux is reintroduced and thumps beneath the scene.

POLO. I'd walk and walk – and I'd try and find some quiet and I'd always end up at the river. There was a jetty, with an old party boat tied up on it. I'd walk down to the edge, get down on my hands and knees and put my ear against the beaten wood. I could hear the waves slapping against the struts, the black water gulping beneath me. I'd lean over and put a single finger in the water. She walks at night, she likes to paddle, to sit and watch the sea go out, knowing that it will always come back in. I knew, somehow, that if I was touching the water here and she was there then somehow we were in the same soup. Somehow, I was near her, we were under the same moon, part of the same sea.

POLO *exits, running. The music crescendos to an almost unbearable level then cuts.*

Twenty-Six

The beach, gone midnight, it's almost black. Through silence we hear faint singing. TWITCH *enters, slowly, singing 'She Said' by Plan B in whispers. She is soaking wet.*

TWITCH *sees something offstage, the singing stops, suddenly – she stands.*

TWITCH. Polo?

POLO *enters, also drenched. He approaches* TWITCH, *she takes a step back. He stops.*

Long pause.

POLO. There was only one heart between us and I couldn't see it go to waste like that.

TWITCH (*barely audible*). Polo?

POLO. People never think about it, really. But it's the longest relationship you'll ever have. Together, you outlive your parents and you know each other for years before you ever meet your husband or your wife. You know your brother, your sister for longer than you know your own children; for ever.

TWITCH. Polo.

POLO. Everything else is so temporary, fleeting barely lasts at all, and who can bear to be forgotten?

TWITCH. No.

POLO. You want something you can hold on to.

TWITCH *bends down to the sea edge. Lights dim to almost black.* POLO *looks on.*

TWITCH. His eyes are still, in the dark all their colour has gone. The moon reflects in a single spot in each one, like someone's frozen stars into the middle of marbles. I slide my hand into his palm and it's cold. There is a moment, a single second, less than – when the tide stops coming in and before it starts to go out. A fraction of a second when the sea stays still – the top of the tide, the top of the curve – and I always want to hold it; to press pause, to make it last. But flood tide always turns to ebb tide; the last wave coming in always turns around and becomes the first wave to go out. You can't stop it. That one wave, lifts his other arm up and off the pebbles and lays it down again. It looks like half his body is dancing. I can't move him, he's too heavy, it's like he's full of sand. I lay my head on his chest and I can hear the stones moving beneath him. I put my ear to his lips but the only thing moving is the sea.

Beat.

POLO. Happy birthday, Twitch.

TWITCH. Happy birthday, Polo.

Beat.

Polo Calvino was not looking to be loved.

POLO. Looking? No there was no need to look. I'd found her. They gave her my heart at birth.

TWITCH. Never let it go.

POLO. Indelible.

TWITCH. Mayday, mayday.

POLO. We've found a – off the coast of –

TWITCH. The sea, it comes in from every angle – it keeps us calm, it holds us tight, it tucks us in.

POLO. The great adventures of –

TWITCH. Lifeboat men, trying to save boys that thought they were bigger than the waves.

POLO. She used to say –

TWITCH. The island would sink with all those stories.

POLO. Like the one they used to tell.

TWITCH. About Polo and me.

POLO *steps towards* TWITCH, *she steps back. A pause, she walks slowly over to him, they hold each other. This is the first time they have touched.*

The End.

PMQ

PMQ was first performed as part of *Coalition* at Theatre503, London, in November 2010. The cast was as follows:

SPEAKER	Gwendolen Chatfield
DAVE	Richard Lintern
Director	James Dacre

Characters

SPEAKER
DAVE
OFFSTAGE VOICE

SPEAKER – *a young woman – sits in a large green-leather armchair suspended approximately six foot above the stage, against the back wall of the theatre. She holds a guitar.*

Beneath her, a dressing room/office. A suit jacket hangs on a hanger, a deep-blue tie, a mirror.

DAVE *waits to enter the House of Commons.*

DAVE *is looking over notes, pacing, practising hand gestures, facial expressions in the mirror. He shoots small, uneasy glances at* SPEAKER *whilst he prepares. He pulls a chair out to face the audience, he is imagining he is in the House of Commons; he practises sitting and standing several times, the effect is comic – he sits. He takes a large breath, as if he's about to stand –*

A polite knock at the door; DAVE *jumps a little.*

OFFSTAGE VOICE. Fifteen minutes, Mr Prime Minister.

DAVE. Right-o.

> DAVE *sits, look dead at the audience, smiles – a long beat – several seconds, his smile twitches, weakens slightly.*

SPEAKER. We're waiting. What have you got for us?

> DAVE *smiles, tolerates her; he stands fully, pulls his shoulders back, he takes one large preparatory breath.*

> SPEAKER *strums hard; the opening bars of 'Little Lion Man' by Mumford & Sons;* DAVE *clenches.*

> DAVE *stamps his foot.*

> SPEAKER *stops.*

> DAVE *takes a breath.*

> SPEAKER *strums.*

DAVE *stops*.

DAVE *stamps his foot*.

SPEAKER *stops*.

DAVE *takes a breath*.

SPEAKER *strums*.

DAVE *stops*.

SPEAKER *prepares to strum again* – DAVE *pips her to the post, stands quickly*.

DAVE (*rushing*). I've prepped pretty much every predecessor I've ever had.

SPEAKER (*sniggers slightly*). P – p – p – p – p.

DAVE. Prepared… previous…

SPEAKER. P – p –

DAVE. Prime Ministers.

SPEAKER. P.

DAVE. For P –

SPEAKER. P –

DAVE. For P –

SPEAKER. P –

DAVE. P –

SPEAKER. P –

DAVE. For PMQs. Shadow Cabinet – Leaders of the Ppposition. It's my area of expertise.

SPEAKER. Teeease.

DAVE. Lamont, Howard, Major.

SPEAKER *makes a snoring sound, bored*.

It's my area – I remember the brat pack, when we were trying to get Grey-face in, ten, twelve hours a day – sleeping at campaign HQ, it was thrilling –

SPEAKER *mouths 'thrilling' in mockery.*

They bumped me up to Lamont's right-hand man. I held him steady, I was his rudder. P –

SPEAKER. P –

DAVE. PMQs – it's what got me here. So today... is... my... crowning –

OFFSTAGE VOICE. Mr Prime Minister, would you like anything before we go in, sir? Coffee, tea?

SPEAKER *signals, as if to say 'I'll have a – '. Gives up. Miffed.*

DAVE. No, no. I'm fine thank you, just fine.

He smirks, he straightens his tie. Confident.

Where was I, oh yes – It's my area. My... a... *je ne sais...* uh... *pièce de... crème de la...* yeah? My area.

DAVE *pulls his shoulders back, lifts his chin slightly, if there is a lectern, he places one arm nonchalantly across it, he leans forward.*

It's in the posture, the poise –

SPEAKER. P – p –

DAVE. It's something you pick up at public school –

SPEAKER. P – p –

DAVE. It's where the well-educated place their confidence – in the firm knowledge that –

SPEAKER. Posh tosser.

DAVE. Style is as important as content; understanding the power of a well-worded sentence, the armour of being articulate.

Small beat. SPEAKER *raises her eyebrows, once, quickly.*

Combine that with – conviction – and you're – unstoppable.
The House is yours. Conviction, heart, balls – (*Clenches his
fist, he looks at it.*) Do you follow? The sense of total
assurance that holds your entire body taught, it makes you –
lighter – (*Tiny beat, he captures the room.*) Understanding
that when I stand in front of the House, in there, for my first
PMQ's – my words become – currency, coins, to be
exchanged for… faith. I give you my words; you give me
your faith… and it makes me… fly.

DAVE *lands the ending sentence with charm, with
confidence.* SPEAKER *looks momentarily captivated, then a
wry smile crosses her lips – suddenly –*

SPEAKER *sings the first two lines of 'Little Lion Man'.*

(*Quickly, with gusto.*) Blackpool, oh-seven, an army of
wildly promising young men thronging the corridors –

SPEAKER *mouths 'thronging' in mockery.*

It was in the length of my stride, my teeth shone, the whole
conference was sweating with collective belief in – me. I
stood at the lectern for that speech and looked out across the
crowd and the loyalty was tangible, it was binding them
together. I was chasing down Brown's cowardice and I knew,
I knew I could win. I was at my beginning, I was pure
potential and I swear to God, that speech, that day, no
notes… I felt my feet pull up against the tops of my
brogues, the laces straining, I swear to you, it may only have
been a matter of millimetres, but I flew.

SPEAKER *sings the next two lines of 'Little Lion Man'.*

Fire belly, the gut – that way that your soul and your speech,
the words are so connected, that you're not even thinking it,
it just comes out as pure… prophesy, as a, a – ray of, a –
steam, a river of – you shine. You're a cardinal, a magician, a
maestro. The divine right of – you sweat it. I remember
Blackpool. I was pure potential.

SPEAKER *sings the first four lines of 'Little Lion Man'.*

DAVE *swallows*.

One shouldn't expect that to last forever. It's not healthy for it to do so; one ages and becomes experienced and –

SPEAKER *snorts*.

You can't do a hundred speeches and have each one have the *crème de la* – the *je ne sais* – there comes a time when the real skill is in stitching it together. It's a – a craft – to be able to offer the likeness, the effect, of all that – fire – but really just to be – skimming, slightly. It's a skill. It's a necessary, skill. Harder, actually... more impressive in many ways than all that... chutzpah.

SPEAKER *strums the previous verse, sings softly.* DAVE *interrupts her.*

Too much heart, it isn't any good to anyone, it it's not metered, it's just idiocy.

SPEAKER *sings the next two lines.*

Craft. You have to learn to rely on your craft.

SPEAKER *sings the next two lines.*

SPEAKER *smirks.*

DAVE *recovers, straightens, his tie, puts on his suit jacket – brushes himself down, pulls himself up and goes to leave. He places his hand on the door handle, takes a deep breath, clears his throat –*

Right. I'm ready – I'm ready to –

SPEAKER. There's a stain on the crotch of your trousers.

DAVE (*speaks under his breath, aware he's speaking into a void*). No, there's not.

SPEAKER. There's food round your mouth – greedy at breakfast, slap your hands, greedy boy.

DAVE *breathes, tries to ignore.*

Your bald patch is shining – baldy boy. Your hands are shaking – shaky boy. You've wet yourself –

DAVE *suddenly snaps his head round to stare at her; this is the first time he's looked at her.*

I'm joking, you haven't really. You have left your flies undone though.

DAVE *restrains from looking down.*

DAVE. No, they're not.

SPEAKER. Yeah they are.

DAVE. No, they're not.

SPEAKER. Suit yourself; let the TV crews tell you.

DAVE. They're not. I know they're not.

SPEAKER. Fine.

DAVE. I know they are done up because I checked.

SPEAKER. That's good, go ahead then.

DAVE. I will.

SPEAKER. Go address the House as Leader for the first time with your cock hanging out, set the tone.

DAVE *flicks a look down, quickly.*

SPEAKER *sniggers.*

DAVE *turns away from the door back into the room.*

SPEAKER *smirks and strums a few lines, nonchalantly.*

DAVE. You hone your craft so that even when you're feeling a little –

SPEAKER *keeps strumming,* DAVE *fights to talk over it.*

(*Builds through this, gets back in his stride.*) For example, there are only four types of questions you can ever really be asked in PMQs – there are tricks, there are tools, so you're never left looking – so you never slip you can learn the technique to – four types –

One: 'The Regional'; schools, roads, Social Services, Mrs Bloggs next door, it's tedious, small-town, but fuck it up and the catastrophe will expand from the local to the national so pay attention to detail; repeat names, show a vested interest, bring up case histories, make them feel like you are so invested that might as well be sitting on their knee with your tongue in the ear of the parish county council minute-taker.

SPEAKER *laughs overly loudly at the joke, pretends to be in creases and then stops suddenly.*

DAVE *glares.*

SPEAKER. Sorry, it was a really good joke.

DAVE. Two: 'The *Daily Mail* Special'; some incendiary wanker of a backbencher will pick a topic that middle England is getting its knickers in a twist over and he'll think he's frightfully clever for doing so. For example –

DAVE *takes a breath* – SPEAKER *cuts in.*

SPEAKER. 'Should we take the Prime Minister's Papal welcome as affirmation of his support for the Catholic position on paedophilia, abortion, homosexuality and little white hats?'

DAVE. Nothing more than lighting fires and playing bully.

SPEAKER *smiles weakly.*

Always begin 'The *Daily Mail*' response with a small, subtle, humble – but derisive laugh – (*He does so.*) Then unravel the idiocy of it: 'Does the honourable lady suggest that one should only enter into dialogue with those of a like mind? Because if she does, I suggest the House of Commons may not be the place for her.'

Beat. SPEAKER *has nothing.*

You see, craft, it's all you need. No fire necessary.

Beat. SPEAKER *goes to strum the guitar and doesn't, can't. She seems a little defeated.*

Three: 'The Teaser'; it looks limp and unexciting on paper but can elicit the most interesting response; they'll use housing to expose immigration, immigration to expose foreign policy, foreign policy to worm you into racism; it's essentially verbal backspin. Take your time, identify the question and the question's camouflage, answer both with facts, numbers, statistics – do not get it wrong. If you're going to try for truth you cannot afford to get it wrong.

OFFSTAGE VOICE (*knocks politely*). Mr Prime Minister, time to go. Are you ready, sir?

DAVE. Yes. Very.

DAVE *turns to the door, confidently. Pulls down his sleeves, dusts his shoulders and straightens his tie – he walks out…*

On the very edge of the stage, SPEAKER *catches him –*

SPEAKER. Four?

DAVE. Hm?

SPEAKER. The fourth type of question – you said four.

DAVE *stops, just short of the door.*

DAVE. Did I?

SPEAKER. Yes.

DAVE. Well, there's no time – so –

SPEAKER. You said there would were four types of question –

SPEAKER *strums lightly on the guitar.*

DAVE. 'The Wife-beater.' The fourth type of question is the wife-beater, the question to which there is no answer.

SPEAKER. For example –

OFFSTAGE VOICE. Mr Prime Minister – ?

DAVE (*to* OFFSTAGE VOICE). One minute, please.

SPEAKER. Mr Prime Minister, your proposed budget cuts will so underfund the armed forces that you will be putting our soldiers, your country's soldiers, in danger?

DAVE. Craft won't carry you through the wife-beater… so you have to – to –

SPEAKER. Mr Prime Minister, the welfare reform you are suggesting will see thousands of families fall beneath the poverty line?

DAVE. To fly – fly by the seat of your –

SPEAKER. Mr Prime Minister, do you not agree that we could fund life-saving developments in the NHS by removing money from a nuclear defence initiative that will cause genocide should it be used?

DAVE. Trust your –

SPEAKER. Mr Prime Minister –

DAVE. You have to speak with blind –

SPEAKER. Daddy, where did Ivan go?

Long beat.

SPEAKER *sings the first four lines of the second verse of 'Little Lion Man'.*

(*Speaking.*) Mr Prime Minister?

DAVE. I don't know.

OFFSTAGE VOICE. Mr Prime Minister?

SPEAKER. Mr Prime Minister?

DAVE. I don't know.

SPEAKER. Mr Prime Minister?

DAVE. What if I don't know?

SPEAKER. Mr Prime Minister?

DAVE. What if I don't know? (*Beat*.) People are losing their homes, their jobs – some people will actually become hungry because of me. Worse than. Death, people are – men are – Afghanistan... Trident. What if I don't know?

SPEAKER *sings the next two lines of the second verse of 'Little Lion Man'.*

(*Seems small, child-like.*) Do you remember that trick? Where they pull the coin out from behind your ear, like it's been there all along. He would do that – all the time. Even when we were older, men, I was a man, last Christmas even and my dad's pulling a coin out from behind the ear of the Prime Minister. (*Laughs, softly.*)

Beat.

I never once thought about how he did it; never questioned it, just believed it was – I don't know, I just believed it was – so I never learnt how to do it. I've never pulled a coin out from behind my kids' ears. I don't suppose they think I can do magic. I mean, I can't so –

SPEAKER *sings the final line of the second verse of 'Little Lion Man'.*

Watching Dad's coffin go in the ground, it made me think of no man's land – Churchill, how can one man put the right words in the right order to make thousands of men throw themselves into walls of bullets? But I can't even pull coins out from behind my children's ears?

SPEAKER *sings the third line of the second verse of 'Little Lion Man' again.*

His words were – currency, coins, to be exchanged for... faith – coins that levitate behind children's ears, that appear and disappear, words that can conjure – mine, my words are so heavy with fraudulence that they fall out of my mouth like – pouring, clunking – like a broken fruit machine and all I can do is try to catch them before they make that terrible noise – catch them and try to throw them back up into the air, but I can't catch them all and besides, they're too heavy.

So I scrabble around on the floor and collect them up as best
I can and I try to hide them, in my pockets and up my
sleeves like tissues in church, and I try to sew them into the
seams of my suit, and I try to hide them behind my ears, like
some successful magic trick –

Beat.

I wonder, I sit and wonder whether it's magic, or heart or
craft, or being able to pretend well or getting your words in
exactly the right order, is it content or style, that makes men
believe in you – and then I wonder if it's just the kind of man
you are.

SPEAKER *sings the chorus of 'Little Lion Man'.*

OFFSTAGE VOICE. Mr Prime Minister, we really need to go.

DAVE. I'm coming.

DAVE *straightens his tie.*

I've prepped pretty much every predecessor I've ever had.

SPEAKER *strums.*

SPEAKER (*softly now, not mocking*). P – p – p – p –

DAVE. I'm an expert. I am at my beginning, I am pure
potential, I swear to God, today, no notes – I'm well-
prepared, well-planned. I'll open with condolences, soldiers
lost, Afghanistan, murders in Cumbria... I'll address the
deaths of good men... and then I'll begin... the whites of a
hundred eyes will say –

SPEAKER. We're waiting. What have you got for us?

DAVE. And I'll feel my feet pull up against the tops of my
brogues – the laces straining, I swear to you, it may only be a
matter of millimetres, but I am going to... because I
understand, I understand that to believe in what you're
saying... I understand – my words are currency, coins, to be
exchanged for... faith. I give you my words; you give me
your faith... and it will make me... fly.

DAVE *smoothes down the front of his suit, turns, takes a breath and exits.*

As he goes, the lights fade to black, SPEAKER *plays –*

SPEAKER *speaks the last two lines of the chorus of 'Little Lion Man'.*

The End.

PRECIOUS LITTLE TALENT

For Simon
With thanks for his optimism

'The difficulty is that the English are finding it impossible to give any account of themselves except for identities that they are dragging up from the past. There has never been a time when some coherent account of English National Identity was more needed.'

Krishan Kumar

'American Democracy: a tradition based on the simple idea that we have a stake in each other and that what binds us together is greater than what drives us apart and if enough people believe in the truth of that proposition and act on it then we might not solve every problem but we can get something meaningful done.'

Barack Obama

'*E pluribus unum*' – 'Out of the many, one.'

Motto on an American one cent coin

Acknowledgements

I would like to thank, first and foremost the Jameses; James Dacre for his relentless energy and commitment to high standards and James Quaife for his super-human ability to make things happen at short notice. I thank them both for working round the clock, for keeping the faith and for having the tenacity and tolerance to have maintained a sense of humour when things have got tough.

I would like to thank Simon Ginty, Emma Hiddleston, John McColl, Cat Hobart, Xander Macmillan, Polly Bennett and Jessica Winch. Much of the original script was influenced by conversations with these people. I consider myself hugely lucky to have worked with such talented collaborators.

I would like to thank Katherine Mendelsohn, David Greig, Carol Tambor and Kent Lawson.

Finally, my thanks go to Jess Cooper and my family for their unfaltering support.

Precious Little Talent was first performed at the Bedlam
Theatre, Edinburgh, on 6 August 2009, as part of the Edinburgh
Festival Fringe, with the following cast:

SAM	Simon Ginty
JOEY	Emma Hiddleston
GEORGE	John McColl
Director	Ella Hickson
Technical Manager	Xander Macmillan
Stage Manager	Cat Hobart
Movement Director	Polly Bennett
Producer	Jess Winch for Tantrums Ltd

A revised full-length production transferred to the Trafalgar
Studios, London, on 5 April 2011, with the following cast:

SAM	Anthony Welsh
JOEY	Olivia Hallinan
GEORGE	Ian Gelder
Director	James Dacre
Designer	Lucy Osborne
Lighting Designer	Mark Jonathan
Sound Designer	Emma Laxton
Producer	James Quaife for Tantrums Ltd

Characters

SAM, *nineteen, American*
JOEY, *twenty-three, English*
GEORGE, *sixty-one, English, Joey's father*

The play takes place in

New York, December, 2008
New York, February, 2009
London, April, 2011

ACT ONE

One

Late night.

Christmas Eve, 2008.

A rooftop – New York City.

SAM (*to audience*). It's Christmas Eve in the winter of two thousand eight and the night is cruel and beautiful and it feels like it's the first time it's ever been that way. I'm sitting on a rooftop, downtown New York City; in front of me midtown, pouring out into the night like a million luminous toothpicks, but right around me is black, black and death. I'm nineteen and I've got an erection, right tight into the front of my pants 'cos I can feel a woman's breath on the left side of my neck. This nervous little breath, panting, just beneath my ear; the moisture in it licking at me in the dark night and I so desperately want to turn around and suck that in, so desperately – but I keep my hands on my thighs, just like this and I say 'hey'.

JOEY. Hey.

SAM. What's your name?

JOEY. Joey.

SAM. No shit, mine too!

JOEY. Really?

SAM. No, it's Sam. I'm sorry – I don't know why I just said that.

(*To audience.*) She laughs this funny little laugh and it sounds funny so I say –

You sound funny.

JOEY. I'm English.

SAM (*to audience*). She says, all like that, all 'I'm English', like that.

(*To* JOEY.) So you're British, eh?

JOEY. No, I'm English. No one's really British. People who say they're British are just embarrassed about being English.

SAM. What about the Scots and the Irish?

JOEY. They're Scottish and Irish.

SAM. And isn't there Wales?

JOEY. Everyone sort of forgets about Wales.

SAM. Tough to be Welsh, eh?

JOEY. I guess.

Pause.

SAM. Politics makes for bad sex.

JOEY. What?

SAM. Um – sorry, it was something my dad always used to say – I – I don't know why I – um… So… you're up here for, um – a little air?

JOEY. Yep.

SAM (*to audience*). So I'm thinking 'a little air', like taking a turn on the veranda, like a midnight, moonlit stroll, like Audrey Hepburn at dawn before breakfast time at Tiffany's; like this is the moment you might tell your kids that you met and she says –

JOEY. Hepburn.

SAM. Hepburn?

JOEY. Hepburn.

SAM. How did you do that?

JOEY. I just – how old are you, Sam?

SAM. How old are you?

JOEY. Twenty-three.

SAM. No freaking way – me too!

JOEY. Really?

SAM. No, absolutely not, I'm nineteen. I'm sorry, I don't know why I – you can check my driver's license if you want.

(*To audience*.) And she only fucking does! She slides these little British, English, fingers right into my back pocket, so as I can feel the bump of her ring dig in against my butt cheek – and then BAM; I stare her right in the face, eyeball to eyeball, and that little licky breath is all over my face and my lips, all warm and moist but I don't flinch an inch… she has this pale skin and pink cheeks like she's been out in the snow…

(*To* JOEY.) Your hand is in my pocket.

JOEY. It's warm.

SAM. Okay, keep it there. That's fine by me.

(*To audience*.) And then I'm sure you won't believe this, I'm sure you will have heard this said a thousand times before but piano music starts to play. A really well-known tune, I know, but it was, I swear to you –

Beethoven's 'Moonlight Sonata' starts to play.

That's it! That's exactly the one! I swear, I swear, ladies and gentlemen, it came swinging up over the fire escapes like a beautiful baboon and fills right up all the air around us like it's smoke and ashes and she looks at me, right dead smack in the eyes. She has beautiful eyes, like two tiny tiny fires and she pokes out her little tongue all pinky in the night sky and she… licks me. Right across my top lip; and I feel like it might just be the end of the world if she leaves.

And suddenly we're running fast as our feet will take us, stamping down fire escapes, looking in on late-night offices where tired and desperate men are sitting and watching dollars dropping like flies but we're running, fast and quick and furious. We're headed down Bleeker where the lights are kind and the windows are crowded up with smart stuff and slutty stuff and it's cold, you see, so cold that my fingers get numb so as they might be tempted to let go of the very best thing that they have ever had the pleasure of holding on to –

(*To* JOEY.) You want to take the subway?

JOEY. Sure.

SAM (*to audience*). We take the uptown 6 train that goes all the way up and down Manhattan, scratching its back along the side of Central Park – we take it all the way up through Astor and Union and 59th and 96th and all the way on up to Harlem and when we get to the top we just come right back again and on our way back down we just can't stop looking at each other and we laugh and we put our hands over our faces like kids in a bathtub –

JOEY. I want to get off.

SAM. Okay.

(*To audience*.) I take her hand and I lead her off that train and I've judged my timing right because we emerge right into the middle of Grand Central Station.

Have you ever been there? Oh, I'm sure you have in movies once or twice or probably a thousand times but can I ask you to try and imagine it as if you were seeing it for exactly the first time? As if you hadn't seen a single movie, like you've never enjoyed Cary Grant running through or De Niro on his Midnight Run – imagine please that you had never even bought a picture postcard. Imagine all those chandeliers as if you had never seen a single thing twinkle in your life ever before.

And do you know what I did – right then, right in the middle of Grand Central Station? I pulled her right around and I kissed her, real hard. And when I stopped, when I stopped and stood back and I looked at her, she said the strangest thing, she said… 'I don't believe in you.'

Two

Earlier that evening.

An apartment beneath the rooftop.

TriBeCa – New York City.

SAM *and* GEORGE *are playing a game of chess.*

GEORGE. Your move.

SAM. I got nothing. I can't see what you did there.

GEORGE. I blinded you with skill.

SAM. Pretty much.

SAM *begins to pack up the chessboard.*

GEORGE. What are you doing?

SAM. I'm packing up.

GEORGE. Why?

SAM. It's bedtime.

GEORGE. Don't be a quitter.

SAM. It's bedtime.

GEORGE. I'll decide when it's –

SAM. I got to do it before I go, George.

SAM *goes to put a tabard on.*

GEORGE. Refill my Scotch before you go putting that thing back on.

SAM *refills the glass.*

SAM. Anything else?

GEORGE. You could fetch me the paper but you are, no doubt, permitted to do that in your official capacity.

SAM. Tea or Ovaltine?

GEORGE. Tea.

SAM. You know, they think tea's got more caffeine in it than coffee.

GEORGE. 'They' have begun to talk nothing but bollocks. I don't want that piss-weak stuff either.

SAM. I just don't want you not to –

GEORGE (*interrupting*). Milk first! Let the milk cool the tea, don't let the tea heat the milk.

SAM. I've already put milk in there.

GEORGE. Hm.

SAM. Your blister pack's empty for today, you already taken your meds?

GEORGE. They're called pills and yes I have.

SAM. Are you sure?

GEORGE. Yes still means yes.

SAM. Okay. I ironed some clean pyjamas if you –

GEORGE. These are fine.

SAM. You've been wearing them for –

GEORGE (*interrupting*). They're fine.

SAM. You want a hand shaving?

GEORGE. No.

SAM. It's been a while since –

GEORGE (*interrupting*). I do apologise, am I offending your sensibilities, Sam?

SAM. I just thought it might be itchy.

GEORGE. Well, it's not, and if it is, I'll itch it.

SAM. Okay, I'm just going to turn your blanket on and then I'll –

GEORGE. I can flick a switch!

Beat.

SAM. George, did Marina come in this morning?

GEORGE. Yes… you know she did, I know she did, we all know she did. She wrote her name nice and large on the timetable in big pink felt-tip because, of course, I can't understand standard English letter formations unless they are the size of small countries and the colour of reconstituted flamingos.

SAM. Just checking, George.

GEORGE. And once it's written, MA-RI-NA – wipes the rest of the timetable clean as if she imagines that in that act of reading it I spray it with the various products of my various incontinences. Does she? Hm?

SAM. George?

GEORGE. Does she think that the neon letters are so cryptically befuddling to my addled brain that in a fit of confusion I violently secrete on the thing? Bafflement, confusion and consternation – I've just spat, snotted and dribbled all over this shiny timetable, I do hope – M… M–

SAM. Marina.

GEORGE. I do hope Marina is back in tomorrow to wipe it clean.

SAM. George?

GEORGE. Yes?

Beat.

SAM. She's just trying to keep things clean. She's just got habits.

GEORGE. Well she can un-habit, uninhabit my bloody kitchen and stop wiping the sodding timetable.

SAM. I'll tell her to stop wiping the timetable.

GEORGE. I'd be most obliged. (*Beat.*) Are you in tomorrow?

SAM. It's on the timeta… yeah, I'm in.

GEORGE. Why don't you have somewhere better to be?

SAM. It's double pay.

Pause.

GEORGE. What about your – uh –

SAM. Family?

GEORGE. Yes.

SAM. There are enough of them to look after each other.

GEORGE. Right, well, in which case you should probably buy a bird.

SAM. Yeah?

GEORGE. Ham sandwiches run the risk of being a little depressing.

SAM. Okay.

GEORGE. Nothing large.

SAM. You want me to bring any decorations or a cake or wear anything fancy or – I could get a tree or –

GEORGE (*interrupting*). No.

SAM. No?

GEORGE. No – business as usual; no ham.

SAM. Right. (*Beat.*) George, are you sleeping alright?

GEORGE. Yes.

SAM. Marina said she came in early this morning and you seemed a little disoriented.

GEORGE. Disorien-ta-ted.

SAM. What?

GEORGE. Disorien-ta-ted. There's an extra syllable in there, we gave you the bloody language, the least you can do is use it properly.

SAM. She said you seemed a little –

GEORGE. You can tell MA-RI-NA that I'm perfectly orientated, thank you.

SAM. I said that to her, I was just –

GEORGE (*interrupting*). I'm going to orient myself toward bed now if you don't mind.

SAM. Sure.

GEORGE. So if you'd kindly orient yourself toward leaving.

SAM. Sure, just after I've tided up.

GEORGE. It's tidy.

SAM. And then I might head up onto the roof for a smoke.

GEORGE. It's rather late, Sam.

SAM. Hell, George, it is late, it's almost Christmas Day; Merry Christmas, George.

GEORGE. Merry Christmas. (*Beat.*) Are you in tomorrow?

SAM. Sure I am.

Beat.

GEORGE. If you come to check on me I'll disembowel you.

SAM. Wouldn't dream of it.

GEORGE. You might as well have this cup of tea as well, it tastes like piss.

GEORGE *leaves the cup of tea on the side and exits.*

SAM *waits a moment, gets his coat and leaves.*

Some time passes.

GEORGE *goes into the sideboard and gets out a small gift box.*

GEORGE *opens the gift box to reveal earrings.*

GEORGE *holds them up and nervously inspects them.*

GEORGE *abandons the idea of them and puts the box back in the cupboard.*

Three

Late night.

Christmas Eve, 2008.

A rooftop – New York City.

JOEY (*to audience*). All those windows; tiny lights holding tiny lives… all in rows and columns, like a massive crossword, with none of the clues filled in yet.

SAM. Hey.

JOEY. Hey.

SAM. What's your name?

JOEY. Joey.

SAM. No shit, mine too!

JOEY. Really?

SAM. No, it's Sam. I'm sorry – I don't know why I just said that.

JOEY (*to audience*). Weird.

SAM. You sound funny.

JOEY. I'm English.

SAM. So you're British, eh?

JOEY. No, I'm English. No one's really British. People who say they're British are just embarrassed about being English.

SAM. What about the Scots and the Irish?

JOEY. They're Scottish and Irish.

SAM. And isn't there Wales?

JOEY. Everyone sort of forgets about Wales.

SAM. Tough to be Welsh, eh?

JOEY. I guess.

   Pause.

SAM. Politics makes for bad sex.

JOEY. What?

(*To audience*.) What?

SAM. Um – sorry, it was something my dad always used to say – I – I don't know why I – um… So… you're up here for a little air?

JOEY. Yep. (*Burps*.) Sorry, heartburn –

SAM. Hepburn? How did you do that?

JOEY. Heartburn… the plane – food.

SAM. Oh.

JOEY. How old are you, Sam?

SAM. How old are you?

JOEY. Twenty-three.

SAM. No fucking way – me too!

JOEY. Really?

SAM. No, absolutely not, I'm nineteen. I'm sorry, I don't know why I – you can check my driver's licence if you want.

JOEY (*to audience*). Sure, why not.

JOEY *puts her hand in* SAM*'s pocket.*

SAM *snaps his head around, they lock eyes.*

SAM. Your hand is in my pocket.

JOEY. It's warm.

SAM. Okay. Keep it there. That's fine by me.

JOEY (*to audience*). And we're sitting there, stony-still, not moving a muscle and suddenly as if we were in some old-fashioned movie, my hand in his back pocket has managed to turn his iPod on and out of his earphones, right across the freezing night, comes the 'Moonlight Sonata'. Americans, what are they like?

And he's looking so sincere and earnest and he won't look away and somehow, it's too much and I just want to sort of, pop the moment and so I –

JOEY *licks* SAM *across his top lip.*

Lick him.

(*To audience.*) I grab him, and I start running. Down these fire escapes and down all these streets I've never seen before, and I keep going, you know in that way, when you're a bit drunk and you're totally convinced that you should be in the Olympics or you're Rocky or – so my feet just keep going and going and – have you ever felt that? Like you just want to run so fucking badly and nowhere is far enough? So I just keep running, faster and faster and the cold hurts my chest and my teeth ache and –

SAM *stops* JOEY.

SAM. You want to take the subway?

JOEY (*to audience*). The train feels good, the windows flashing and the faces going past – it lets you think for a second, lets you breathe. And he's still sitting there, still smiling at me, like a, I don't know… a – dog. And then the wine from the plane and the cold and the – and I think I'm going to be –

JOEY *puts her hands over her face.*

SAM *puts his hands over his face as if it's a game.*

(*To* SAM.) I want to get off.

SAM. Okay.

JOEY (*to audience*). So he grabs me and drags me through the turnstiles and up – up into the middle of Grand Central Station. People aren't lying when they say that place is beautiful. It's got the kind of grandeur that makes you feel like you can borrow a life that's better than yours, just for a moment, reminds you what fairy stories felt like – with all those chandeliers and it all beating, softly, with whispers of old movies, love affairs worth waiting for and great lines said at the right time – it makes you feel like –

SAM *grabs her and kisses her.*

I don't believe in you.

Four

It's ten o'clock in the morning.

The morning is fresh, cold and bright.

It's Christmas Day.

GEORGE *is dressed in his Sunday best.*

SAM *enters.*

SAM. Good morning, George, and a very merry –

GEORGE (*interrupting*). Please be quiet.

SAM. I didn't realise we were dressing up.

GEORGE. It's not for –

SAM. Is everything okay?

GEORGE. You need to leave.

SAM. What?

GEORGE. I don't need any help today.

SAM. You've done your buttons up wrong.

GEORGE. Did you hear me?

SAM. Yes. (*Beat.*) You look like you haven't slept.

GEORGE. Leave, please.

SAM. Why?

GEORGE. I need you to leave.

SAM. Are you okay, George?

GEORGE. Yes.

SAM. Have you taken your –

GEORGE (*interrupting*). I'm sorry but you can't stay.

SAM. I'm serious, if something has happened you need to stop being cranky and just tell me.

GEORGE. You are my employee. I am telling you to leave the premises.

Pause.

SAM. You're going to tell me or you're going to have to throw me out.

Long pause.

GEORGE. I have a guest.

SAM. You have a guest.

GEORGE. Yes.

SAM. You haven't had a guest in two years, George.

GEORGE. Well, I have a guest.

SAM. Okay. Okay –

GEORGE. Don't use that tone.

SAM. Tone?

GEORGE. Suggesting I am of unsound mind.

SAM. It wasn't a tone – I'm just saying a guest is unusual.

GEORGE. Sam, the d-defence for sanity is much the same – p-proof for insanity so we're going to be here all bloody day if you d-don't–

SAM. Breathe.

GEORGE. Leave.

SAM. Where is your guest, George? Show me your guest.

GEORGE. She's sleeping.

SAM. Yeah?

GEORGE. Yes.

Pause.

SAM. Oh. (*Beat.*) Wow.

GEORGE. 'Wow'?

SAM. She must have got here pretty late if I missed her?

GEORGE. She did, rather, yes. I'm not sure what this has to do
with –

SAM. It's not very wholesome, it being Christmas and all.

GEORGE. What?

SAM. She a whore?

GEORGE. No, she bloody well is not!

SAM. Sorry, that was way out of line.

GEORGE. Yes, it was.

SAM. You need me to leave.

GEORGE. Yes!

JOEY *enters in her pyjamas, rubbing her eyes.*

JOEY. Morning. Happy Chr–

JOEY *spots* SAM.

Pause.

GEORGE. Morning. Would you like a cup of tea?

JOEY. Yes; please.

SAM. Hey.

JOEY. Hey.

GEORGE. This is Sam.

JOEY. Hello, Sam.

SAM. I'll get it, the tea.

JOEY. He knows where the kettle is?

SAM. Yes.

JOEY. Right.

GEORGE. Did you sleep well?

JOEY. No, not very, jet lag.

SAM. Valerian.

JOEY. Sorry?

SAM. Valerian tea, for jet lag, works like a dream. Merry Christmas, by the way, I forgot to say… just then.

GEORGE. Tea would be lovely.

SAM *leaves to make tea*.

It'll wear off.

JOEY. What?

GEORGE. Jet lag.

JOEY. How long has he been here?

GEORGE. Sam?

JOEY. Yes.

GEORGE. Here?

JOEY. Yes.

GEORGE. Oh – not long.

SAM (*from off*). Sugar?

GEORGE *and* JOEY. No.

JOEY. It looks different in daylight.

GEORGE. It's a little –

JOEY. I should get changed. Do you know him?

GEORGE. Yes.

JOEY. Right.

GEORGE. If you're going to have a shower I'll need to turn the –

JOEY. He's your... neighbour?

Beat.

GEORGE. Yes.

SAM *enters with tea.*

SAM. Here we go – one for George and one for Joey.

JOEY. Thank you.

GEORGE. Joey?

JOEY. Yes?

GEORGE. Joanna.

SAM. Milk, Joanna?

JOEY. Thank you.

SAM. George?

GEORGE. Yes. Thank you.

JOEY. Do you know what, I should – uh, have a shower and get ready, um –

SAM *(interrupting)*. Second on the left, on the way back toward the bedroom.

GEORGE. We'll put some breakfast on.

JOEY. So you'll still be here when –

SAM *(interrupting)*. Oh, I don't know.

GEORGE. Off you go, Joanna.

JOEY. Right.

JOEY *exits.*

Pause.

GEORGE. Unusually good cup of tea, Sam.

SAM. Thanks.

GEORGE. What's the plan for lunch?

SAM. Lunch?

GEORGE. Yes.

SAM. You're shaking, George.

GEORGE. No.

SAM. Sit down.

GEORGE. Yes. Thank you.

SAM. I'll get some breakfast.

SAM *goes to put his tabard on.*

GEORGE. Don't.

SAM. What?

GEORGE. Don't put that on. Could you put it in the drawer, please?

SAM. Sure.

GEORGE. Sam?

SAM. Yeah?

GEORGE. She can't – um – she can't know anything. It's… vital.

SAM. George, that's going to be –

GEORGE (*interrupting*). Not a thing.

SAM. Right.

GEORGE. I'm sorry for asking you to leave, it's rather complicated.

SAM. I bet it is.

GEORGE. We should have eggs, for breakfast, she likes them a certain way, I can't – I can't – um –

SAM. Scrambled, poached or boiled?

GEORGE. Scr– could I get a whisky?

SAM. It's ten o'clock in the morning.

GEORGE. Yes.

SAM. Scrambled, poached or boiled, George?

GEORGE. Sam, are you –?

SAM. Scrambled, poached or boiled – eggs?

GEORGE. Could you pass me my – my –

SAM (*interrupting*). I know it's not my place but she's very young, she's clearly in some kind of trouble and I don't think that this, you, are the right –

GEORGE (*interrupting*). What do you mean, she's in trouble?

SAM. I – um – I met her, last night and she was kind of, you know, a bit messed up, like just – lost, I guess, and I don't think her ending up here, with a man that is like three times her age, is going to do her any good.

Beat.

GEORGE. She's my daughter.

Beat.

SAM. Oh. (*Beat.*) Shit.

GEORGE. Last night?

JOEY *enters behind* SAM. SAM *doesn't see her.*

SAM. Two years and you never say you have a daughter?

JOEY. Oh.

GEORGE. Joanna, I –

JOEY (*interrupting*). Sam, it is Sam, isn't it?

SAM. Yes.

JOEY. Could you turn that up a second?

SAM. This.

JOEY. Yes. I think it's the Queen's Speech.

SAM *turns the radio up.*

(*Taunting*.) We used to listen to it when I was small, we'd have dinner, eat so much we all felt like we were going to be sick and right before we all fell asleep you'd make us sit down and listen to it, didn't you, Dad?

GEORGE. Yes.

JOEY. Why don't I go and put some breakfast on?

GEORGE. Joanna?

JOEY. Everyone okay with poached eggs?

SAM. Sounds great.

JOEY. Good.

GEORGE. Joanna?

JOEY. Your buttons are done up wrong, Dad.

JOEY *exits*.

Pause.

GEORGE *starts furiously trying to undo and redo his buttons and he can't manage it.*

SAM *watches for several seconds.*

SAM *goes over and helps* GEORGE.

GEORGE *rejects the help.*

GEORGE. I need to go and get some things for lunch.

SAM. I'll go.

GEORGE. No, I need the a –

SAM. I can't let you go on your own, George.

GEORGE. Keep your voice down. I am a grown man, I am going to –

SAM (*interrupting*). I can't let you do that.

GEORGE. You can't stop me.

SAM. I'll come with you.

GEORGE. I don't want her here on her own, she'll find things. You'll stay here.

GEORGE *goes to leave.*

SAM *steps in his way.*

SAM. George, I can't let you go out there on your –

JOEY *enters.*

JOEY. Tea or coffee?

GEORGE. I'm just going to pop out for a minute, get some bits and pieces.

JOEY. I'm doing eggs.

SAM. George?

GEORGE. Sam can help you.

JOEY. I don't need any help.

GEORGE. I won't be long.

GEORGE *exits.*

QUEEN'S VOICE *(from radio).*'Christmas is a time for celebration, but this year it is a more sombre occasion for many. Some of those things which could have been taken for granted suddenly seem less certain and, naturally, give rise to feelings of insecurity. When life seems hard, the courageous do not lie down and accept defeat; instead, they are all the more determined to struggle for a better future.

– I think we have a huge amount to learn from individuals such as these. And what I believe many of us share with them is a source of strength and peace of mind in our own families.'

End of Act One.

ACT TWO

One

JOEY *is dressed for Christmas Day. She has made an effort.*

It is midday.

JOEY *is looking for something in the sitting room, rifling through books and drawers, keeping an eye/ear out for people coming in.*

SAM *enters.*

SAM. What are you looking for?

JOEY. Where's Dad?

SAM. I don't think he's in there. (*Beat.*) You look nice.

JOEY. Thanks.

SAM. You want a drink?

JOEY. No. Thank you.

SAM. Okay. Well, I'll be in the kitchen if you –

JOEY. How come you're not with your family?

SAM. Can't afford the trip home.

JOEY. Where do they live?

SAM. Norfolk.

JOEY. What?

SAM. Norfolk, Virginia – it's just north of Portsmouth.

JOEY. Portsmouth?

SAM. It's like seven hours south, by car. What were you looking for?

JOEY *holds up a framed photograph.*

JOEY. Who are these guys?

SAM. The Romeos.

JOEY. The who?

SAM. Romeos – Retired Old Men Eating Out. It's a bunch of old British guys; he has lunch with them once a week or so.

JOEY. You live next door, don't you?

SAM. No, I live in Hoboken.

JOEY. Oh. Dad said –

SAM. Oh, sure – yeah – my aunt lives in the building.

JOEY. Right.

SAM. He never lets me in his room.

Beat.

JOEY. Okay.

SAM. What I mean is, whatever it is you're looking for – it might be in there.

JOEY. I wasn't looking for anything.

SAM. Okay. Well if you do want a drink, shout.

SAM *goes to exit.*

JOEY. Sam?

SAM. Yeah?

JOEY. Is this the only photo in the apartment?

SAM. I think so.

JOEY. No others, not lying around or in his wallet or – ?

SAM (*interrupting*). He got given that; I doubt he even knows it's there.

JOEY. There aren't any books.

SAM. He reads newspapers and magazines mostly.

JOEY. I had the smallest room in the house until I was thirteen because he refused to give up his bloody library.

SAM. You seem kind of angry.

JOEY. Have you ever considered being a psychologist, Sam?

SAM. Sure.

JOEY. Why are you here?

SAM. Why are you here?

JOEY. I asked you first.

SAM. I was here first.

JOEY. To see my dad.

SAM. Ditto.

JOEY. Are you his – cleaner?

SAM. No.

JOEY. His cook, his student, his –

SAM. I'm his friend.

JOEY. You're nineteen.

SAM. You want to check my –

JOEY. No.

SAM. I come say 'hey' every now and then, we hang out, we play chess, we talk, we watch movies – I just come say 'hey'. No one else does.

JOEY. Meaning?

SAM. Nothing.

JOEY. He's the one that's never mentioned me.

SAM. You never mentioned him either.

JOEY. Oh, I'm sorry – when was I meant to do that? Before or after you rammed your tongue down my throat?

SAM. You licked me.

JOEY. You kissed me.

SAM. I didn't know you were George's daughter.

JOEY. You only kiss strangers?

SAM. No. I don't really kiss people, at all, usually; just you.

JOEY. Oh.

Beat.

SAM. Can I do it again?

JOEY. What?

SAM. Kiss you.

JOEY. They're right about you Americans being greedy, aren't they?

SAM. You're pretty funny; and pretty… and funny.

JOEY. Sam – I –

SAM (*interrupting*). Can I kiss you?

JOEY. Don't ask that, no one asks that, well, Americans probably ask but we don't –

SAM *lunges forward to kiss* JOEY.

JOEY *lurches out of the way.*

I didn't mean do it!

SAM. You said 'don't ask'!

JOEY. I meant 'don't ask' as in read between the bloody lines. My body was not saying 'come hither'.

SAM. Why not?

JOEY. What?

SAM. Why wasn't your body saying 'come hither'?

JOEY. I don't know.

SAM. Last night you put your hand in my back pocket, then you licked my face and dragged me through New York. In American, that means 'come hither'.

Beat.

JOEY. I was very tired.

SAM. Tired?

JOEY. Yes.

SAM. Sure.

JOEY. Look, Sam, I'm sure you're really nice, you seem really nice.

SAM. I am.

JOEY. Okay.

SAM. You seem – amazing.

JOEY. That wasn't quite where I was –

SAM. I think you're a bit amazing. I know it's crazy 'cos I just met you but I think, I think you're kind of amazing.

JOEY. Okay, Sam – why don't we play a game where you say the exact opposite of what you're thinking. I think it might help with the language barrier.

SAM. No.

JOEY. Why not?

SAM. I'd started.

JOEY. Oh right, I see.

SAM. The idea of doing you makes me sick.

JOEY. Good.

SAM. I've never thought about what you look like naked.

JOEY. That's a little easy to decipher.

SAM. English girls are real warm and friendly.

JOEY *gives a sardonic smile.*

Why don't you want me to tell you that I like you?

JOEY. Wait, I can't work out the opposite of –

SAM (*interrupting*). I stopped playing.

JOEY. Yes, I know, I was… I don't know why I don't like it; it makes me feel uncomfortable.

SAM. Why?

JOEY. I don't know.

SAM. It's a shame; I could do it all day.

They look at one another.

Beat.

JOEY. The more you say it the less I believe it.

SAM. That makes no sense.

JOEY. Does to me.

SAM. Guess I'd better shut up.

JOEY smiles.

SAM exits.

Two

The sitting room.

It's one o'clock.

GEORGE *enters, he's out of breath.*

GEORGE *is carrying a bunch of white roses.*

GEORGE *starts trying to arrange the roses.*

JOEY *enters.*

JOEY. Hello.

GEORGE. Were you sleeping?

JOEY. No.

GEORGE. It's a lovely day out, bright sunshine, you should have a roam.

JOEY. It's freezing out there. You want a hand with those?

GEORGE. Not at all.

JOEY. They're my favourites.

GEORGE. God knows where you have to go to grow a rose in bloody December but nevertheless; they look rather good, don't they?

JOEY. Perfect.

Pause.

GEORGE. Why don't you go and help Sam with lunch?

JOEY. No, I'm okay here. I'm reading.

Beat.

GEORGE. That yours?

JOEY. What?

GEORGE. The paper?

JOEY. Oh yeah, I got it yesterday, for the flight.

GEORGE. I see university has had its way with you.

JOEY. What?

GEORGE. *Guardian.*

JOEY. Sure.

GEORGE. How is it?

JOEY. The paper?

GEORGE. University.

JOEY. I graduated. You sent me a congratulations card.

GEORGE (*works hard*). You said you were going to do a Masters in Politics and Religion, focusing on the contemporary relationship between Church and State.

Beat.

JOEY. I didn't get funding.

GEORGE. Why not?

JOEY. Because there isn't any.

GEORGE. Couldn't your mother –

JOEY. Mum didn't have the cash.

GEORGE. And –

JOEY (*interrupting*). I'm not his responsibility. Careful, you'll spill the water.

GEORGE. Surely he could have seen his way to –

JOEY (*interrupting*). I wouldn't have taken it even if he'd offered.

Beat.

GEORGE. You should have rung.

JOEY. I did.

GEORGE. What are you doing for money?

JOEY. I worked in a bar.

GEORGE. Worked?

JOEY. Yes.

GEORGE. What happened?

JOEY. Overstaffed.

GEORGE. From what I remember of the last time the economy nosedived; it didn't stop people from drinking.

JOEY. Overstaffed, Dad. Too many staff; management can't afford to pay their staff.

GEORGE. It's Christmas.

JOEY. Too big to be an elf it turns out; fucking shame because I do suit green.

GEORGE. I don't like your tone.

JOEY. Of course you don't.

Pause.

GEORGE. You could have been unpleasant by phone.

JOEY. I don't want to be unpleasant, I want – can we turn up the carols?

GEORGE. Of course.

JOEY turns up the carols.

JOEY. You should get a tree.

GEORGE. Little late in the day. Have you rung your mother?

JOEY. No.

GEORGE. You should ring her.

JOEY. Why?

GEORGE. It's good manners to let people know where you are.

JOEY. Really. You didn't.

GEORGE knocks over the vase, the water spills all over the table.

GEORGE. Fuck!

JOEY. Language.

GEORGE. Can you get a cloth?

JOEY exits.

GEORGE tries to stop his hand from shaking.

JOEY re-enters.

GEORGE asks for the cloth.

JOEY. I'll do it, sit down.

GEORGE. No –

JOEY (*interrupting*). I'll do it.

Some time passes. JOEY cleans in silence.

GEORGE. How is she?

JOEY. Fine (*Beat.*) They've had another baby, girl, Ahdia-Jessica, cute as hell.

GEORGE. I'm sure.

JOEY. The house is covered in toys.

GEORGE. Bet she doesn't like that.

JOEY. There weren't any decorations. No Christmas tree, no wreath, no presents.

GEORGE. Give me that cloth; you've missed half of it.

Some time passes.

JOEY. It's different. It smells different. They've painted the kitchen orange. They've made my old bedroom into a nursery.

GEORGE. Where does he put his books?

JOEY. He reads them on his computer.

GEORGE. As if there was any further proof needed of that man's –

JOEY. The books aren't the point, Dad.

GEORGE. Would you like a drink?

JOEY. No.

Pause.

GEORGE. Those roses look rather lovely.

JOEY. Mum's started wearing a headscarf, which is fine, it's just, she's my mum so... Dad?

GEORGE. Yes?

Pause.

It must be nearly lunch, my stomach's rumbling.

JOEY. Dad – can I stay, a while?

GEORGE. Sam's bound to be incinerating dinner I'm going to go and –

JOEY. Dad?

GEORGE. Sam!

JOEY. Who the hell is he anyway?

GEORGE. What?

JOEY. It's a bit weird, isn't it? Playing house with a teenager?

GEORGE. Playing house?

JOEY. Well?

GEORGE. He's – he – he helps me around the place, sometimes – he's – he's here because I pay him to be here.

JOEY. You pay him? To clean?

GEORGE. Yes.

JOEY. And to spend Christmases with you?

GEORGE. Please stop manipulating the situation, he helps me – that's all.

JOEY. But I don't get it – helps you do what?

GEORGE. Things your mother used to do!

Beat.

JOEY. I can teach you how to iron a shirt.

GEORGE. Boil an egg?

JOEY. Poach them even.

GEORGE. Oh, I don't want to rush things.

Pause.

JOEY. Dad – please, can I stay just for a –

GEORGE (*interrupting*). Joanna, I haven't seen you for two years.

JOEY. That's hardly my fault.

GEORGE. You should have rung or written or –

JOEY. It's not like you're busy!

GEORGE. You can't just turn up here at four in the bloody morning with no explanation –

JOEY. I'm trying to explain.

GEORGE. Soaked to the skin, make-up all over your face and stinking to high heaven of booze!

JOEY. I didn't *stink* of –

GEORGE (*interrupting*). And this morning I discover that you've spent half the night enjoying all manner of high-jinks with my employee – I'm still braced for the arrival of the police, or the angry lover, or the wail of an abandoned infant from the dumpster.

JOEY. Dustbin.

GEORGE. Dustbin.

Beat.

JOEY. Well, thank you for your welcome.

GEORGE. Thank you for your w-warning.

GEORGE *exits*.

JOEY *is left standing*.

Three

SAM *and* JOEY *are surrounded by boxes*.

SAM *rips off a large piece of tape – it makes a loud noise*.

JOEY. Fuck's sake, Sam, shh! You'll wake him up!

SAM. Sorry!

JOEY. What does it look like?

SAM. I can't open it without making any noise.

JOEY. Do it quietly.

SAM. It's tape!

JOEY. We can put it in the corner – we can make paper chains.

SAM. Popcorn strings.

JOEY. Paper chains.

SAM. Okay.

JOEY. And we'll put the nativity on the table and we'll put a
star on the top of the tree and cinnamon sticks and
decorations and we'll play carols and if we have time we can
make mulled wine and it'll all smell amazing – oooh – it's
exciting. He's going to like it, right?

SAM. You sure he's the kind of guy that goes in for surprises?

JOEY. You think he won't like it?

Beat.

SAM. He'll love it. Course he will, he'll fucking love it. Okay –
so action plan, tree first?

JOEY. Yes. I'll go and get the scissors, you put some carols on!

SAM. Aye aye, captain.

JOEY *exits.*

SAM *impatiently pulls the tree out of the box.*

The tree is bright neon pink.

JOEY *enters.*

JOEY. Oh. You didn't need the scissors.

SAM. Nope.

JOEY. It's meant to be green.

SAM. The one in the shop was green. We could spray it?

JOEY. We don't have any spray.

SAM. We've totally got enough stuff to cover it.

JOEY. There aren't enough paper chains in the entire world to
stop that tree being pink, Sam.

SAM. I guess. I'm sorry – I should have checked the box, but
look, it's totally not the end of the world we can still do all

the other stuff, there's the nativity and the mistletoe and the candles and the wine – it'll be amazing, it'll just be treeless. Who cares about trees anyway? Totally overrated.

JOEY. Yeah, I guess.

SAM. You do the nativity and I'll do the mistletoe; give me the scissors, the nativity is in the newspaper wrap in the blue bag – get it out, we'll set it up on the table.

JOEY. Why are you helping me?

SAM. What?

JOEY. I've been really unpleasant to you ever since I got here and you're still helping me.

SAM. Sure.

JOEY. Why?

SAM. I want to.

JOEY. I just don't want you to… you're not going to get in my pants.

SAM. Your pants?

JOEY. I'm not going to sleep with you.

SAM. Oh, I know, I'm not… I'm helping you because I want to.

JOEY. Right.

SAM. 'Cos you kind of seem like you could do with some help. (*Beat.*) Come on, unwrap – we're against the clock here.

JOEY. Okay, okay.

JOEY *starts unwrapping the nativity.*

SAM. Can you pass me the string, it's on the top there?

JOEY. Sure.

SAM. Oh look, we're both under the –

JOEY. Are you done with the string?

SAM *throws the string at* JOEY.

JOEY *goes to put the string back on the side and spots the blister pack.*

What's this?

SAM. Hm?

JOEY. It's a pill-box thing.

SAM. Oh, I don't know, I can't see it. I thought you were doing the –

JOEY (*interrupting*). It's full of pills, are they Dad's?

SAM. No.

JOEY. Whose are they?

SAM. Mine.

JOEY. What for? Sorry, is that rude, I didn't mean to –

SAM (*interrupting*). ADHD.

JOEY. Oh. Right; gosh – that kind of makes more sense of –

SAM. Thanks.

JOEY. Sorry, I didn't mean to be rude.

SAM. Oh no, don't sweat it. Mistletoe – check. Wine – I'll go and put the wine on, that nativity better be done by the time I get back –

SAM *goes to exit and pockets the medication.*

JOEY. Where did you get the nativity?

SAM. Same place I got the tree, it was the only place open. You know where we put the oranges for the wine?

JOEY. Mary's purple.

SAM. No fucking way, that's cool, man.

JOEY. She's purple and glittery.

SAM. That's not right, right?

JOEY. There's a giraffe.

SAM. That's totally a camel.

JOEY. It's a giraffe. It's in the same bundle as a rhino.

SAM. You don't think that's cool, do you?

JOEY. No.

SAM. I'm sorry – I just, he just said it was all there, so I...

JOEY. None of it looks right. This was –

SAM (*interrupting*). No, come on, come on, you just got to –

JOEY. It's all cheap and new and shit and –

SAM. It's good, you just got to set it up right and get the
    lighting right and –

JOEY. There's a fucking pink tree and a giraffe and fake
    fucking snow, none of it feels or looks like Christmas.

SAM. It's okay, we just got to –

JOEY. Stop saying 'it's okay' when it's not, Sam, it makes you
    sound like a fucking idiot!

    Beat.

SAM. You'll wake George up.

JOEY. He's not a baby.

SAM. I thought you wanted it to be a surprise.

JOEY. It looks like he's been burgled by Elton fucking John.
    Let's pack it away – let's just throw it all away.

SAM. What do you want it to look like?

JOEY. It's meant to look – look – older.

SAM. We could just wait a while.

JOEY. You ever have those memories where you can't work out
    if they ever actually happened or you've just looked at the
    photograph so many times that you think they did?

SAM. Sure – Jenna Jameson.

JOEY. Why can't you be sad?

SAM. It's Christmas, who wants to be sad?

JOEY. We should tidy this shit up before Dad comes in.

SAM. What did it smell like?

JOEY. What?

SAM. Well, photographs don't smell of anything so if the memory smells like something then it's got to be real.

JOEY. Cinnamon, cinnamon and oranges.

SAM. Come here.

JOEY. What?

SAM. Come here.

> SAM *collects a crap candle that's in one of the bags.*

> SAM *lights the candle and gives* JOEY *the orange.*

JOEY. What are you doing?

SAM. Close your eyes, stick your nail in this.

> SAM *gives* JOEY *an orange.*

> SAM *lights the candle.*

> Sniff.

> JOEY *smiles.*

> And we can even get a little fake snow and –

JOEY. Sam – that's aerosol.

SAM. Oh.

JOEY. You'll blow my face off.

SAM. Okay, well – we'll get our glittery Mary and we'll turn her upside down, you don't mind do you, Mary? No you don't. She's real tolerant see? She doesn't bitch all the time and we'll just sprinkle her magic dust all over the place and you look real close and it smells like Christmas and it's pretty much snowing.

> SAM *shakes the Mary and glitter falls off it.*

JOEY *sits, eyes closed, nose above a candle, holding an orange and getting covered in purple sparkly stuff from the crap Mary.*

The glitter falls over the flame.

There is something a little wondrous about it.

Time passes.

Eventually the pair start to tidy.

It seems there is a little peace.

Meanwhile, GEORGE *enters the bathroom.*

In the sitting room, JOEY *blows out the candle.* SAM *and* JOEY *exit.*

GEORGE *is trying to shave.*

This should take a few minutes.

The effort is extraordinary.

His hand shakes badly.

The attempt is unsuccessful.

As frustration culminates, GEORGE *slams the sink, careful not to be overheard.*

GEORGE *wipes his face.*

SAM *and* JOEY *enter the sitting room.*

SAM *is still holding mistletoe.*

JOEY. It's never going to happen.

SAM. I just like the look of it.

GEORGE *enters.*

JOEY. Dad?

GEORGE. It smells of cinnamon.

JOEY. Yes.

GEORGE. That's nice.

SAM. How d'you sleep?

GEORGE. Well, thank you. That meal could've sedated a rhino, mind.

SAM. Thanks.

JOEY. I thought we might play Trivial Pursuit?

GEORGE. God, where did you find that?

JOEY. In the cupboard.

GEORGE. I'm not sure I'm in the mood.

JOEY. Dad, come on – indulge me.

GEORGE. I'm tired.

JOEY. You just had a nap.

GEORGE. Sam, why don't you play?

JOEY. Where's the harm? We play for half an hour, you win by a staggeringly huge lead, I moan about my tiddler of a brain – and the world's natural balance is redressed – perfect.

SAM. Come on, Joey, I can play.

JOEY. I want you to play, Dad.

GEORGE. You sound like a four-year-old.

SAM. Why don't I get some drinks? Wine? Bucks stuff?

JOEY. Wine would be great.

GEORGE. Could you get me a whisky mac?

SAM. Sure. Joey – wine?

JOEY. Thanks – more –

SAM. You sure?

JOEY. Yes. Thank you.

Pause.

GEORGE. That cinnamon really does –

JOEY. Please, Dad, just one game.

SAM. Joey – I don't think –

GEORGE (*interrupting*). One round – no more.

JOEY. Yess.

SAM. George, if you don't want to – I can do it.

JOEY. Shut up.

SAM. He shouldn't have to just because –

JOEY (*interrupting*). You're such a two-faced –

GEORGE (*interrupting*). It's fine, come on, let's give the little madam what she wants.

JOEY. Oh, don't be like that otherwise there's no point.

GEORGE. Come on, set it up. Pass me the cards, I'll shuffle them.

GEORGE *begins to read them.*

JOEY. Shuffle, not read, Dad – no cheating.

GEORGE. Alright.

JOEY. Sam, hurry up – we're ready.

SAM. Okay, good, okay. Let's get involved here – I warn you though, I'm crazy competitive.

JOEY. I'm terrified. Okay, Dad, first question –

SAM. Elvis!

JOEY. No way! How did you know?

SAM. Seriously?

JOEY. No, you twat.

SAM. Whoa.

GEORGE. He was being funny. Let's start again –

JOEY. Right, Dad, without interruption – first question, 'What is the title of J. D. Salinger's most famous novel?'

GEORGE. *Catcher in the Rye.*

JOEY. Yup. Sam, roll. Okay. You won't get this –

SAM. I might.

JOEY. You won't – 'How many muscles are there in your hand?'

SAM. Um,

JOEY. Tick, tick, tick –

SAM. I don't know, like one in each finger –

JOEY. I knew it –

SAM. – none, they're all tendons.

JOEY. What? How did you know that?

SAM. Full of surprises. Right, I'll ask – roll.

JOEY. I don't trust him to ask.

GEORGE. For God's sake.

JOEY. Fine, ask – but I never pretended I was any good at this.

SAM. Okay, right – okay – 'Mick Jagger was lead singer of which –'

JOEY. Rolling Stones.

SAM. The difficulty level of these questions is pretty varied, isn't it?

JOEY. Dad, your go – roll.

GEORGE. Right, four, Arts and Literature.

SAM. Anyone for anything to eat or…?

JOEY. We're playing.

SAM. I just thought… George, you okay for –

GEORGE (*interrupting*). I'm fine, Sam. Joey – ask the question.

JOEY. 'In linguistics, what is the name of the smallest structural unit of meaning?'

GEORGE *searches*.

SAM. You lost me –

JOEY. No shit. Come on, Dad, enlighten the boy.

GEORGE. This whisky's gone straight to my head.

JOEY. Dad, hurry up – come on.

GEORGE. It's right there – it's – it's –

JOEY. Dad?

SAM. Give him a second.

JOEY. Will you just shut up?

GEORGE. Come on, of course, I'm joking – it's too easy for me, it's my field, ask me another – something about the Spice Girls or the – the –

JOEY. No, go on – just answer it, it's fine.

SAM. No, give him another – it's too easy –

JOEY. Dad – answer.

SAM. Just give me the box, I'll take another –

JOEY. No, Dad, just say the answer, take the point.

SAM. Give me the box.

JOEY. Dad!

    SAM *snatches another card.*

SAM. George, 'By what name do Canadians refer to the Union Jack?'

JOEY. No way, he can answer the other one.

GEORGE. Please, can we stop a minute?

JOEY. Dad, answer the original one.

    SAM *mouths the answer to* GEORGE.

    JOEY *catches them cheating.*

    Why the fuck are you cheating?

SAM. Joey –

JOEY. Why?

GEORGE. I'm going to bed.

JOEY. You've only just got up.

GEORGE. And I'm still tired.

JOEY. It's Christmas Day.

GEORGE. Joanna, stop being so childish.

JOEY. A child? I'm barely a fucking guest!

GEORGE. Get out!

> JOEY *grabs* SAM*'s coat off the back of the door and exits.*
>
> *Silence... some time passes.*
>
> GEORGE *turns and heads towards his bedroom.*

SAM. I'm sorry.

GEORGE. It's not your fault.

SAM. She knows something's not right, George, she's a smart girl.

> *Pause.*

I think she needs her dad.

GEORGE. I know that.

> GEORGE *exits.*

Four

The sitting room.

The lights are off.

SAM *is watching television.*

It's ten o'clock at night.

JOEY *enters.*

SAM. Hey.

JOEY. You're still here?

SAM. I couldn't leave.

JOEY. That's kind of you.

SAM. You took my coat.

JOEY. Oh.

> JOEY *takes off* SAM*'s coat.*

SAM. Where have you been?

JOEY. Is he –

SAM (*interrupting*). He stayed up for ages, he was worried, he asked me to stick about, to wait, he –

JOEY (*interrupting*). Yeah. I bet.

> *Beat.*

SAM. He didn't mean –

JOEY (*interrupting*). Sam, you shouldn't have to tell me that.

> *Beat.*

SAM. You must be freezing.

JOEY. Why were you cheating?

SAM. Where you been?

JOEY. Why were you giving him the answers, Sam? Listen to me, why? He's the smartest man I know, he was a professor for twenty years – you know that?

SAM. Yeah.

JOEY. Oh, he told you that? Of course he did. Well, he can win Trivial Pursuit in his sleep, so why the fuck were you cheating?

> *Beat.*

SAM. I wanted to help him.

JOEY. Because that's all you want to do, isn't it? You just want to help; you just want to help everyone!

SAM. What's wrong with that?

JOEY. He didn't need your help.

SAM. I'm sorry.

JOEY. I don't need your help!

SAM. No.

JOEY. So, what are you doing still doing here, Sam?

SAM. He asked me to stay to check you were in safe and you
are so I'm done, I'll go – I'm going.

JOEY. You know what, Sam? I think it's a bit fucked up a
nineteen-year-old boy spending all his time with a sixty-
year-old man.

SAM. Yeah?

JOEY. Watching all your old movies, shuffling around making
Dad his bucks fizz and his tea just the way he likes it, letting
him shout at you and order you about and... do you like it,
secretly? Knowing someone's boss, all wise and knowing;
feeling like someone has all the answers? 'Yes sir, no sir!'

SAM. Is this making you feel better?

JOEY. Yes.

SAM. Fine. Go ahead.

JOEY. Oh, don't go and take all the fun out of it.

SAM. Cutting me down is not going to make you feel any taller.

JOEY. Listen to yourself; you're a walking fucking fortune
cookie!

SAM. You're not angry with me.

JOEY. Aren't I? Aren't I? Because I can't shake the feeling,
Sam, that you, you and all your smiling and your starry-eyed
fucking – I just walked up Fifth Avenue – and it's all big and
shiny and the cars are huge and the buildings all stretching
themselves up into the stars and lights on Broadway all
shouting their success into the night like everyone is just
bound to be a big success! And then you go and sit in a café

and all the waitresses are failed actresses and failed singers and on the subway there are a billion adverts for pissy little classes and you just know those waitresses are going to be serving coffee for the rest of their fucking lives!

SAM. What's wrong with being a waitress?

JOEY. I just can't help but feel, Sam – all that dreaming – it suddenly feels like the most stupid fucking idea you ever had and all those stars and buildings, all those chandeliers and even the kisses; it all feels like lies.

Beat.

SAM. When I moved here, I was sixteen. I was so scared; I didn't think I was going to get anywhere. I knew I wanted to be a doctor so badly but I didn't have the money or the grades or... and I was staying in this shitty shitty little apartment and it was fucking freezing and I used to go to bed every night and I'd just repeat and repeat to myself, 'if you're going to make your way in the world, it's going to take everything you got.'

JOEY. Sam?

SAM. Yeah.

JOEY. You know what that is?

SAM. What?

JOEY. That is the theme tune from *Cheers*.

SAM. Who cares? Who fucking cares? Sometimes a fucking bumper sticker can save someone's life.

JOEY. But it's not real, none of it's real!

SAM. You can't believe in anything, can you?

JOEY. Come on then, Sam, enlighten me, what is it that you believe in, hm?

SAM. God, my country, my family...

JOEY. Where I come from you're a nutter if you think those things even exist.

SAM. Myself.

Beat.

JOEY. I – I've spent my whole life jumping through these
hoops that were meant to lead somewhere, I worked my arse
off at school, at each stage, GCSEs, A-levels, I busted a
fucking gut at uni whilst everyone else was getting pissed
and getting laid and it was all meant to be so that when I left,
I'd – I'd land somewhere. But it's like I made it through the
final hoop, fucking degree in my hand and smile on my face,
ready to enjoy my job and my security and then someone
just smacked me in the face with a fucking spade. I got
sacked from a bar job, there aren't any other crap jobs left, I
haven't landed anywhere.

SAM. So go home.

JOEY. I don't know where to go.

SAM. What about your mum?

JOEY. They eat food that I don't know how to cook and say
prayers before eating that I don't understand, my mum – my
mum wears clothes that I don't know where to buy them. My
bedroom is now the bedroom of a little girl –

SAM (*interrupting*). Your sister.

JOEY. – who speaks a different language to me.

SAM. So learn.

JOEY. I'm scared. I'm scared I'll disappear.

Pause.

SAM. You got to know where you come from if you want to
know where you're going.

JOEY *laughs.*

What?

JOEY. How do you not feel awkward saying that shit?

SAM. I'm not wrong.

JOEY. No.

SAM. Well then.

JOEY. How do you know?

SAM. Where I come from? I'm an American, it's easy, we got it written down.

JOEY. Sometimes I'm jealous of – of – people that are fighting wars.

SAM. What?

JOEY. I watch history programmes about the Second World War or the Civil Rights Movement or I watch the news and see people screaming and shouting and I sometimes want to be among it, sometimes I touch the TV screen and wish myself into the middle of it all. Does that make you angry?

SAM. No.

JOEY. I want to stand in a group and say 'we are this. We know we are this. We can *see* that we are this; we will fight to be this.'

SAM. White people have been doing that for hundreds and hundreds –

JOEY. But I want to be on the other side, I want to be on the right side. I want to be good. I want to be part of good people. I want to be proud.

SAM. You got to be proud of where you come from.

JOEY. But I don't know what it is; I don't know what we, I don't know what I look like.

Pause.

SAM. Dance with me?

JOEY. What?

SAM. Dance with me?

JOEY. How – how do you say the things you do and believe them, like, how do you keep a straight face?

SAM. What have I got to lose?

JOEY. Pride.

SAM. Will you dance with me?

JOEY. No.

SAM. Dance with me.

JOEY. There's no music.

> SAM *switches on the radio.*

> *'Fairytale of New York' by The Pogues plays.*

SAM. Now there is. Dance with me.

JOEY. To this? You must be fucking kidding.

> SAM *takes* JOEY*'s hand.*

SAM. Shut up.

> *The music kicks off.*

> JOEY *dances.*

> JOEY *is wild with it.*

> *They dance, they jig, they stomp and spin with wild abandon.*

> *Youth in all its optimistic fury flails bumps and grinds across the stage.*

> GEORGE *enters.*

> GEORGE *has a large gash from shaving down his face.*

> GEORGE *is dripping blood.*

> GEORGE *doesn't know where he is.*

JOEY. Dad?

SAM. Turn the music off.

JOEY. Dad?

SAM. I've got it, don't worry – turn the music off!

> JOEY *goes to turn the music off.*

> George, what are you doing, buddy?

GEORGE. I don't… I don't…

GEORGE *is on the verge of tears*.

SAM. Come on, buddy. Come on.

SAM *and* GEORGE *exit*.

JOEY *stands*.

End of Act Two.

ACT THREE

One

GEORGE (*to audience*). A man, I have always felt, has his
mind, whereas a woman has her heart; a fact that has caused
much heartache and many headaches through the years.
When disaster strikes, a gentleman, such as myself, runs to
his cool and calm and satisfying arsenal of rationale, indeed
my mind was my occupation, my brain my bread and butter,
after all. And now – there – like a sh, sh – shadow – the connection. And I am lost. And I am lost.

She left me for a Muslim man, this I understood – stand. He
knew who he was, you see, he had history – his culture was
potent, he was validated, located, connected, reinforced. I
was somewhat awash, at sea – wishy-washy – and I learnt
that this can be a little unnerving for a mother, a wife, my
lover.

My wife had been my greatest achievement. There comes a
time, the elder gentlemen will concur, when, when one faces
– *struggling* – the reckoning. When one weighs – his wife,
his cars, his houses, his wage – you weigh your present
against the dreams you had as a child and woe betide the
man that falls short. For to arrive at a destination that doesn't
satisfy – well, there is little room left now for improvement.

What I have is what I have – well, not exactly. What I have –
is what I had. It is less and less every day and I was not
satisfied with what I had when I started. So you see it is a
bleak and terminal affair, if I let it cross my mind. Mind. At
times I don't mind.

And then there is her. I can suffer the panic of a dark night,
the claustrophobia of an irreparable situation – I can suffer
that, but were she to get even a glimpse of this; a glimpse –
if she should see her father as a fool, that, I don't think I
could bear. She should leave – take with her her precious,

talented youth and hide it from me. I sleep with tens of photographs of her, surrounding me, so I can try to keep her in my head. But – I am aware, I – one day I will have the in-in-indecency to forget her, to misplace her and no child should have to suffer that. She should leave, leave me before she realises I will be leaving her.

JOEY *enters*.

JOEY. Dad?

GEORGE. Yes.

JOEY. What are you doing sitting in the dark?

GEORGE. I'm sorry if I startled you.

JOEY. Would you like a cup of tea?

GEORGE. No, no.

JOEY. Are you okay?

GEORGE. Yes.

JOEY. Whisky?

GEORGE. I'm fine.

Pause.

JOEY. Dad – what's –

GEORGE. Just a scratch. I cut myself with the bloody razor.

JOEY. No I –

GEORGE. Why don't you pop that lamp on?

JOEY *turns the lamp on*.

JOEY. I got you a present.

GEORGE. Oh, you shouldn't do that you –

JOEY. Don't worry, didn't break the bank.

JOEY *gives* GEORGE *the present*.

It's a bit egotistical really.

GEORGE *unwraps the present – a photograph of* JOEY.

Thought you could put it up, around somewhere. Just so I'm saying 'hey', even if I'm not here.

GEORGE. Thank you. It's lovely. (*Beat.*) Look in the sideboard, there, there's a box.

JOEY *finds the parcel.*

I was going to send it – I…

JOEY *unwraps the present, she holds the earrings up.*

JOEY. They're lovely.

GEORGE. I was going to get a book, like normal – I just thought – something that sparkles, why not?

JOEY. Why not.

They smile.

Why won't you tell me?

Beat.

GEORGE. Give us a hug.

JOEY *hugs* GEORGE.

Sorry for being such a beast, JoJo.

JOEY. You smell like Dad. Well done.

GEORGE. Oh, thank you, gold star.

JOEY. Yes; definitely.

Beat.

I think Sam and me –

GEORGE. I –

JOEY. I think Sam and I are going to sit on the roof for a bit before bed, look at the lights. Would you like to come?

GEORGE. No, you're alright. Have fun.

JOEY. Will do.

GEORGE. Tell Sam it's about bloody time he went home.

JOEY. Oh, I think he was going to stay tonight.

GEORGE. What?

JOEY. It was a joke.

GEORGE. Right. Well –

Beat.

It would of course be fine if that was the case.

JOEY. Sleep well, Dads.

GEORGE. Nighto.

JOEY *exits.*

Two

JOEY *and* SAM *sit on the roof and look out across New York City.*

JOEY. Don't you think it looks like a massive crossword.

SAM. Crossword? How?

JOEY. Look, all the windows with their lights on are like the empty squares ready to put the letters in and all the windows with lights that are off look like the black squares in between.

SAM. I don't see it. I always think it looks a bit like toothpicks.

JOEY. Toothpicks? What the fuck kind of toothpicks do you use?

Beat.

What's wrong with him, Sam?

SAM. He's ill.

JOEY. I'd got that far.

SAM. He – he –

JOEY. Please.

SAM. He doesn't want you to know.

JOEY. He's my dad, Sam.

SAM. He has early onset Lewy body dementia.

JOEY. Dementia?

SAM. Yeah.

Beat.

JOEY. What does that, um, does that –

SAM. It comes in bursts, sometimes he's fine and other times he hears things or sees things or forgets things; he gets confused, he has trouble with movement, he –

JOEY. No, I mean, um – is he… is he going to get better?

SAM. No.

JOEY. Right.

Pause.

How long?

SAM. You can't really tell.

JOEY. Roughly, give or take –

SAM. Life expectancy following diagnosis is between five and seven years.

JOEY. And when we was he, um – ?

SAM. Just over –

JOEY (*interrupting*). Two years.

SAM. Yeah.

JOEY. I thought he was embarrassed, by Mum and work and – I thought he was a coward.

SAM. He doesn't want people to know.

JOEY. He's just going to sit over here, miles away from anyone, and disappear?

SAM. I don't know, I –

JOEY. I need him. I – Sam, I don't want him to forget me.

Three

JOEY (*to audience*). It's a movement, isn't it? That's what they call it. When people feel the same thing in their soul at the same time – they call it a movement. I've always been jealous that I never got to ban the bomb, or burn my bras, jealous of people that lived through the war because, well, they had a common enemy and that'd make you want to fight and it'd make it clear what you were fighting for and it might even allow for a hero or two.

I said this to Sam, who, it transpired, one got used to over time – sure there were differences; sex, for example. I liked the British kind, angsty, passionate but essentially joyless and for him, well it was sort of like going to the Oscars, lots of tears and thank-yous and I felt he struggled with an overwhelming urge to clap at the end.

We sat with Dad, and played board games and talked and – Sam would take over when Dad forgot things, or when I found dirty plates in the cupboard or his shaving stuff in the cutlery drawer, or once when he struggled for my name – Sam stepped in at times when I just couldn't really stop myself from finding it all horribly sad. (*Controls tears.*)

In January Sam took me away for the weekend – and when we got to Washington, strangers were high-fiving each other and smiling and everyone seemed so – excited. It was that same feeling I'd had, on that rooftop on Christmas Day, right in the pit of my stomach, looking at all those tiny lights holding tiny lives and knowing that they were part of something – but that something was bigger than them – and it was good. And when it came to it, with the sun peeking itself out behind the Washington Monument, and looking down The Mall and seeing two million people waiting, exercising the muscle of – faith – well, I thought that it didn't really matter what you believed in – just as long as you knew how to believe.

And just as he appeared and all the flags started waving and young kids started whooping and older men and women shed some quieter tears, Sam turned to me and he wrapped me right up in his scarf and he said –

'Now, you've got to believe in this – right?'

And I looked at him, and he had this stupid smile on his face, grinning ear to fucking ear, and suddenly I realised what kind of balls it takes just to think that the world isn't such a bad place.

But of course, Sam, Dad, even that new President of theirs, they weren't really mine to believe in, not for ever anyway. No, us British, English – well, me – I'm not like them, I'm not flying the flag of revolution, I don't have fire in my belly or idealism on my tongue and I'm not singing the song of change and why? Because I don't know the words yet; but I will, we will. I won't be forgotten.

Barack Obama's inaugural speech is heard.

VOICEOVER. 'It's the answer that led those who have been told for so long by so many to be cynical, and fearful, and doubtful of what we can achieve to put their hands on the arc of history and bend it once more toward the hope of a better day. It's been a long time coming, but tonight, because of what we did on this day, in this election, at this defining moment, change has come to America.'

EPILOGUE

SAM (*to audience*). It's the spring of 2011 and the night is clear
and promising and it feels like it's the first time it's ever been
that way. I'm twenty-one and in front of me, London Town;
the sun is real low in the sky, the clouds are pink and the
birds are black and the river's running gold.

Evening-dinner people are drinking beers and eating burgers,
rude boys on BMXs, swanky-looking people, skanky-
looking people – and right in the middle of it, sliding
between the clowns and the couples and the conversations –
walking right this way, almost here, almost close enough to
touch, not knowing I'm looking right at her...

Hey.

JOEY. Hey.

Beat.

You look different.

SAM. Do I?

JOEY. Older, I guess.

JOEY *kisses* SAM *on the cheek.*

SAM (*to audience*). She smells the same.

JOEY. Have you had a tiny stroke?

SAM. No.

(*To audience.*) We sit – riverside. The lights in the trees look
like luminous fruit; she bends her head back and looks up – I
want to run my tongue along the line of her neck.

JOEY. It's hot, eh?

SAM. It's hotter at home; sweaty as hell.

JOEY. I can't imagine it not being cold.

SAM. How are you?

> (*To audience*.) She doesn't look at me. She watches a bird picking over an ice-cream cone. She has three freckles on the left side of her nose, I remember being in bed and putting my fingers on them as if her head was a bowling ball.

JOEY. Tired, but okay. You?

SAM. Good, it's good to see you. I got – these are –

> SAM *gives* JOEY *a small bunch of white roses*.

JOEY. Thanks.

SAM. They're from the – they covered the whole place in them. Hundreds and hundreds all over the –

JOEY (*interrupting*). Sure.

SAM. I'm sorry if getting your number was –

JOEY. It's fine.

SAM (*to audience*). She looks me straight in the face for the first time.

JOEY. I should have – I meant to, but I – I just in the end, I –

SAM. It's fine.

JOEY. It's not really. I bet people thought –

SAM (*interrupting*). Who cares?

JOEY. Was my mum –

SAM (*interrupting*). I spotted her immediately. You look just like her. She's beautiful.

> JOEY *laughs*.

> (*To audience*.) Bang, right there. Teeth and eyes; it's so good it makes my stomach hurt.

> What?

JOEY. I forgot how easily you –

SAM. Maybe I'm just used to beautiful women.

JOEY. Maybe. (*Beat*.) Was she –

SAM. She was alone.

JOEY. She gave you my number?

SAM. I asked. I – I really wanted to see you.

(*To audience*.) I want to cook my mum's bolognese for her, tomorrow evening I'll cook my mum's bolognese for her.

JOEY. I have to get back to work, Sam.

SAM. What time do you finish?

JOEY. I've two jobs I go to –

SAM. Where you working?

JOEY. That place, there – with the white awning.

SAM. You're serving coffee?

JOEY. In the daytime.

SAM. And in the night-time you're –

JOEY. I work for a travel magazine, for free – just experience – I'm an expert on Puerto Rico.

SAM. You get to travel, that's great, that's amazing –

(*To audience*.) My head is full of five hundred Puerto Rican men and flight-transfer timetables – Puerto Rico to JFK.

JOEY. No, I get to Google.

SAM. Oh.

(*To audience*.) Heathrow – JFK.

JOEY. Sam – I really have to –

SAM. I have some things for you – he wanted me to give you some –

JOEY (*interrupting*). I don't want them.

SAM. Joey?

JOEY. You started med school yet or –?

SAM. Oh – almost, yeah, real close – just I broke my leg beginning of the year and –

JOEY. Jumping down fire escapes?

SAM. Sure, something like that. It kinda blew my savings so – I need to work just a little longer just to –

JOEY. Shouldn't be buying plane tickets to England.

SAM. I wanted to, it seemed like a good way to –

JOEY. You staying around long?

SAM. I don't know.

JOEY. Few days or –?

SAM. Yeah, I guess, I'll take a look about.

JOEY. Where are you staying?

SAM (*to audience*). I want to wake up with her hair wrapped round my thumb.

North.

JOEY. Really? Whereabouts? I live in the north.

SAM. It might be west, some hostel, place.

JOEY. It's good to see you.

SAM. Yeah, you – you too.

Beat.

You want to bunk for an hour or so – we can go take a look at the city, take a stroll – what's that?

JOEY. What's what?

SAM. The church – the –

JOEY. It's St Paul's – Sam –

SAM. We should go there, we can go for a run – we can head over the bridge and grab some drinks, and take the subway.

JOEY. I'd lose my job – I really have to –

SAM. What about tomorrow?

JOEY. I don't have a day off until Sunday – we could grab a coffee then, if you're still –

SAM. When we missed you we used to shout at each other and one of us would storm out and slam and the door and scream 'screw you', you know, to pretend – and then we'd fucking piss ourselves laughing and he'd tell stories about when you were small.

(*To audience*.) She looks at the roses in her hands, she starts pulling the petals off.

(*To* JOEY.) Why won't you look at me?

JOEY. Sam, I'm really –

SAM. He told everyone about you after you left, wouldn't shut up about you. His room was fucking full of photos, the whole, time – I never knew, he used to sleep with like fifty fucking photos around his bed.

JOEY. Sam, I'm late.

SAM. I had to fucking dust those things every day.

JOEY *stands up*.

SAM *grabs her hand*.

Your mum said you hadn't spoken to her in –

JOEY. I have to go.

SAM. I love you.

JOEY. That's not the point.

SAM. How can it not be the point?

JOEY. How does it work?

SAM. What?

JOEY. How does it work, what do I *do*?

SAM. You come with me.

JOEY. What?

SAM. Come back to the States with me, make me home. I'll
work for a while to get the money together and then I'll train
for med school and you can find a job, there are fucking
truckloads of travel magazines, and we can rent a place, and
we'll cook in our fucking pyjamas – we'll get a dog, we'll
drink beer and we'll – yeah – we can have a kid, and we'll
make sure it only speaks to you so it sounds good, and I can
teach it – I can teach it something useful – and – and – it will
be amazing, it will be –

JOEY *takes* SAM*'s face in her hands as if he's a little boy.*

JOEY. I don't believe you.

SAM. Why?

JOEY. Because I don't think it's going to happen that way.

SAM. It could –

JOEY. I don't think the odds are very good.

SAM. You got to try.

JOEY. I've got to work.

JOEY *stands up.*

SAM. I'll show you – two years, two more years and we'll meet
here and –

JOEY. Don't, Sam, please don't do that.

SAM. For God's sake, what is wrong with you?

JOEY. Nothing.

SAM. Come with me. What have you got to lose?

JOEY. A shitty unpaid magazine job and a job in a café, a flat
that I can't afford, a routine that stops me going mad, three
friends that took me six months to make and stopped me
feeling so lonely that I thought I was going to break in half, a
lifestyle that keeps me busy enough that I don't think about
the fact my dad got buried yesterday, Sam – that, that is what
I have to lose. So no, I won't go running through London, I

won't – dance until dawn – I won't run off to America –
because you end up starstruck in a station or on a rooftop –
with your mouth open, looking at the world and it feels
amazing, it feels like everything is possible and it feels like
just believing that, just feeling that, in your stomach is
enough – but it's not enough, it's necessary but it's not
enough. Because eventually you have to close your mouth,
stop staring, get the fuck off the rooftop and go to work and
that's what you have to believe in, you have to believe in
getting up at dawn, and you have to believe in fourteen-hour
shifts, you have to believe being alone is okay, you have to
believe that shit magazine job might be the first step to
something else. Rooftops, stars, midnight runs – they're just
going to make it harder to get up in the morning.

SAM. I can't believe you've given up.

JOEY. I'm not giving up, I'm just getting started.

End of play.

GIFT

Gift was first performed as part of *Decade*, commissioned and produced by Headlong, at Commodity Quay, St Katharine Docks, London, on 1 September 2011, with the following creative team:

Director	Rupert Goold
Set Designer	Miriam Buether
Costume Designer	Emma Williams
Lighting Designer	Malcolm Rippeth
Composer and Sound Designer	Adam Cork
Associate Director	Robert Icke

The ensemble cast of *Decade* was as follows:

Jonathan Bonnici
Leila Crerar
Emma Fielding
Kevin Harvey
Tom Hodgkins
Samuel James
Arinzé Kene
Amy Lennox
Tobias Menzies
Claire Prempeh
Charlotte Randle
Cat Simmons

Chloe Faty
Isabella Mason
Charlotte St Croix

Characters

JASON

WOMAN

KAREN

WOMAN 2

Jason is dark-skinned.

Jason is from Panama but passes as Arab.

Jason is in his mid-twenties.

Jason grew up in the southern states of America.

Jason wears a WTC TOUR cap and T-shirt.

One

JASON *stands at the gift counter. A pale* WOMAN *approaches.*

JASON. Hi. How can I help?

WOMAN. The tours – are – uh –

JASON. Quarter past, half past and quarter to; if you stand by the meeting point just in front of the blue door a guide will come to collect you at the appropriate time.

WOMAN. Do I buy tickets from you?

JASON. No. I can do you gold and silver lapel pins, patches, caps, coins, tribute pens, postcards, ornaments for your tree – in season; we got books, beer mugs, magnets, T-shirts and right now we have a special on these pins right here –

WOMAN. Thanks but I'm good.

JASON. Okay.

WOMAN. Just a ticket for the walking tour.

JASON. The cashier, by the blue door.

WOMAN. Thank you.

JASON. No, no – thank you.

The WOMAN *exits.*

JASON *stands.*

Beforehand they look – right through me. You see her, look right through me? Perfect and made-up, arranged a little... like... a doll – and they appreciate the chivalry, with the coats, the manners they like... sure, but beforehand they, they – look right through me.

Two

JASON (*voice-over, with real ring-a-ding*). 'Ladies and
gentlemen, today's tour will be taken by Karen. Karen is one
of our longest running guides here at The Tribute Centre, she
has been working the Ground Zero tour here for a little over
six years, yes six years, so you will be very well looked after
indeed; couldn't be in better hands. Please gather by the blue
door where Karen is waiting for you. She will be able to
answer all of your questions. We do hope you enjoy the tour
and have a good day.'

Three

JASON. The woman with the pale face joins the back of the
group. She's alone... minus her coat she looks a little...
skinned; like she might burn, somehow. She seems kinda in a
rush, this is on her list and she'd like to get it ticked – that's
what Karen says, Karen says you can spot a list-ticker... but
I'm not so sure – she seems a little – a little...

It was her husband, Karen's – I mean. Karen still cries, every
tour, every time. Six years; same spot. She points up at the
space in the sky where the window that he jumped from
should be. She gives a few statistics, smiles at them...
silence... then tears. They have to have personal stories of
the event, the tour guides, so I wasn't allowed – I was gift
shop only because on the day, at the time of the – I was
playing RuneScape and then later jerking off which I guess
people wouldn't pay ten dollars to hear about.

Sometimes on my break I follow the tour a while. Today I
hang back a little so as Karen can't see me. My girl – the
pale-faced – is part of the silence. She doesn't seem in a
hurry any more. I think – yeah, she – I think I can see her...
crying, a little.

Four

JASON. Hi.

WOMAN. Hi.

JASON. How was –

WOMAN. Yeah.

JASON. Would you like a –

WOMAN. How much are the pins?

JASON. Plain silver – ten dollars, plain gold are twelve – the flags are –

WOMAN. That's kind of expensive.

JASON. The 'Never Forget' ones are less; limited edition – end of line.

WOMAN. Right.

JASON. Are you – ?

WOMAN. Oh yeah – I'm fine.

JASON. Would you like a tissue? Your face is still damp.

Beat.

WOMAN. Thank you.

JASON *hands the* WOMAN *a tissue. He threads his fingers through hers a little and holds on a little longer than he should. The* WOMAN *takes a sharp little breath inward.*

Beat.

It's the bit at the window – that – the idea of looking down and – deciding to – deciding that doing something is better than just… waiting.

JASON. You think of the lovers right?

WOMAN. What?

JASON. All the people you've slept next to. I always think, in that situation, I'd measure my life by the heartbeats of the people that I'd slept alongside.

The WOMAN *seems suddenly cold.*

Would you like your coat? I can get your coat for you, if you'd like – or a baseball cap – you know you lose ninety per cent of your heat from…

The WOMAN *smiles.*

WOMAN. You know any place nearby that does tea or hot chocolate or – ?

JASON. Sure. (*Beat.*) I mean – I'm nearly done here – so I – can – show you if –

Five

JASON. There's this woman that stands, oftentimes, at the back in Karen's tours. I've seen her once or twice but the guys have said she's in like once a month, only ever for Karen. And when Karen is at the window point – talking about how her husband jumped, and she starts to cry – this other woman gets this look – this look of like, pure angry and then she starts crying too and the two of them just stand there and stare at each other with wet faces. I watch from the gift-shop window, and sometimes I think that one day, when the tour has stopped and the grass has grown and there are hover-boards or some shit, Karen and that woman – will still be standing, just staring at other, pure angry and crying – neither one of them wanting to be the first to stop. I feel like they'll just be there, face to face, for the rest of time.

Six

A bar – they have not had tea. There are drinks on the table.

JASON. Karen says I sell so much because I'm the only thing in the whole shop with a heartbeat and that's what people want when they come out – they want something with a heartbeat that's able to smile at them.

WOMAN. Put you in their pocket.

JASON. That's what Karen says.

> WOMAN *puts her hand onto his chest.*

WOMAN. You make me look whiter.

JASON. Yeah, I guess I do.

WOMAN. What do you sell most of?

JASON. Erasers.

WOMAN. That's funny.

JASON. Is it?

> JASON *slides his hand up her thigh.*

WOMAN. Where are you from – your family, originally?

JASON. I – uh –

WOMAN. Are you a – ?

> JASON *kisses the woman.*

Seven

JASON. I think about it sometimes, like – why. And I figure it's like if you went round Auschwitz – I suppose – you know – if you were a Jew you might be inclined to fuck a German just to – just so – so you didn't just stand there staring at each other pure angry and crying for the rest of time, you know?

Eight

JASON. Hey Karen.

KAREN. Hey Jase – how you doing today, honey?

JASON. Good thanks.

KAREN. How's your mum doing? She still here?

JASON. No, she's gone back home.

KAREN. Panama, right?

JASON. Yeah, Panama.

KAREN. You know I didn't even know where Panama was, couldn't 'a told ya – it was just the hats in my head.

JASON. Yeah – people do that.

KAREN. Your ma showed me – right at our back door, and I had no idea. I always thought you were from – from – ya know – over – in a – over – ya ma, I liked her, she was nice, I liked her.

JASON. Yeah, she's good.

KAREN. How's things selling?

JASON. Good. The stationery is still going real well.

KAREN. Yeah? Them limited-edition pins?

JASON. Still got a whole heap.

KAREN. Look at that smile.

JASON. Tch – stop it Karen.

KAREN. You found yourself a nice young lady yet, Jase? You need a nice young lady – you know? It matters.

JASON. Yeah?

KAREN. Matters more than anything else.

JASON. You think so?

KAREN. Like I always say – end of the day – you measure your life by the heartbeats of the people that you've slept alongside. Huh? (*Kisses* JASON *robustly on the cheek and ruffles his hair.*) You find yourself a nice young lady – okay?

JASON. Okay Karen.

KAREN. Get home safe.

JASON. Okay Karen.

Nine

WOMAN 2 *approaches*.

WOMAN 2. Hi can I get a postcard?

JASON. Sure – we got the double icon right here, the towers and liberty – or we got the flag, or the panoramic sunset – in blue or red – or the 'far but not forgotten' which is the liberty again but kinda… miss?

WOMAN 2. Um – I – I'm not – uh –

JASON. Sure. Are you –

WOMAN 2. Sorry?

JASON. Would you like a tissue?

WOMAN 2. Well – yeah – thanks.

JASON. You just done Karen's tour?

WOMAN 2. Yeah – it's um – it's real – real – um –

JASON. The bit by the window –

WOMAN 2. Yeah. I just don't know how you – what you – uh –
to be able to – the things you'd think – I –

JASON. I think you'd think of the lovers.

WOMAN 2. What?

JASON. All the people you've slept next to. I always think, in
that situation, I'd measure my life by the heartbeats of the
people that I'd slept alongside.

WOMAN 2. You think?

JASON. Yeah.

*JASON hands her the tissue and holds her hand a little long.
He wipes a tear from her face and she takes a sharp little
breath inward.*

Ten

JASON. I'd say two-in-ten success rate or thereabouts. I think
there have been now, working here five years, about seventy,
in all. I know the ones to try with; their faces are still a little
damp. Like dolls, plastic – like someone held 'em over a
flame, they've melted a little.

Beat.

You have to get used to them crying during – it's kind of – I
don't know, they just do that.

Beat.

I sometimes think what they'd look like all together – all laid
out on their backs – like – if it would fill a football field…

like, they'd look like – like swimmers – their legs all bent back – gasping – dolls – melted a little – then set all crooked; their bones too… unforgiving.

Beat.

I don't hear from them again ever.

Like not one. I sometimes think that's weird.

They know where I work, right?

Beat.

Recently I try to slip one of the 'never forget' pins in their pockets, before they go.

I think it's nice.

They're not selling that well anyways.

Beat.

And I always put their coat back on for them – real gentle –

And they appreciate the chivalry.

They're real grateful… for the kindness.

They are.

BOYS

For the brilliant young men and women of
Stafford Street and 320 Basement

'No man is an iland, intire of it selfe; every man is a peece of the Continent, a part of the maine; if a clod bee washed away by the Sea, Europe is the lesse, as well as if a Promontorie were, as well as if a Mannor of thy friends or of thine owne were; any mans death diminishes me, because I am involved in Mankinde...'

John Donne
Meditation 17: Devotions upon Emergent Occasions

'The crisis of modern society is precisely that the youth no longer feel heroic in the plan for action that their culture has set up. They don't believe it empirically true to the problems of their lives and times.'

Ernest Becker
The Denial of Death

Acknowledgements

I would like to thank Rob Icke for his hard work and his unfaltering faith, right from the first draft to the first night, it wouldn't have happened without him. I would like to thank the cast and crew for their ideas, commitment and conviction, it has been a pleasure. My thanks go to Lindsey Alvis and all at Headlong, HighTide, Nuffield and Peter Wilson for their generous support. I am indebted to Jess Cooper, Simon Stephens and all at the Lyric Hammersmith for their continued help and advice.

I would like to thank the inhabitants of Stafford Street, Edinburgh, and 320 Basement, London, for their friendship and for great times spent around the kitchen table.

My thanks to Tim for letting me talk it through, for taking the time to give good advice and for adding to the argument that we don't have to do it alone. Milk.

Boys was first by HighTide Festival Theatre, Nuffield Theatre, Southampton, and Headlong at the HighTide Festival 2012 at The Cut, Halesworth, on 3 May 2012, before transferring to Nuffield Theatre, Southampton, and Soho Theatre, London. The cast was as follows:

MACK	Samuel Edward Cook
BENNY	Danny Kirrane
CAM	Lorn Macdonald
TIMP	Tom Mothersdale
LAURA	Alison O'Donnell
SOPHIE	Eve Ponsonby
Director	Robert Icke
Designer	Chloe Lamford
Lighting Designer	Michael Nabarro
Sound Designer	Tom Mills

Characters

BENNY
MACK
TIMP
CAM
LAURA
SOPHIE

A forward slash (/) in the text indicates interrupted speech.

Square brackets [ ] *indicate unspoken speech.*

ACT ONE

Scene One

The kitchen of a five-man student flat, Edinburgh.

An unusually hot summer.

Rubbish bags pile up in the corners.

There are five chairs; one of these chairs is never touched unless indicated.

The kitchen is thick with the usual debris: tobacco packets, Rizlas, wine bottles and beer cans, dirty washing lies around, ashtrays are overflowing, pizza boxes and kebab boxes are scattered, plates and pots pile up in the sink.

On top of this – this morning – there are remnants of a party the night before: helium balloons populate the ceiling, there are streamers and party hats about, a fake pirate's sword is stuck into the middle of the table, a 'Barclay's' sign is propped up on the side 'We'll loan you the best years of your life'.

CAM *sleeps curled beneath the table. He is wearing dinosaur pyjamas and still has a pirate hat on from the night before.*

BENNY *enters in his dressing gown; he winces against the morning sun, he doesn't see* CAM. BENNY *collects a bowl, some milk and a spoon. He goes to his cupboard and takes out a packet of Coco Pops, pours himself a bowl – a toy lands in his bowl.* BENNY *is delighted, he unwraps the toy as if he was a kid – he holds up a tiny toy soldier and then thinks to tell his best friend. An acute sadness falls.* BENNY *places the little soldier out in front of him on the table and stares at it. He puts the toy in his dressing-gown pocket.* BENNY *approaches another cupboard – pulls the bin over to it and braces himself. He breathes in deeply – and begins to unpack the cupboard into the bin: jams, mouldy bread, noodle packets, tins of baked beans – he reaches a packet of Coco Pops and looks at it.*

He takes the soldier from his pocket – puts it into the box of Coco Pops and puts the box on the table. He returns to the cupboard.

BENNY *stands.*

BENNY *takes a balloon – pulls it down and then lets it float back up to the ceiling.*

BENNY *climbs up on top of the fridge and looks out across the kitchen.*

TIMP – *impish and toned, tattooed, pierced and sporting a Mohican – wears a pair of tight pink boxers with 'Spank' written across the arse. He has an eyepatch over one eye. He walks stealthily over to the kettle and begins making two cups of tea, two pieces of toast.*

BENNY. Morning… Captain.

   TIMP *startles slightly, turns and notices* BENNY *on top of the fridge.*

TIMP. Oh 'ello.

BENNY. What happened in here then?

TIMP. What do you mean?

BENNY. The balloons.

TIMP. Party.

BENNY. Oh really. (*Beat.*) Laura here?

TIMP. No – why?

BENNY. Who's the other cup for?

TIMP. Oh – this? Cam.

BENNY. He up?

TIMP. Yeah – rehearsing. What you doing up on the / (*Notices that the cupboard has been opened and is half-cleared out.*)

BENNY. I thought I'd /

TIMP. Should have fucking been here last night, Benny-boy!

BENNY. Funny being up here at this height.

TIMP. Pirate party for the new intake!

BENNY. It's end of term.

TIMP. Prospective students, looking around, open day – fresher than freshers.

BENNY. Feels like you can control everything.

TIMP. Fresh meat, Benny!

BENNY *puts his hands out as if he is conducting the kitchen.*

BENNY. I'm magic, see; I'm making your tea turn into steam.

TIMP. Well, stop it – I'll come and tell ya all about it, one sec.

BENNY *keeps his hands out, trying to move the objects of the room about.*

As TIMP *goes out the door slams behind him. The noise wakes up* CAM *who bangs his head on the bottom of the table.* BENNY *is startled, thinking he has done it.*

CAM. Whathafuareyouwhyisthe.

BENNY. Cam?

CAM *crawls out from under the table, looks woozily around the place.*

CAM. Oh fuck.

BENNY. Aren't you rehearsing?

CAM. Fuck off. What time is it?

BENNY. Elevenish.

CAM. Oh fuck.

TIMP *re-enters holding just one cup of tea and sees* CAM – *a beat whilst* TIMP *creates his story.*

TIMP. There you bloody are.

TIMP *hands* CAM *the cup of tea.*

CAM (*befuddled*). Cheers.

BENNY. Where's yours?

TIMP. What?

BENNY. Tea?

CAM. You want this?

TIMP. Drank it.

BENNY. But you were –

CAM. Don't fancy it; too hot.

> CAM *hands* BENNY *the tea.*

> Why you on the /

BENNY (*takes the tea*). Thanks.

CAM. Anyone got any idea what I did with my /

TIMP. You seen the kiddiewink this morning?

CAM. What?

TIMP. The old ankle-biter.

CAM. No.

> CAM *sees that the cupboard is open and that it has been half unpacked, he stops in his tracks.*

> Oh.

> CAM *stops and looks at the cupboard.*

BENNY. I thought I'd /

TIMP. I regret to inform you, Benny-boy, that you may have missed what was almost certainly the best party of the year last night.

BENNY. Again. What time is the concert, Cam?

CAM. Later.

TIMP. You're right – now I think about it all the very great parties happen when you are very not being there and it is deeply suspicious.

BENNY. You alright?

TIMP. Yeah.

> CAM *pulls his violin out from under a pile of rubbish – a smiley face has been drawn on it in squirty cream.*

CAM. Oh, for fuck's sake.

TIMP. Oh dear.

CAM. Most important concert of my life and I'm going to smell like a fucking yogurt.

BENNY. What is wrong with you?

TIMP. Why nothing, kind sir, could I interest you in a beverage?

CAM. Are you…? Oh – yeah – right.

BENNY. What?

CAM. I was meant to remind you that you put your E in your aspirin bottle last night.

TIMP. Did I?

CAM. One of the girl's rape alarms went off; you thought it was the police – you put all your drugs into your painkillers.

TIMP. Oh fuck – I'm high.

BENNY. You didn't notice?

TIMP. Yep – yep – now I come to think of it – yep that is what this feeling is.

> TIMP *clips* CAM *round the ear.*

CAM. Ow.

TIMP. Course I fucking know I'm high, you mutant ninja retard; couldn't be arsed with a hangover – that's all – besides I'm highly entertaining when I'm highly high. (*Searches around on the table and picks up two more tablets.*) Anyone else?

> CAM *goes to take one.*

BENNY. Cam?

CAM. What?

BENNY. You're playing violin in front of three thousand people and a fuck-ton of TV cameras in about five hours.

CAM thinks about it for a minute.

TIMP. Oh, come on – that's a TV show I'd watch.

BENNY. Cam? That's your whole career – don't be a dick. What are you doing?

CAM. I'm dead tired of being nervous.

TIMP. Sort you right out, that will.

BENNY. Timp – shut up!

TIMP. Come on – it'll calm him down.

CAM. I really want to.

TIMP. I want a party pal.

CAM. Haven't you got to go to work?

TIMP. You can come – you can practise – we'll have you instead of the radio. Doesn't that sound lovely?

BENNY. Timp?

TIMP. What? Why are you crawling inside your own arse?

BENNY. He's on the front page of the newspaper – he's meant to make fucking history this evening – not dribble on himself with a full fucking orchestra behind him.

CAM. Imagine – not caring, aw just for a second – just imagine…

BENNY. I can't watch this.

BENNY turns to go.

CAM puts the pill in his pocket.

TIMP. You fucking mentalist – you joker – I can't believe you just did that!

BENNY *turns back and goes ape-shit.*

BENNY. What? What the fuck – tell me you didn't just – spit it out – spit it out –

BENNY *launches himself at* CAM *and starts trying to get his fingers in his mouth before attempting an approximation of the Heimlich on him.* CAM *pretends to choke it up once – twice – but then it is clear the noises are those of sexual gratification –* BENNY *is confused –* CAM *and* TIMP *start rolling about with laughter.*

TIMP. We're having you on, you fucking spanner!

BENNY *stands angry and red.*

CAM. That was nice though – will you do it again?

TIMP. Aren't you lovely when you're angry – you're like a very troubled tomato.

BENNY. You're such a pair of – fucking – (*Growls.*)

TIMP. Ooo – look there's another one – Benny-boy? Lighten you up?

BENNY. Not before me cornflakes thanks.

TIMP. Well – in for a penny – in for a pound! (*Sinks the second pill.*) Benny, you're being a bit of a grumpy fucking frowner. Is it not a time of celebration? Did you not get your hexam results?

BENNY. Yes.

CAM. How d'you do?

BENNY. First.

CAM. Nice one, man.

TIMP. We shall have bubbles!! Bubbles for breakfast.

TIMP *goes to the fridge and cracks open a beer and hands it to* BENNY.

BENNY. Cheers.

CAM. Cheers!

BENNY. You done any practice?

CAM. Not much.

BENNY. Shouldn't you /

TIMP. Will you two stop fucking bleating – tell him about last night, Cam!

TIMP has put on some pretty serious dubstep.

BENNY. Timp, man?

TIMP. Oh come on!

TIMP puts on 'Keep Young and Beautiful'. He starts grooving around the place a little.

You want to hear what happened last night then?

BENNY. Will you stop blinking like that you're making me feel ill.

TIMP. First, a toast.

BENNY. What are we toasting?

TIMP. You. I fucking love ya, ya grumpy brainy faggot!

CAM. Aye-aye.

BENNY. Cheers.

TIMP. World of work, Benny-boy, just you wait till you start – it's like lighting a match – sort of exciting for a minute then you realise you can't un-strike it – so there's nothing else to do but get up at dawn every fucking day and wait till it's burnt! Ha!

TIMP lets out a wild laugh right up in BENNY's face – BENNY smiles.

Just saying, buddy – beginning of the fucking end!

BENNY. Thanks, Timp. Thanks.

TIMP. Here is to a beautiful bloody rainbow.

They put their cans up.

BENNY. Contract's up at the end of the week we should think about clearing up, getting out. Maybe tomorrow we should /

TIMP. Tomorrow, tomorrow – I'll love yaaaa... don't go and summon the fucking evil 'Leprechaun of Dawn', Benny-boy!

BENNY. Leprechaun of Dawn?

TIMP. Tomorrow says you are giving in to the God of morning, saying it's okay for him to come and shit his horrible daylight all over us, tearing us apart. No one says tomorrow. Them's the rules or the Leprechaun of Dawn will arrive and stick his pointy teeth into your horrible little wrinkly bollocks and nibble them off.

BENNY. Right. Glad I cleared that up.

CAM. To tonight!

BENNY. What's tonight?

CAM. My concert is done, you guys have your results – and Timp... doesn't need an excuse – we thought we'd have a party; a sort of end-of-an-era thing.

BENNY. To tonight.

The three boys raise their cans and drink.

TIMP. Gluggedyglug. Now, yesterday – however, is a different matter altogether.

BENNY. Can you try and be less –

TIMP. Less what?

BENNY. Just. Less.

TIMP jumps up onto the table and starts to pretend to be walking down the street, a little like a Victorian gentleman, tucking his thumbs into his boxer shorts as if they were trousers.

TIMP. No. So – young Cameron and I are in George Square having a gentlemanly peruse of the prospective students of the gentler gender, wondering if they might like a more mature hand to guide them through this troubled time of change – were we not, Cameron?

CAM. We were.

BENNY. You two tour guides for students?

TIMP. Yes indeedio.

BENNY. Neither of you went to the fucking university.

CAM. We know the basics.

BENNY. How?

TIMP. We've seen you go to lectures.

BENNY. Fucking hell.

TIMP. I snaffled myself a garment –

CAM. He nicked a T-shirt from the university shop.

TIMP. Split the tour guide in two – cocks to the right, tits to the left – I'll take the left.

CAM. Ta very much.

TIMP. And we set off on our merry way. Four hours later and Cameron arrives home –

CAM. Having spent all fucking afternoon fielding questions about the rugby team and Greyfriars fucking Bobby /

TIMP. Miserable little mutt.

CAM. One of the pricks said 'Do you hactually know anyone who's hactually Scottish?'

TIMP. But when he arrived home much to his delight the flat was overfloweth – with young tail. Was it not, Cameron?

CAM. Aye it was.

TIMP. And were you not eternally grateful?

CAM. I had half a pint and went to sleep because I've got a very important concert.

TIMP. As if you did. Now we arrive at the rub.

BENNY. I'm not sure I want to know about your rub, Timp.

CAM. Listen, eh – this is so fucking cool, right – so /

TIMP. Wait, wait – the youth are so hasty. We'll get to it. So, she's called Margaret /

CAM. Megan.

TIMP. Was it not Mégane – like the car?

CAM. Like a Renault Mégane?

TIMP. No, you're right – it was Megan. I think – anyway – she's hot, right? Impressive honkers – long hair, big eyes – lovely looking; she's Australian or something –

CAM. Austrian.

TIMP. She's Austrian.

BENNY. Right. Is this /

CAM. And she's quite funny – actually, you know, a laugh – but a bit loud.

TIMP. And she's so fucking excited by the prospect of us – she's all over Cam, right /

BENNY. *You* got laid?

TIMP. Don't be daft. / So we get back here and –

CAM. What the / ?

TIMP. Don't sulk.

CAM. I get laid /

TIMP. Don't lie /

BENNY. Carry on!

TIMP. And we're all in here. Beers out, smoking a bit – music – all these fucking girls, I mean fuck knows what we were talking about but you know they were excited and we were experienced and they liked my dancing and it was, all in all a lovely atmosphere. You know, sort of a crèche, sort of a stable, sort of heaven – and this Renault girl – she's sixteen, seventeen maybe – just done her Highers, straight into uni – stands up and says 'I'm a virgin. I don't want to start university a virgin. Will one of you have sex with me?'

CAM. 'Please' – I distinctly remember her saying – please. I remember thinking... good manners.

BENNY. Whoa. Sixteen.

CAM. It's not that young.

TIMP. All things are relative, Cameron.

CAM. And she's pissed.

TIMP. Not that pissed.

CAM. Pissed enough not to notice that earlier Timp had put his cock in her pint whilst she was telling a very interesting story about Kirkcaldy.

BENNY. Who fucked her?

CAM. He just plopped it in there – like a fucking water snake and she's telling this story with this pint in one hand and everyone's fucking killing themselves – I mean – really laughing and she thinks it's because of her bus-stop story and everyone's really screaming about Timp's magnified fucking bell-end.

TIMP. Magnified my arse.

CAM. Poor cow. And when she turns to look he's wopped it out and put it on her shoulder – everyone's still screaming right – now she's confused so /

BENNY. She's pissed, your cock's in her pint and she's sixteen –

TIMP. Seventeen – maybe.

BENNY. She's a pissed teenager!

TIMP. Moral fucking dilemma right?

CAM. No – I think he means /

BENNY. You fucked her?

TIMP. But she's standing there and she is pretty, and she is legal /

BENNY. Timp!

CAM. And she did say please.

BENNY. Who fucked her?

The door slams open and MACK *enters, he is latently thunderous – silent – somehow completely impervious to the action that he's walked into.*

Beat.

MACK *starts making himself a cup of tea.*

Silence.

MACK. Morning.

CAM. You making tea?

MACK. Yes.

CAM. Can I have a cup?

MACK. I don't know – can you?

BENNY. Carry on.

TIMP. I'm late for work.

BENNY. I want to hear the end of the story.

TIMP. We'll tell you later.

BENNY. I want to know who /

CAM. Sugar please, Mack.

MACK *hands* CAM *a cup of tea.*

Beat.

MACK *sits.*

BENNY. Cam – carry on.

CAM. I should be practising really – I /

MACK. Don't let me stop you.

CAM. I wasn't there for all of it.

BENNY. Spit it out.

CAM *freezes*.

CAM. I don't really – I can't remember – very /

MACK *starts to laugh*.

BENNY. Tell me who fucked the girl.

TIMP. May I?

MACK. You already were, weren't you?

Beat.

BENNY. Timp?

TIMP. Room's silent – Mack stands up, walks over, takes her hand and takes her to his bedroom. She just goes with him, like he's fucking Obi-Wan Kenobi –

CAM. It was brilliant – fucking brilliant.

CAM *slaps* MACK *on the shoulder.* MACK *looks at* CAM. CAM *removes his hand*.

TIMP. We don't see either of them for the rest of the night. Alacazam – there it is!

Beat.

MACK *claps* TIMP*'s story*.

Thank you – thank you, kind sirs – I have been delighted to have been your entertainment for this brief time but if I may now –

MACK. Are you fucked?

TIMP. I think the question is, Mr Mackenzie – are you?

TIMP *sniffs* MACK.

BENNY. Are you?

MACK. Drugs, no – don't touch 'em.

BENNY. How old was she?

MACK *looks up from his tea. Beat.*

CAM. I swear that shite is starting to fucking crawl – it's doing my head in – I can smell it from my fucking bedroom. They said when they're picking it up yet?

TIMP. You're such a fucking drama queen. You fucking love it, us all sitting here with our tongues out – come come on, how old?

MACK. Haven't you got a concert to go to?

CAM. Later.

MACK. Shouldn't you be rehearsing?

TIMP *starts giggling.*

Something funny, Timp?

TIMP. Nothing.

MACK. Tell me, Benny – why are you looking at me like that?

BENNY. Like what?

They hold the stare for a few second more – it is latently aggressive.

TIMP. You totally did – you're such a bad boy, Mack – such a bad – bad – bad /

MACK. And what exactly is it that you think is bad?

BENNY. Are you joking?

MACK (*suddenly grave*). No.

CAM. It's just funny cos – she's sort of, young and /

MACK. Seventeen.

TIMP. Did you draw her a map?

CAM. Yeah but –

MACK. But what?

CAM. You're twenty-three.

MACK. So? What's age, eh, Cam?

TIMP. Without anything to compare it to your cock probably looked quite big.

BENNY. She was a virgin.

MACK. We all were once.

TIMP. Bet she'll be a Pringle.

CAM. What's a Pringle?

TIMP. Once you pop you just can't stop. Has anyone got any chewing gum?

MACK *throws* TIMP *some chewing gum.*

TIMP *pours himself a glass of water and chugs it down.*

BENNY. It's wrong.

CAM. Has anyone seen my bow?

MACK. Why? Why is it wrong?

CAM. I think we're just saying it's a bit – you know, risky, I guess – she's –

MACK. Let's all be precise, shall we?

BENNY. You took advantage.

MACK *and* BENNY *hold the tension between them – there is a beat.* CAM *and* TIMP *try to recover over the top but it brews beneath.*

TIMP. Can someone please explain to me – why when you two are sitting there having just polished off four years a studying with shiny old marks and you – (*Pointing at* CAM.) are about to get your tiny magical musical arse kissed by half the world and we are going to have a blinding fucking knees-up – I am the only one that is having a lovely old time?

CAM. Because you had drugs for breakfast, Timp.

TIMP. Right.

CAM. I need to go for a slash.

TIMP. Oh – careful –

CAM. What?

TIMP. Nothing.

CAM *exits*.

Pause.

BENNY. She have any mates with her?

MACK. What?

BENNY. The girl, last night – she have any friends with her? Looking out for her?

TIMP. Right – tonight – I'll bring back the food – chip in for the booze – and I'll /

BENNY. Did she?

TIMP. Benny, we were having laugh? No need to /

BENNY. Wonder if she is, right now? Having a laugh with her mates – or maybe she doesn't have any up here yet, so she's just sitting on her own somewhere with a sore head and sore fucking – wondering what /

MACK. She asked calmly and rationally for someone to sleep with her. She had come to that decision on her own. To say no, would have meant that I thought I knew more about what was good for her than she knew herself. Now – I'd say that would be pretty patronising. No?

BENNY. Sometimes people don't know what they want.

MACK. So what – we should make their decisions for them?

BENNY. She was seventeen. You're twenty-three.

MACK. Seventeen-year-olds have brains.

TIMP. Not all of them. I didn't. Still don't.

MACK. They can get married, they can drive cars –

TIMP. They can ride, Mack.

MACK. If she wanted to, and she did want to.

BENNY. She'd never had sex before.

MACK. Are you saying she wasn't capable of making the decision?

BENNY. But you were in a position of –

MACK. Of what? Hm?

Beat – BENNY *doesn't respond.*

I don't expect anyone to take responsibility for me. I don't expect to take responsibility for anyone else. I think it would be patronising. That's very clear to me.

BENNY. She was vulnerable.

MACK. You can't possibly know that.

Beat.

TIMP. Come on, lads – calm down – party tonight – eh?

CAM *enters – stopping* BENNY *from leaving.*

At the sight of CAM, TIMP *suddenly remembers it's time to go and starts scurrying to collect his things.*

CAM. Timp?

TIMP. Cameron, my little angel – I'm a bit late.

CAM. I just went for a piss.

TIMP. That's nice.

CAM. In the bathroom.

TIMP. Best place for it.

CAM. Why is there a naked girl in the bath?

TIMP. She isn't going to have a bath with her clothes on, is she?

CAM. She laughed when I got my cock out.

TIMP *trying not to laugh.*

TIMP. How unkind.

CAM. And made me jump so I pissed all over myself in front of a naked girl who was already laughing at me.

TIMP. Your cock.

CAM. What?

TIMP. From the way you told it it seemed clear that she was laughing at your cock specifically rather than you – as a whole.

CAM. Was she from last night?

TIMP. No, no – she's from work.

BENNY. The restaurant?

CAM. Did you sleep with her?

TIMP. Now, listen – here's the thing – right – so actually, quite a interesting story – she's one of the waitresses –

BENNY. She works with Laura?

TIMP. Sort of –

BENNY. Fuckin' hell, mate.

TIMP. No but listen – right – (*Takes to the floor – charm a-go-go.*) She turned up after her shift, looking for some green – I had this Afghani stuff she was after. She doesn't speak much English though, Polish or something – but older – you know – late twenties –

MACK. Doesn't bother me what you do, mate.

TIMP. And she turns up when I'm in the bog, right? And it's been one of those days – burritos – so I've laid a pretty impressive pile in there – and it won't flush, you see? I've tried and I've tried and then there's a knock at the bathroom door. I open it and it's this nice Polish girl and I think she's going to come in there and think I've left it for her, that I'm the kind of man that might do that, leave a browny staring her in the eye – and I'm not that kind of man? Am I?

CAM. Why has your shite got anything to do with that girl in the bath?

TIMP. Well, that's this Polish girl innit?

BENNY. Why did she need a bath?

TIMP. No, no, you dirty bugger – listen.

CAM. Carry on.

TIMP. I say 'I'm really sorry – I've done a massive turd and it won't go away.' But she can't understand me, you see, no comprendez. So I'm in a bind? So I mime the situation – I do a little face and a little squat and I mime the flush a few times and then sort of try and show it won't go.

CAM. Looks like funky chicken.

BENNY. You did a poo-dance at a girl that doesn't speak any English?

TIMP. Well, she didn't understand either, right?

BENNY. But it was so clear.

TIMP. So I have to take her by the hand and I show her over to the toilet, I show her what I've done and then to show her that it won't shift I pull the chain, right?

CAM. Right?

TIMP. And the thing only fucking flushes, doesn't it? It just disappears. Ala-fucking-cazam. I turn to her and she's looking at me – wide-eyed like I'm a fucking freak. As far as she's concerned I just opened the door – did the funky fucking shitting chicken, then all proud showed her my turd and just flushed it away. Like a little ceremonial doo-daa, bet she thinks it's fucking cultural. Them British and their big shits – I bet she thinks – and I'm so fucking embarrassed, so overcome with shame, the only thing I could do – was –

CAM. What?

TIMP. I mean – it's obvious –

CAM. Is it?

TIMP. What else could you do – I had to kiss her. To apologise, to defend the name of the British gentleman in her head; it was basically an act of patriotism. All things considered – I slept with her – for Queen and country.

CAM. Right.

BENNY. And Laura?

TIMP. See – there was nothing else I could have done.

MACK. Clearly.

Beat.

TIMP. See – not that bad at all, mind you – not as funny as you shagging a nipper though. (*Beat.*) That's really fucking funny – (*Looks at his watch.*) and I'm really fucking late.

CAM. What about the – ?

TIMP *kisses the top of* CAM*'s head.*

TIMP. I'll come back with food – and drink, but buy extra, alright?

BENNY. Shouldn't we start thinking about shifting this before we /

TIMP. What if we stayed.

CAM. What?

TIMP. Couple of them freshers said – last night – this place was on the list for them to come look round – move in, like – and I thought – fuck off – this is ours, this is where we have our fun, keep your hands off. (*Beat.*) Just cos you two are graduating – doesn't really mean anything has to change – right? We could just renew the lease – we could stay?

Beat.

BENNY. Our lease ends in a week.

TIMP. So – we'll renew.

BENNY. We can't.

CAM. If they haven't found new tenants yet.

TIMP. Mack?

MACK *shrugs.*

We do have a lovely fucking time?

Beat – a strange silence falls.

BENNY *holds his silence – several seconds pass – no one can respond.*

LAURA *enters.*

LAURA. I thought you'd be at work by now.

TIMP. 'Ello.

LAURA. Hi, boys.

BENNY. Hey, Loz.

CAM. Hi.

LAURA. I left my spare swipe-card in your room and I left mine at work last... are you high?

TIMP. Took a pill by mistake when I woke up.

LAURA. How?

TIMP. Thought it was aspirin.

LAURA. You're a fucking idiot, I can just go and /

BENNY. I'll get it.

LAURA. What?

BENNY. You two – catch up.

TIMP. No, no – you wait here; I'll go and grab it.

TIMP *exits.*

Beat.

LAURA. You lot have a party last night then?

CAM. Yeah – some freshers' thing.

LAURA. Isn't it the end of term?

CAM. Prospective students – seeing if they want to /

LAURA. Spend four years getting fucked... yes please. You alright, Benny?

BENNY. Yeah.

LAURA. Were you at the party?

BENNY. No. I was out with Sophie.

MACK *stands, removes himself from the table.*

LAURA. She alright?

BENNY *nods.*

It happen here? (*Beat.*) The party – the party happen here?

MACK. Ended up here.

LAURA. Wish I could have come.

CAM. Ach, you didn't miss much –

CAM *opens the freezer to get some ice out – and finds his bow – he takes it out and hides it quickly.*

I was in bed early – big concert – you know /

LAURA. Oh my God yeah the big concert; my mum's got your face on her fridge. I put it there. She's so excited to know you – she keeps telling everyone – 'my daughter is friends with Cameron Robertson, you know, that wee musical lad' – were there lots of people?

CAM. What?

LAURA. At the party?

CAM. Yeah, few.

Beat.

LAURA. Be so weird won't it, you not all being here, not being able to pop round. Bet you'll be glad – no more fucking motormouth.

BENNY. Don't be daft.

LAURA. Maybe you'll all come back one day and visit and have a big reunion and you'll go round all the bits of the house – like old pictures and be like, I looked at that and – I was sick on that, and I – you know – and if Cam gets really famous maybe they'll put one of them blue plaques up on the wall and I can be like, I used to hang out with them.

CAM. Yeah.

LAURA. I used to look at my teddy when I was small and be like 'teddy, I wonder where you'll be when I'm ninety' and I used to think about him rotting and get really sad.

CAM. Oh.

LAURA. I'm just going to use the loo – tell Timp when he /

BENNY. Laura?

LAURA. Yeah?

BENNY. It's broken.

LAURA. Oh. Oh well... I'll use the one at work.

TIMP *re-enters.*

TIMP. Ready?

LAURA. Yeah.

MACK. Don't forget to let your bath out.

TIMP. Be an angel, Cam – let it out for me. Don't get in it though – it's filthy.

TIMP *laughs a little nervously.*

LAURA. What you doing having a bath, it's boiling?

TIMP. Fancied it.

LAURA. See you tonight, guys, can't wait!

TIMP. Come on.

LAURA. You've scratched your back, babe.

TIMP *and* LAURA *exit.*

Silence falls.

CAM *takes a toke on a joint that has been smouldering, it's long and deep.*

CAM. Better let that bath out.

CAM *exits.*

BENNY *and* MACK *are left alone – neither speaks – time passes.*

MACK *eventually gets up to leave*.

BENNY. I'd get in that bath straight after – have a good wash.

MACK *stops*.

Beat.

MACK *laughs*.

MACK. Toilet's broken of course.

BENNY. You'd have let her walk in?

MACK. Wonder if she'd thank you. Guess we'll never know, oh great protector.

Beat.

BENNY. Sophie was out last night.

MACK. Yeah?

BENNY. Drinking – dancing.

MACK. Sounds like a laugh.

BENNY. No – the kind that makes you think someone's probably a bit, you know… broken.

MACK. Could mean either though, couldn't it? Could mean fine.

BENNY. Could mean falling apart.

Beat.

MACK *stands up abruptly from his chair, it scrapes along the floor –* MACK *grabs as many of the rubbish bags as he can carry and storms out of the kitchen – the door slams closed behind him.* MACK *returns to grab another handful.*

What are you doing?

MACK. Moving it.

BENNY. Where to? You can't put it on the stairwell the other tenants will /

MACK. I don't want to sit and look at it.

BENNY. I'll call the council.

MACK. Fuck – I wish we'd thought of that when they stopped collecting. Will you ring the rest of the city at the same time and just let them know that they'd been ignoring the blindingly fucking obvious?

MACK *kicks the door open and throws the bags out of it into the hall.*

MACK *continues to move it all – aggressively – until all the bags are out of the kitchen.*

BENNY *gets out his phone and makes a phone call – the automated voice comes on and* BENNY *confuses it for a human.*

BENNY. Hello – oh.

He sits on the phone – he is clearly been asked to wait, we can hear the tinny sound of 'Greensleeves' or something similar.

MACK *exits.*

BENNY *sits. The sun rises – the tinny music plays.*

Scene Two

Hot orange summer sun cuts across the dust that lies thick in the air.

There is no birdsong; there is no breath – the heat sits.

CAM *enters.*

BENNY *watches from on top of the fridge.*

CAM *wears his tails ready for performance.*

CAM *holds his violin.*

CAM *checks for anyone in the kitchen, but he fails to see* BENNY.

CAM *walks over to the far wall and stands with his face to it, his back to the room.*

CAM *takes a large breath.*

CAM *tries to play – he is too nervous – he cannot.*

CAM *lets his violin and bow fall to his side.*

CAM *bangs his head against the wall three times.*

CAM *takes another large breath.*

CAM *lifts his bow and his violin.*

CAM *plays half a note, fails.*

CAM *bangs his head against the wall.*

CAM. Fuck. Fuck. Fuck.

Beat.

CAM *takes a pill out of his pocket and places it in the palm of his hand he looks at it – he is on the verge of taking it...*

BENNY. What you doing?

CAM. Fuck, Benny, you scared the shit out of me.

BENNY. Shouldn't you be off by now?

CAM. My palms are sweating – my fucking /

BENNY. Don't take that.

CAM. My room's too fucking hot; Mack's playing his music full fucking volume – outside everyone's in the sun, having a great time –

BENNY. Go to the college or the concert hall – they'll be quiet.

CAM. Stinks of fucking rubbish everywhere.

BENNY. You alright, Cam?

CAM. You'll all be having a party whilst I'm gone; getting the beers in.

BENNY. And you'll be making history.

CAM. All I can see out my window is fucking students –
throwing flour and eggs all over each other. You seen how
warm it is out there?

BENNY. You should go, mate, you don't want to miss it.

Beat.

CAM. Don't I?

Beat.

BENNY. Course you don't.

CAM. You just jump through the hoops and it works out –
exams, degree – job – there's a path. There's no maybe –
maybe not – or tonight's the fucking night. All on one
moment, all on one person – fucking…

BENNY. You've got instructions.

CAM. What?

BENNY. The music – that's instructions, isn't it. Don't get that
in an exam. (*Beat.*) Nice up here – like being above
everything – you can control it, calmer – cooler somehow.

CAM. Cooler?

BENNY. Yeah.

CAM. You're on top of a fucking fridge, Benny.

BENNY. The top of a fridge is actually… I thought you were
meant to be leaving?

CAM. I'll go in a minute.

BENNY. You're going to be late.

CAM. I've got ages. You want a drink?

BENNY. No thanks.

CAM. Come on – have a drink?

BENNY. I'm alright.

CAM *picks up a ball and chucks it at* BENNY, BENNY
catches it.

CAM. Come on – we'll chuck it about a bit? It'll help me calm down.

BENNY. What time are you meant to be there?

CAM. Don't know.

BENNY. Cam?

CAM (*snaps*). What?

BENNY. Go.

BENNY *throws the ball back.*

CAM. It's easy for you – you've got a piece of paper saying you know it and that's that. Imagine if tonight I could just walk on stage and in front of that whole fucking crowd and just roll out a piece of paper and go – look – this says I can do it so there we go. And then everyone cheers and claps.

BENNY. It's just pressure – there's always going to be /

CAM. Exactly fucking right – it's always going to be there.

BENNY. You don't get to be excellent without there being pressure. It's a pay-off.

CAM. Who says I want to be excellent?

BENNY. Fifteen years of eight hours' practice a day.

Beat.

CAM. There's this guy coming, tonight – he's a Russian virtuoso called Viktashev; he's come up from London. He's pretty much it – you know? The big balls.

BENNY. Nice.

CAM. And he sends me this email the other day – it's like two pages long, saying he's heard my stuff and how now is a vital time for me. How there's this competition in Belgium; it's called the Queen Elizabeth and it's, you know –

BENNY. The big balls.

CAM. Aye – and this Viktashev guy won it when he was nineteen, youngest ever – and he wants me to go and break his title. He says he's going to ship me over to Vienna and train me – just me and him. And he keeps going on and on about how there's this window, this right age – and if you can get through it – you'll go somewhere great but if you miss it – you won't get it back.

BENNY. You got to not listen to all that /

CAM. And then at the end he writes this little story about how the lowliest and youngest inmates in Russian prisons tattoo stars on their knees.

BENNY. Why?

CAM. To say they won't kneel to anyone.

BENNY. Bit much that.

CAM. I'm meant to do what he tells me and not do what anyone tells me – you know what I mean?

BENNY. Yeah, it's a bit much. Got to do it for you I guess.

CAM. If I was doing it for me I'd stay here and have a pint with you.

BENNY. Right. (*Beat*.) Can't waste it though, Cam.

CAM. Why not? My choice, isn't it?

BENNY. Right now I reckon I know more than I ever will again. Iteration, deconstruction, reification, homogeneity /

CAM. Show-off.

BENNY. I'm never going to use those words ever again. So I might as well not know 'em. It's a waste. You though, you'll go on getting better and better and you could be – great, you know? Like – really really get to the top of something – get close to – inch of God.

CAM. What?

BENNY. That's what my dad used to call it, 'inch of God', the extra inch that takes you from great to – really being the dog's fucking bollocks. You got a shot at that. Not to be sniffed at.

CAM. Don't sniff at the dog's bollocks?

BENNY. Do not, Cameron.

CAM. You can keep learning words – keep studying.

BENNY. Thanks.

CAM. PhD – teach or something.

BENNY. It's all criticism though… not sure that's something you want to be great at, is it?

CAM. Come up with your own ideas can't you?

BENNY. What's the point in following something hardly anyone else can follow? I reckon you just end up somewhere no one else is ever going to visit.

CAM. Hardly anyone is great at the violin.

BENNY. But everyone's got ears.

CAM. I don't want to do it.

BENNY. You have to.

CAM. I don't want to.

BENNY. I don't know if that really matters.

CAM. What?

BENNY. Bigger than you somehow; maybe.

CAM. It's my fucking fingers.

BENNY. You believe in God, Cam?

CAM. No.

BENNY. Not even in primary, like nativities.

CAM. Snow.

BENNY. What?

CAM. Imagine, a bit of snow right now – how good would that be?

BENNY. There's no snow in the nativity.

CAM. It's about Christmas.

BENNY. It's Bethlehem, it's red.

CAM. Alright, God squad.

BENNY. That's just geography. I miss it sometimes.

CAM. Geography?

BENNY. The idea of something above you. I used to imagine him just sitting up there at night-time, made you feel a bit safer.

CAM. You don't believe in him any more?

BENNY. Don't think so.

CAM. Why not?

BENNY. Learnt too much, I guess.

CAM. Can't you just decide?

BENNY. It's like you get two books by well-known people, credible people, out the library and they say opposite things but they're both meant to be right. What are you meant to do about that?

CAM. Choose one.

BENNY. Just like that?

CAM. Yeah – why not?

BENNY. Then you always know you chose it, so it's just a choice rather than a knowing.

CAM. What's the difference?

BENNY. You chose it – so you know can just un-choose it – flimsy. It's one option but it could have just as much been the other one, it's like TVs inside TVs – they eat each other – like all the facts sort of chase each other, round and round – all the articles and books and blogs and papers and journals and they just keep running round and round and – You remember *Little Black Sambo* –

CAM. Sounds a wee bit /

BENNY. It is – but that's not the point. It's this story where this little kid meets these tigers and he gives them all his best most colourful clothes so that they won't eat him and they like those fancy clothes so much they chase and chase each other so hard that they just melt into butter.

CAM. Tigers turn into butter?

BENNY. I guess I just miss – you remember when you had a question, any question easy or hard, you know – what's ham through to why are we alive – and you knew the absolute best place to get a right answer was your dad.

CAM. Yeah.

BENNY. When your dad was like Google but better and with hugs. (*Beat.*) You'll be alright. You've got to go though, you got to try – it matters.

CAM. Can't I choose not to.

BENNY. You've got to go – one of us – has fucking got to – I won't let you give up. I won't let this flat make you give up.

Pause.

CAM. I'm sorry, Benny.

BENNY. I just think you should try, that's all.

Beat.

CAM. But what if I do?

BENNY. What? What if you try? Then you'll know you did your best.

CAM. Exactly.

Pause.

BENNY. You're going to miss it.

CAM. Sometimes think I'd be much happier if I'd never picked the fucking thing up.

CAM *picks up his violin and starts to pack it away,* BENNY *watches silently.*

BENNY. Knock 'em dead?

CAM *nods*.

BENNY *nods*.

CAM *exits*.

BENNY *looks at the kitchen, rolls his sleeves up and defiantly heads over to the half-emptied cupboard. With confidence he begins to put the things into a bin bag – he is full of confidence when –*

CAM *enters*.

CAM. I cannie go.

BENNY. What?

CAM. The whole of the fucking landing is stacked up – I can't get out! I can't get out down the stairwell.

BENNY. What? It's not that many bags – it was only /

BENNY *exits and checks the front door.*

(*Off.*) Mack!

CAM *opens a beer – looks at it – doesn't drink it.*

BENNY *re-enters.*

How did that happen?

CAM. I don't know.

MACK *enters.*

MACK. What?

CAM. I can't get out the front door for all that shite you put out here.

MACK. Come on – it was only a few bags.

BENNY. He needs to go.

CAM. I have to go, I'm late!

MACK. Well – move it then.

CAM. I can't get past it to move it, it's at waist height.

MACK. That's not all ours.

CAM. No shit, Sherlock.

MACK. Well then.

BENNY. They clearly dumped it because we – you – did.

MACK. I put ours out there; there was more than enough room
    to get past.

CAM. Mack, it is a wall – I'd have to wade through it to be able
    to move it and I'm in a fucking suit already sweating my
    balls off, I shift that lot I'm going to stink like a rat's arse.

Beat.

BENNY. We'll help you.

MACK. Will we?

BENNY. I'll help you carry it.

CAM. Thank you.

> MACK *shrugs. The kitchen door is wedged open and bags
> start flying in –* CAM *and* MACK *passing what seems like
> an endless stream of rubbish into the kitchen, bag after bag –
> in they come,* BENNY *works hard to try and find space for
> them but they start really taking up space, the kitchen starts
> to feel much smaller.*

BENNY. Go on – go. We'll sort it.

CAM. Thanks, Ben.

BENNY. Come back a superstar.

CAM. Do my best.

> CAM *goes to leave.*

MACK. Cam?

CAM. Yeah.

MACK. Good luck, man.

CAM. Thanks.

CAM exits.

MACK *and* BENNY *stand and look at the rubbish.*

MACK. Council didn't answer then?

BENNY. It was automated.

MACK. Really?

MACK nods.

BENNY. Have you got something you want to say?

MACK. No, no.

BENNY. It is their problem; I mean it is their job to sort this out.

MACK. Okay.

BENNY. You pay for it to get picked up and the council pick it up.

MACK. Right.

MACK goes to make himself a cup of tea.

BENNY. I'll put it back out then.

MACK. We don't.

BENNY. What?

MACK. We don't pay for it. We're students, we don't pay council tax.

Beat.

BENNY. Cam and Timp aren't students.

MACK. They don't pay, that's why they live with us. That and cos we're fucking lovely to look at.

BENNY. Yeah fine – but we're still entitled to the same services.

MACK. Entitled?

BENNY. Deserve – we're /

MACK. We're – ?

BENNY. We're going to give it back… soon.

MACK. Oh right. Okay. Here's to hoping it gets better soon.

BENNY. What's the other option then?

MACK. Not saying there is one.

BENNY. You think we should get rid of it ourselves?

MACK. Can't see how we'd do that.

BENNY. Then what?

MACK. Then nothing.

BENNY. If we don't 'deserve' to get it picked up and we can't get rid of it ourselves – Mack? Then what are you offering, what are you – suggesting? You think we should eat it, fucking breathe it in?

MACK. Calm down, Benny.

BENNY. Stop acting like you've got a fucking answer.

MACK. No – no – I haven't got any answers, Benny, none at all.

BENNY *picks up several bags of rubbish and takes them out of the front door.*

MACK *makes his cup of tea, cleanly – almost rhythmically – from 'off' we can hear* BENNY *in the stairwell, he is having an altercation with someone. As first we can hear him speaking calmly – and then it bursts into a much larger, more aggressive argument.* MACK *listens to the argument and leans, nonchalantly against the counter.*

BENNY *comes back in with the bags that he was carrying.*

BENNY *looks at* MACK.

BENNY *puts the bags down.*

Tea?

BENNY *doesn't respond.*

Bicky?

BENNY. No.

MACK. I thought you were going to put them /

BENNY. Guy opposite's on the landing – he said I couldn't dump it out there.

MACK. Really?

BENNY. It's a common stairwell.

MACK. True.

BENNY. You want to live like this?

MACK. It's just trash.

BENNY. It's crawling – we can't get it out – we can't dump on the street, we'll get fined, we can't put it in the stairwell and no one is coming to pick it up – we're going to fucking drown. I don't want it in here. I shouldn't have to live with other people's crap all over me – we didn't make this mess!

MACK. I think you're getting things out of proportion, Benny.

BENNY. Am I?

MACK. I think you should breathe.

BENNY. I think you should try and be less of a selfish cunt.

MACK (*laughing*). You're the one that wants to post it back through people's letter boxes, piece by piece, Benny.

BENNY. I'm going to ring the landlord.

MACK. Oh yeah?

BENNY. They have to do something, it's a health hazard.

MACK. No they don't have to do anything – don't you see?

BENNY. No I fucking don't!

MACK. How many students do you think are moving out this week? You think they're going to let it cost them to move it, you kidding?

BENNY. We'll call the police.

MACK. Look out the fucking window – How many houses do you see? Hm? Ringing the council, ringing the landlord, going to have a gentle word with the neighbours – if there was a solution do you not think someone would have thought of it over a week ago when they decided to stop picking this shit up and it started rotting under our own fucking noses?

BENNY. Someone has to take care of it.

MACK. Who?

BENNY. They won't just leave us here to /

MACK. Who?

BENNY. Because that's how things work, there are people, organisations –

MACK. Who?

BENNY. Systems that make sure /

MACK. Who?

BENNY. This is Britain, you idiot, they won't just leave us to rot! It's not fucking /

MACK. I'd love to take a look at your world, Benny; I bet it's lovely.

Beat.

BENNY. I'm going to be out of here. I'll just leave it with you.

MACK. Where you going?

Beat.

BENNY. London.

MACK. Sounds expensive.

BENNY. Get a job.

MACK. Hear there's hundreds going.

BENNY. Got a first – haven't I?

MACK. Oh, you should have said – you'll be fine then.

Pause.

BENNY. What if I'm not?

MACK. What?

BENNY *comes in close to* MACK.

BENNY. What if I'm not fine – what would you do about it – pal?

Pause.

MACK. You got to learn to look after yourself, mate.

BENNY. You've been crying.

MACK. Red-eye – I had a joint.

BENNY. Your face is wet.

Beat.

MACK. Redemption.

BENNY *earnest – looks at* MACK *– long pause.*

MACK *starts to laugh a little –* BENNY *immediately defensive but unsure what is going on.*

Red. Dead. Redemption. I forget to blink when I'm gaming if I'm high. Sorry to disappoint.

BENNY *lunges at* MACK *and smacks the bottom of his cup of tea – the tea flies up and all over* MACK.

MACK *freezes a moment – looks at* BENNY.

Just trying to do you a favour – Ben, make sure you don't fall too far.

Beat.

BENNY *goes to leave as he does so the kitchen door opens,* SOPHIE *enters.*

SOPHIE. Hello.

BENNY. Sophs?

SOPHIE. Hey. (*Kisses* BENNY *on the cheek.*) Mack.

MACK. How did you get in?

BENNY. You get home alright last night?

SOPHIE. What?

MACK. Who let you in?

SOPHIE. The door was open.

BENNY. Must have bounced off when I slammed it.

SOPHIE. Bloody hell – it's worse in here than it is out there.
Why don't you put it in the stairwell?

MACK. Not very neighbourly.

SOPHIE. Having all this in here in this heat isn't good for you.

BENNY. We know.

SOPHIE. Well, you need to move it.

MACK. What would we do without you?

SOPHIE. I'm not being funny.

BENNY. Sophie – we realise /

SOPHIE. You know you have to pay.

BENNY. What?

SOPHIE. Can't settle the strike so private companies have
stepped in in the interim. We have to pay to get it picked up.

BENNY. How much?

SOPHIE. Tenner a bag.

BENNY. What? No way.

SOPHIE. Everyone has to pay.

BENNY. What the fuck? Ten pounds a bag – they're taking the
piss.

SOPHIE. Cheaper than dumping it if you get caught. One of the
boys next door to us, they were trying to clear out their flat

and he gets a two-hundred-quid fine for dumping a bag not in a communal bin – but the bins are fucking rammed, there's no space left in any of them. It's an infringement of civil rights.

MACK. What, the inalienable right to dump your shit on someone else?

SOPHIE. He had no other choice.

MACK. He could have paid to have it picked up.

SOPHIE. He might not have the money.

MACK. Then he should make less mess.

BENNY. Mack?

SOPHIE. I can see you've done really well at keeping it to a minimum.

MACK. Everyone starts dumping on the streets and it's chaos in seconds.

SOPHIE. Everyone keeps it in their houses and you get illness that costs as much as the clear-up would.

MACK. Got any stats on that? Sounds pretty spurious to me.

SOPHIE. Spurious? That's a complicated word, Mack.

MACK. What are you going to do with yours then, Little Miss /

BENNY. Mack – back off.

Beat.

SOPHIE. We moved out yesterday. I leave tomorrow morning.

MACK. What? Why? (*Realising he's betrayed himself.*) Bet Daddy came and sorted it all out for you.

SOPHIE. Yes.

Beat.

BENNY. Fuck, Sophs – you can't just leave.

SOPHIE. End of term, isn't it. I'll be back for graduation – can I get a glass of water?

BENNY. It'll be weird not – um – you're going to London though, right – so, we'll all still /

SOPHIE. Of course. Course we will.

Pause.

BENNY. I'm going to go and check the contract – see what it says about deposits. You alright in here?

SOPHIE. Yeah I'm alright.

BENNY *exits.*

'How did you get in?' What was that?

MACK. Better I ask than Benny.

SOPHIE. Just say you lent me your spare keys.

MACK. Why would I have done that?

Beat.

Guess I'd better have them back.

MACK *hands* SOPHIE *her water.*

SOPHIE. Thank you. I don't –

MACK. You're going – tomorrow?

SOPHIE. Why did you cancel last night?

MACK. Had to.

SOPHIE. Why? It's none of my business what you do.

MACK. Cam and Timp ended up bringing a party back – I couldn't – um –

SOPHIE. Right.

SOPHIE *tries to give* MACK *the keys.*

MACK. Keep 'em.

SOPHIE. What for?

MACK. I don't know – just – keep them.

Beat.

SOPHIE. I could put them back in your room for you.

Beat.

MACK. I said keep them.

SOPHIE. We could watch a movie.

MACK. He's getting /

SOPHIE. What /

MACK. Shaky.

Beat.

SOPHIE. Aren't we all? (*Beat.*) We can have a joint – just – talk and /

MACK. You want tea?

SOPHIE. I've got water. (*Picks up her glass of water.*) Pussy.

SOPHIE *pours the glass of water down her front, it makes her T-shirt go see-through.*

Shall we have a nap?

MACK. No.

SOPHIE. What are you scared of?

MACK. Nothing.

SOPHIE. You're terrified.

MACK. Women love to tell men how they feel, don't they?

SOPHIE. Men?

SOPHIE *looks around trying to see one.*

MACK. Think you've 'interpreted' something – think you've discovered a feeling, think you can stick a flag in it – own it, irrespective of whether it's total bullshit or not.

SOPHIE *stares at him.*

SOPHIE. Have you got a boner?

MACK *turns away from her.*

MACK. Fuck off. I haven't got a fucking /

SOPHIE. Why turn away then?

MACK. I'm making myself – a – piece of /

SOPHIE. Cock.

MACK. Biscuit.

SOPHIE. A piece of biscuit – what's that then?

MACK. I'll smack you in a minute.

SOPHIE. Oh yes please.

MACK. Right –

> MACK *turns back around.*

SOPHIE. Careful you'll have my eye out.

MACK. Come here –

> SOPHIE *backs off.*

SOPHIE. No – no, Mack.

> MACK *crouches and prepares.*

> Benny'll come in.

MACK. I'm just taking the trash out.

SOPHIE. Take that back.

MACK. No!

> MACK *lunges at* SOPHIE *and gets her over his shoulder easily – she screams –* MACK *panics – and puts her down quickly – 'shhing' her all the while.*

> Shh-shh.

SOPHIE (*serious*). Take that back – I'm not trash.

> *Beat.*

MACK (*looks at her – humble*). You're not trash.

> *Beat.*

BENNY *enters*.

SOPHIE *reacts as if* MACK *has just poured water right down her front*.

BENNY. What the fuck's going on?

SOPHIE. He just poured water all over me!

BENNY. What? Why?

SOPHIE. He just fucking drenched me!

BENNY. What are you doing?

MACK. She – it was a joke.

BENNY. What the fuck is wrong with you?

MACK. I thought she was going to /

SOPHIE. Will you get me a T-shirt please, Mack?

MACK *exits*.

BENNY. I'm sorry.

SOPHIE. It's fine.

BENNY. He's been a cunt ever since /

SOPHIE. No he's not.

Beat.

BENNY. Dad sent his love – hoped you were alright. Said you should pop by if you're ever /

SOPHIE. Yeah – yeah.

BENNY. Said he'd like to see you.

SOPHIE. Mm – it's really fucking hot, Ben.

BENNY. Yeah.

SOPHIE. Excited about tonight?

BENNY. Can't wait.

MACK *enters*.

MACK *hands* SOPHIE *the T-shirt, she turns away from* BENNY *and* MACK *to put it on.*

We got them T-shirts in Amsterdam.

MACK. Yeah.

Meanwhile we see SOPHIE *smell the T-shirt. She seems small, soft for a moment.*

Beat.

SOPHIE. What does it say in the contract?

BENNY. It has to be cleared before we can leave or they take our deposits; six hundred quid each.

SOPHIE. That's outrageous – they can't /

BENNY. And under Scottish Law it's joint responsibility – one of us doesn't pay and everyone else and their guarantors are responsible. Looks like we're in it together, eh, Mack?

Beat.

MACK. I'd double check the signatories.

BENNY. What?

MACK. Front page.

BENNY *reads the front page of the contract.*

BENNY. You're not fucking on here? What the fuck?

MACK. We turned the sitting room into my room – remember?

BENNY. You don't live here.

MACK. Never liked contracts.

Pause – BENNY *sees the keys on the floor.*

BENNY. They your keys, Mack?

MACK. Oh yeah – must have dropped them.

BENNY. You alright?

SOPHIE. Fine, why?

BENNY. You look a bit… has he been having a go?

SOPHIE. No.

BENNY. Don't let him.

SOPHIE. I'm alright, Ben.

Beat.

BENNY. You remember last night, Sophs? It was so hot out – you could have taken your shoes off, carried them like flip-flops. Everyone out, everyone with their skin out – all having finished exams – all smiling and high-fiving – and saying hi to all these people, fucking hugging them – people I've seen every day for four years, people who have seen me – and I'm hugging them thinking – I've got no fucking idea what your name is. Four years, seeing them every day – and you still don't even know their fucking name… hardly know them at all.

Beat.

BENNY *walks over to the window to look out.*

SOPHIE *and* MACK *look at each other – unseen by* BENNY.

We'll throw it out the window – fuck it, we'll just throw it out the window.

BENNY *tries to push the sash of the window up.*

BENNY *tries again –* BENNY *looks up at the window lock.*

MACK. They're locked.

BENNY. What? Since when?

MACK. Landlord didn't want any more accidents.

BENNY. I didn't give the say-so –

MACK. Your dad did.

BENNY *stands, lost – confused, overwhelmed, he bites his finger.*

Scene Three

The surface of the kitchen table has been cleared. Around the kitchen are the remnants of food preparation, pots, pans – there are yet more rubbish bags piled around the circumference of the room. The lights have been switched off, there is only evening gloom from the window – it is nearly dusk. Along the length of the table lies a body covered in a black sheet.

Behind this MACK, SOPHIE *and* BENNY *stand.*

SOPHIE *is dressed as Snow White,* BENNY *is dressed as a lion. They are blindfolded.*

In front of the body, on the opposite side of the table to the other three, stands TIMP, *dressed as Peter Pan.*

TIMP *climbs up onto a chair.*

TIMP. One –

The three prepare to take their blindfolds off.

Two –

TIMP *lights a match and it burns brightly in the dusky light.*

Three. You were blind but now you can see!

SOPHIE, MACK *and* BENNY *take their blindfolds off – the light from* TIMP's *single match half-illuminates the gloom.*

There is an intake of breath.

BENNY. What the fuck is –

SOPHIE *and* MACK *take a step backwards as if a little haunted.*

TIMP *holds the match up close to his face – the three stare at him – not being able to quite see the body in front of them.*

TIMP. What lies before you here, my friends, is a land of untold dreams, it's everything you ever hoped for, everything that flickered behind your lids on a lazy afternoon – and it can be yours, all yours – you just have to reach out and touch it. So be brave, my little warriors – steel yourselves for an onslaught of pleasure like you have never considered before – a battle of loveliness, a skirmish of delight – arm yourself with your weapons – and prepare to devour – the lovely – the jubbly – oo – oo fuck – ouch –

The match has burnt down and TIMP *starts waving it about manically trying to stop it from burning his fingers – the match goes out – all is dark.*

BENNY. Timp – what the hell is /

BODY (*in an intentionally spooky deep voice*). Hello.

TIMP *turns the lights on.* BENNY *pulls the black sheet off from over the body, there is something hopeful in his face.*

TIMP. どうぞめしあがれ [*Pronounced: Douzo meshiagare! Meaning: Help yourself!*]

What is revealed is LAURA *in a makeshift Little Mermaid outfit, covered from head to toe in carefully placed sushi. She has chopsticks in her hair, soy sauce in her belly button and wasabi and ginger in either palm.*

LAURA. Hiya!

SOPHIE. Is that sushi?

LAURA. No, it's me, you idiot.

TIMP. It's the best fucking sashimi dream you ever fucking dreamt, right? Am I right? We got maguro, ikura, saba, ebi – and sake!

SOPHIE. What the –

TIMP. Tuna, salmon roe, mackerel, shrimp and salmon –

LAURA. I'm like a mermaid –

TIMP. It's a marvel.

LAURA *sings a few lines from 'Part of Your World' from Walt Disney's* The Little Mermaid.

BENNY. You've got soy sauce in your belly button.

TIMP. Fucking great, right? Come on – dig in. There's chopsticks in her hair /

LAURA. Ginger in my right hand and wasabi in my left.

TIMP. Chuck us some beers, Mack.

MACK *turns to the fridge to get the beers.*

BENNY *wanders over to the window* – TIMP *passes him a plate and it falls to his side.* BENNY *stands apart, looking out at dusk across the city.*

SOPHIE. This is amazing; this must have taken hours.

TIMP. Why do you think you lot have been stuck in my room playing dress-up – talking of which, Mack, where's your fucking costume?

MACK. I'm wearing it.

LAURA. I can't see him what are you wearing? Timp, will you tell me what he's wearing?

TIMP *goes to get* BENNY *from the window.*

TIMP. Come on – tuck in, Benny – poor cow's been there for ages already.

BENNY. I'm alright.

SOPHIE. Are you naked?

MACK. She's got a bikini on.

SOPHIE. Alright, hawk-eye.

MACK. No harm in paying attention to detail.

TIMP. There is when that detail's my girlfriend.

MACK. You dressed her up like a fucking goldfish.

TIMP. Everyone else has dressed up, mate? Look at him – fucking Simba over there.

BENNY. I'm Mufasa actually.

TIMP. Party's a funny time to have a gob on, that's all.

MACK. I'm fine.

TIMP. Come on!

MACK. I said I'm fine.

TIMP. Just come and have some food.

MACK. Don't much like sushi.

TIMP. What music do you fancy?

LAURA. Can we have some Disney – for the theme – can we?

SOPHIE. As if Timp's going to have a bunch of Disney tunes on his /

LAURA. He's got loads. He's got all the movies as well.

SOPHIE. What – why?

TIMP. You're asking a recreational drug user whether he likes multicoloured talking animals? Fucking love 'em.

BENNY (*still over by the window*). There are loads of white vans – driving down Princes Street.

SOPHIE. It'll be the rubbish collection.

BENNY. There's fucking loads of them though.

TIMP. What is wrong with you all?

LAURA. I'd dance with you, babe – if I could stand.

BENNY. Will someone help her up?

TIMP. She's dinner.

BENNY. She's clearly uncomfortable.

LAURA. I'm fine.

BENNY. She's not – she can't see anything or eat anything.

MACK. She said she's fine.

Beat.

BENNY. The sunset – it's made the whole city – pink.

LAURA. Red sky at night shepherd's delight – red sky in morning, shepherd's warning.

TIMP. We'll let the shepherds know – Come on, Ben – come eat.

BENNY. You can see it slipping; last tiny fraction of it.

SOPHIE. This is really good, Timp.

BENNY. Can't be going far though, eh? Stays fucking light all night – drives you mental. You reckon it hides just below the /

MACK. Benny?

BENNY. Yeah?

MACK. We're having a laugh.

BENNY. Are we?

MACK. Yep.

BENNY. What's your costume?

MACK. I'm Tinkerbell. I've just got very tiny wings. I'd prefer it if you didn't draw attention to them – I'm pretty self-conscious about it.

Beat.

TIMP. Look! Fucking look at that – (*Spots a crumpled up old ironing board under all the mess.*) You remember this?

SOPHIE. Tobog-ironing!

MACK. The tobog-iron!

LAURA. I can't see – show me!

No one shows her.

Timp – can – we, can I /

TIMP. Calton Hill – fucking king of the slopes on this bad boy; could have gone professional.

LAURA. That was the night we had the snow party.

SOPHIE (*sings*). Snow-body does it better!

TIMP (*kissing and playing with* LAURA). You got your little party-Nazi out.

LAURA. Can I get up now?

MACK (*robot voice*). 'Dance. Dance, everybody dance or I'll kill you, what's the point of a party unless you dance. Ahhhh, do not sit down, I will annoy you. Do not sit down, I will annoy you.'

SOPHIE. Wasn't the only thing you got out.

LAURA. Oh God don't.

SOPHIE. If you don't dance I'll get my rat out!

LAURA. What can I say? I'm a woman of my word. Please can I get up? Timp, it's starting to itch.

SOPHIE. Right in the middle of the dance floor.

TIMP. That you did, I was so proud.

SOPHIE. Benny, didn't you get off with Cat Logan that night?

BENNY. Did I?

BENNY *walks over – silently whilst the hubbub goes on around him and he begins to take all the sushi off* LAURA. *There's something gentle about it – he removes it all – plates it all up and helps her up to her feet. When he's done –* LAURA *looks at him a moment – kisses him on the head, he nods at her.*

SOPHIE. She'd come dressed as the devil – which made no fucking sense, bless her – and was completely covered in red paint.

TIMP. Fuck – yeah I remember this. It was fucking brilliant! Cam had taken those mushrooms and was going all spacky trying to lift up the carpet looking for little people. Little people! Oooh, little people – you remember that, Mack? (*Suddenly pointing to* MACK.)

MACK. Fuck off.

TIMP. We're at – at – aaa fuck where was it, it was brilliant –

MACK. Massa.

TIMP. We're in Massa – sittin' in those booths, you know – all dark – and this one is fuck-faced – and he's talking to this girl. She's like, you want to come home with me – Mack's all – yeah yeah – so she shimmies out of the fucking booth and his eyes nearly pop out – she's only a fucking little person – a dwarf – she was tiny – very fucking funny that was.

SOPHIE. Benny – don't you remember you got off with Cat Logan in the shower and all her body paint went everywhere?

MACK. Cam burst in here – turns the music off and is like 'There's been a murder! There's been a murder in the shower!' He fucking believed it too – look on his face.

BENNY. That wasn't Cam. It wasn't Cam that took the mushrooms and ran in, it was /

TIMP. Then you walking in looking like you'd gone five rounds with a fucking Rottweiler.

LAURA. Which basically you had. Cat Logan is a dog, no two ways – she fucked Mike Elliot and tried to use Scotch as lube.

MACK. Fuck off?

TIMP. He had to go to A+E. Stingy todger.

LAURA. Poor wee guy – worst thing about it was it was a bottle of Balvenie twelve-year-old his dad had got him for his twenty-first. If I were him I have spent the next three weeks sucking on my bedsheets.

TIMP (*sings*). Once, twice – three time a laydeee – and I looove you!

LAURA. Fucking Balvenie twelve-year-old, you know what that costs?

TIMP. Who wants more disco biscuits?

TIMP *starts handing out pills.*

BENNY. It wasn't Cam that ran in.

TIMP. Come on, you!

BENNY. No.

SOPHIE. I remember you two meeting. It was in Stereo; we'd only just met you.

MACK. I met you at football.

TIMP. I remember thinking fucking students – bunch of fucking layabouts no thanks.

MACK. Right.

TIMP. Never done an honest day's fucking work.

SOPHIE. Anyway – you looking across the bar and going 'Oh shit – that's it – I'm fucked.' I took a step back cos I thought you meant you were going to be sick.

LAURA. You said that?

TIMP. Can't remember.

SOPHIE. I remember it exactly – you said it like there was nothing you could do about it. It was amazing.

LAURA. Oh, Timp. That is, Timp – that is /

TIMP. Alright alright it's not fucking Jeremy Kyle.

BENNY. We have to get rid of this.

TIMP. I told you we're waiting till we all come up – we'll be like twenty times faster. We'll have it all done in no time – all of us lot – if we're high, five minutes, tops. Like Billy Whizz.

MACK. Billy the Kid?

TIMP. Billy Whizz – the fucking Beano.

MACK. Who's Billy Whizz?

BENNY. All of us – we have to all lift it, because I can't – not on my own.

SOPHIE. You alright, Ben?

MACK. He's fine.

A pissed, hazy drunken hum continues – dancing, laughing –
MACK *looks on,* TIMP *cackles and jokes –* LAURA *fawns
over* TIMP. *As they get high – and smoke fills the room – it
gets hotter and hotter – they start sweating, gurning, sweat
pouring off them – it sweats, it thumps – laughing, smoking –
sitting, eyes rolling. There is a sense that it could always be
this way – nothing forward, nothing backwards – there is
something utopian and yet claustrophobic, this should last for
just long enough that we feel it may never change.* BENNY
just sits – looking at it all – feeling increasingly desperate.

CAM *enters, still in his suit – carrying his violin, he is
excited – bursting with success. He looks at the scene – he
seems so composed, so smart. For a moment the others do
not see him – they continue to sway and stagger and for a
moment it looks as if* CAM *might want to leave.*

BENNY. Cam! Cam! Cam! Cam!

CAM. Alright, Benny?

BENNY. How was it?

TIMP *spontaneously rugby-tackles* CAM *to the floor.*

LAURA. You look like a little penguin! Doesn't he look like a
little penguin?

CAM *tries to get up,* TIMP *rolls around laughing –* CAM
can't help but laugh.

Like he's on ice – look at him – trying to, it's like Bambi.
Bambi!

CAM. What the hell happened in here?

TIMP. We're tidying; we're just at the bit where it gets worse
before it gets better.

SOPHIE. How was it? How did it go?

BENNY *goes over and takes his hand – desperate to hear
him speak.*

BENNY. Tell us it went okay.

MACK. Anyone want another beer?

BENNY. Will you tell us?

SOPHIE. Give him a second.

CAM. God – it's nice to be back here. It was fucking intense.

BENNY. Will you tell us?

TIMP. Go on then – tell us how it went, you little homo.

CAM. It was – pretty amazing. I've never – I was really fucking nervous but… I don't think I've ever seen that many people – I mean except for football matches, but…

BENNY. Did you play well? The stars – the guy with the stars on his knees – the Russian – did he – did you impress everyone? Did they clap?

CAM recounts the evening but there is something about his passion, his excitement that cools everyone else a little – as if he has brought a draught in from outside.

CAM. I was so fucking nervous, I kept having to dry my hands, I swear I was actually sweating through my fingertips and I was so worried I was going to… but you know waiting to walk out there and you can just about see all those people and the lights are real bright and – fuck, my heart's still beating like the fucking – and you stand there and you see the glint on glasses and the odd grin but not much else so you're not really sure that they're there and – they start clapping and man – that many people – and the noise, the noise was so loud it make the stage shake a little bit, I felt it through my feet, the clapping, it was mad. And all the moisture goes out your mouth and suddenly you're standing in front of them and it's dead dead silent and – that was sort of the best bit – just when I was about to play and my bow is just a wee way off the strings – just waiting there – hovering – and it's there and you're still and then you hear this little tiny noise, this little fucking seat creak and you realise that fucking hundreds of people just leant in – just a fraction – to hear what you're going to do next – waiting for you to start.

Beat.

TIMP. You did your thing?

CAM. Aye – I did my thing.

TIMP. Big old hoo-ha after?

CAM. Aye – big old hoo-ha after.

TIMP. Well there we go – lovely jubbers. Pass me a beer, Mack.

Everyone goes back to their own business – CAM *stands a moment, unsure whether to join in.* BENNY *sits still looking at* CAM *wanting more.*

MACK. What am I a fucking vending machine?

TIMP. Well if you will stand by the fridge.

LAURA. Come dance – Cam.

LAURA *grabs him and spins him round and round, then puts him down and wanders back to* TIMP.

CAM (*almost shouting*). Everyone fucking talking to me and offering me shit and that guy – the Russian –

SOPHIE. Oop – exotic.

CAM. He wants to teach me – one on one – in fucking Vienna – I don't even know where that is!

TIMP. It's not anywhere near here.

CAM. They all stood and clapped and – it was – it was – great. It was really really great. (*Pause.*) You guys are totally fucked.

BENNY *nods.*

TIMP *hands* CAM *a rolled note and indicates a plate with coke on it.*

TIMP. Go on – get your snout in that, wonderboy.

CAM *does a line.*

BENNY *sees that* CAM *is a little disjointed – apart –* BENNY *goes to hug* CAM. CAM *steps back – takes his tie off and directs his attention to the rest of the group.* BENNY *stands alone.*

CAM. Let's fucking party!

LAURA. Are we going to get to say we knew you when you were younger when we're older?

BENNY *looks out of the window.*

BENNY. Cam, did you see what the white vans were? Cam?

CAM *parties in with the rest of them, not wanting to be left out.*

CAM. They're police vans.

BENNY. What? Why?

CAM. Don't know – they're parked right down Princes Street – helmets and batons the lot. Must be a march or something; fuck knows.

TIMP. Benny – come on!

TIMP *holds out a pill on his finger.*

Come on – gobble gobble.

BENNY. Why are there police vans? Is something happening?

TIMP. Come on – swallow some smiles.

MACK *still at one side watching* BENNY *all the time.*

SOPHIE *approaches* MACK *– drunk – dancing – being overtly provocative.* MACK *desperately tries to contain her – to shut her down.*

SOPHIE. Come on, grumpy – let's dance.

MACK *looks at* SOPHIE *with threat.*

Change the track, Timp.

MACK. I'm alright, Sophs.

SOPHIE. Come on.

TIMP. Batting above your average, Mack.

MACK. I'm alright – thanks.

SOPHIE. Don't make a girl beg.

MACK. Honestly – I'm –

SOPHIE *begins being pretty explicit with* MACK.

Stop it.

LAURA *catches sight and tries to pull* SOPHIE *away.*

SOPHIE. I'm mucking around.

LAURA. Sophs? Don't.

BENNY *catches sight.*

BENNY. I wouldn't touch him with a bargepole, Sophs – you might catch something.

TIMP. Bargepole? You joking? Toothpick more like.

SOPHIE. As if I would.

TIMP. I bet you're horrible in the sack, Macky.

MACK. Horrendous.

BENNY. I bet it's with his eyes closed and his teeth clenched and thinking furiously of his mother.

MACK. Spot on.

LAURA. You ever been in love, Mack?

TIMP. Ah, come on – as if!

MACK *starts to laugh.*

BENNY. Have ya – have you ever been in love?

TIMP. Only with toddlers.

SOPHIE. What?

CAM. Didn't you hear about last night? He fucked a seventeen-year-old.

Beat.

SOPHIE. You did what?

BENNY. Go on Mack – tell us.

Pause – the others, excited – willing MACK *to speak.*

MACK. You won't guess what Timp did.

SOPHIE *pours herself a shot and knocks it back.*

TIMP *glares at* MACK.

Timp was fucking hilarious he /

LAURA. What did you do, babe?

BENNY. Mack fucked a drunk seventeen-year-old. Didn't you, Mack?

SOPHIE. Did you? That's funny – God, Mack – what are you like?

MACK. I – I –

MACK *stands looking at* SOPHIE, *a glass in his hand not able to move.*

BENNY. Proud of it 'n' all – thinks he did her a favour, gave her what she asked for. Didn't ya?

CAM. She did say please.

SOPHIE. Oh, in that case.

LAURA. What did you do?

TIMP. I got my cock out.

LAURA. Boring.

SOPHIE. Was it good?

BENNY. Yeah – was it?

MACK *throws his glass against a wall and it smashes.*

CAM. Fucking hell!

MACK *laughs wildly.*

SOPHIE *stands stock still.*

TIMP *throws a bag of icing sugar all over* MACK.

TIMP *stares at* MACK, *the threat of violence is palpable.*

Beat.

They break – they laugh.

TIMP. You're a fucking mentalist!

MACK *gasping – gulping for air, still stares at* SOPHIE.

MACK (*snapping – wild*). You want to dance – let's fucking dance!

BENNY. Did it make you feel like a man?

MACK. Shall we – shall we! Turn it up – Timp – come on! Hey! You fucking remember – down south we went to Alton Towers for the day – we fucking remember this and I'm sitting next to Benny-boy – and we're waiting for this ride to kick off right and he's so fucking scared of this rollercoaster, such a fucking softy – he starts – he starts singing to himself – he starts singing – (*Sings a couple of lines from 'I Just Can't Wait to be King' from Walt Disney's* The Lion King.) Fucking put it on, Timp, find it, let's dance – let's have a fucking dance!

TIMP *starts looking for the track –* CAM *delighted by the hysteria starts leaping around with* MACK *– they start singing the song –* MACK *knows the words.*

You remember, Benny – you remember how you cried?

SOPHIE. Stop it, Mack.

BENNY. You know the words.

MACK. Like a little lion all scared and /

BENNY. You took my hand and you sang it with me and you said I'd be alright – cos you knew I fucking hated heights.

There is a beat – MACK *and* BENNY *look at each other for moment whilst the dancing leaps around them, there is something impossibly tender about it – but* MACK *can't stomach it – he belts out another line of the song. Pandemonium ensues –* MACK *drags everyone into the song – they are all singing.* MACK *gets to* SOPHIE *who looks up at him intensely – with one arm he pulls her up and close to him so their faces are almost touching – and he shakes his head to say 'no' –*

No one else sees this – MACK *then turns her away and carries on chanting for people to get up and dance. He is wild, untameable – a chant begins that sees him leaping from chair to chair – the distances are dangerous, the act is daring.*

ALL. Mack! Mack! Mack!

He leaps.

BENNY *stands apart, silently watching.*

BENNY. It wasn't Cam that ran in from the shower…

MACK. Come and dance – Benny-boy.

ALL. Mack! Mack! Mack!

He leaps.

BENNY. I don't want to dance.

ALL. Mack! Mack! Mack!

He leaps.

BENNY (*louder*). I don't want to dance!

ALL. Mack! Mack! Mack!

He leaps.

BENNY (*louder still*). I don't want to dance!

MACK *tries to leap a final time but he has arrived at the chair that has not yet been touched.* MACK *goes to leap and he can't – he can't touch it – everybody stops – the moment is too great to ignore.*

Beat.

I want to know why my brother killed himself.

Lights down.

Scene Four

It still isn't dark – the husky blue of twilight lingers in the air.
Debris from the party can be seen but the kitchen is empty,
except for BENNY *who sits alone at the kitchen table. He gets*
up and goes over to look out of the window.

CAM *enters – he's still in his shirt from the concert but has now*
paired it with shorts.

CAM *lingers by the door.*

BENNY. Eh-up.

CAM. Hi.

BENNY. Y'alright?

CAM. Yeah.

BENNY. Where you all hiding?

CAM. Bathroom. Not hiding – just they wanted a bath. Cold
water or –

BENNY. Probably figured lions don't like water, big cats, aren't
they?

CAM. What?

BENNY. Nothing.

CAM. It's nice, it's like kids – we're doing bubble beards. You
should come.

BENNY. I'm alright.

Beat.

CAM. Those pills were shit, eh? Can't feel a thing – Timp
reckons they're duds. Everyone's mellow as fuck.

BENNY. I guess there's a mood.

Beat.

CAM. I wanted to say thank you.

BENNY. What for?

CAM. Earlier – for making me go.

BENNY. You would have gone anyway. You seen this?

CAM. Are there more than earlier?

BENNY. Yeah – been building all night; hundreds of them. (*Beat*.) Exciting, Vienna though – great that is. Only way is up. It's good.

CAM *comes over and looks out the window with* BENNY.

CAM. What are they doing? They're just standing there.

BENNY. I saw one of them earlier, pop his baton under his arm and lift his visor up and eat a whole fucking hot dog.

CAM. So?

BENNY. Why do you need riot gear to eat a hot dog?

CAM. You don't.

BENNY. Then why are they wearing it?

CAM. I don't think he put it on just so he could eat the hot dog.

BENNY. I know that, you flaming idiot.

CAM. What's your point?

BENNY. Why are they there if there's no riot?

CAM. Waiting for one I guess.

Beat – CAM *looks out of the window a moment.*

They'll fuck off home when they run out of hot dogs.

BENNY. Makes me angry.

CAM. Don't let it.

BENNY. You sure those pills were shit?

CAM. What?

BENNY. You're gurning like a bloody washing machine. Here.

BENNY *gets a piece of chewing gum out of his pocket and gives it to* CAM; *he puts his fingers on either side of his jaw and starts to massage it.*

CAM. Probably just a bit tense.

BENNY. Oh yeah?

CAM. I wanted to ask you something, Benny?

BENNY. What?

CAM. It's stupid really.

BENNY. Go for it.

CAM. It's tiny – it's just – after the concert –

BENNY *finishes massaging* CAM's *jaw and ruffles his hair.*

BENNY. There you go, munchalot.

CAM. We were talking at a table after the concert, me and Viktashev, right? And he's saying all this stuff about how exciting things are going to be and how I need to watch out because everyone is going to want a piece of me –

BENNY. Did he put his hand on your leg? I'll fucking kill him if he did.

CAM. No – he didn't put his hand on my leg.

BENNY. He put his hand on your cock?

CAM. No – (*Laughing.*) listen –

BENNY. It's no fucking laughing matter – I'll chop his cock off, if you need someone to –

CAM. No. No – listen, I'm being serious.

BENNY. Shame.

CAM. This old guy comes over to us. He's got this camera. He's dressed like an old-school artist – this silk-scarf thing and the soles of his shoes were thick and his coat was heavy, you could tell it had been really expensive. (*Beat.*) He says 'Viktashev?' He's Russian, I think, Eastern European anyway. Viktashev seems not to recognise him – but the old guy asks if he can take our picture. Viktashev looks at me with his eyes wide and he raises his eyebrows and then he turns to the old guy and he says 'no thanks'. Like fucking wincing and smug – (*Imitates*.) 'no thanks' and then, I think, he adds something like... buddy. Then Viktashev turns his head away from the old guy's face really quickly and laughs a bit and smiles at me and his eyebrows go again and he says 'so where were we?' like he and I were on the same team against this old guy. But I didn't want to be on Viktashev's team. You know what I mean?

But the old guy didn't move – he just stood there, looking at us, then he starts rooting around in his bag. Viktashev gets a bit loud and says 'look' – with this hard 'k' that makes the old guy blink like he's startled – and a bit of Viktashev's spit lands on this old guy's coat, but the old guy just keeps blinking and rummaging and Viktashev again 'look' – with the hard 'k' and buddy – 'we're having a meeting'. Like the old guy couldn't see we were having a meeting? And I wanted to smile at the old guy to tell him it was alright but who the fuck am I to try and smile him out of the situation? So I don't smile at him and I just look at the table.

The old guy eventually finds this book and takes it out of his bag and he places it on the table – and immediately Viktashev puts his hand on it and I see that Viktashev's wedding ring is new, really shiny and clean and I – somehow that makes me think – 'what the fuck do you know?' Viktashev tries to push the book off the table – but the old guy doesn't even notice, he's got his thumb wedged in between two of the pages and he's opening it and I realise it's his like album, his portfolio – and he's smiling because he thinks the second we see it we'll understand, so he's smiling. Viktashev is calling for security and I can see photos of all these ballerinas that I think I recognise and an actor and musicians, and then right at the end there's fucking Picasso, this amazing photo of him – when he's just about to start painting, the paintbrush is like seconds away from the canvas – it's class – and I think, fuck me, this guy's taken Picasso's photo.

Beat.

BENNY. Did security come?

CAM. Aye but before they got there the old guy just smiles –
he's got yellow squares for teeth, really square like Travel
Scrabble pieces, the little magnetic ones, no letters though,
obviously – anyway – I say – 'I think they're really good.'
(*Beat.*) Benny – who the fuck am I to say – 'I think they're
really good'? I'm a fucking kid compared to him. Why isn't
anyone looking at him? He's taken Picasso's fucking picture.
He's done a whole life. (*Beat.*) What would you do if
someone told you – if you knew – if the look in some old
guy's face told you that being young was as good as it ever
fucking gets?

Beat.

BENNY *looks at* CAM. BENNY *doesn't respond.*

*There is an explosion outside the window – it's dulled by
distance but we can feel it.*

ACT TWO

Scene One

There is an explosion outside the window – it seems closer now, the room shakes.

BENNY. What the fuck was that?

They both go to the window to look out.

CAM. It's burning.

BENNY. Fucking hell.

CAM. Fuck – that policeman's on fire – look at him. Look.

Beat – they stare.

How did… (*Stops himself from asking the question.*)

BENNY. Police vans don't just explode.

CAM. Must have overheated.

BENNY. Engines were off, been there for hours. No way.

CAM. Then /

BENNY. Don't know.

Orange light continues to reflect through the window – the police van burns.

CAM *continues to chew, it's manic, it's tense.*

Take that fucking gum out, man… you're killing me.

CAM. I'm going to tell the others.

BENNY. They won't care.

CAM *exits.*

BENNY *stands at the window.* BENNY *climbs up on top of the fridge. In the distance we can hear* CAM *telling the others about what has happened, no one enters.*

Long pause. BENNY *looks out of the window.*

We can hear laughter from off.

BENNY *sits.*

TIMP *enters, he is looking for weed, he finds some and sits at the table and begins to roll a joint.*

TIMP *doesn't see* BENNY.

LAURA *enters soon afterwards and sits down next to him.*

LAURA *goes to go and look out of the window.*

LAURA. You seen the /

TIMP. Come here.

TIMP *beckons* LAURA *to him and she immediately goes over, forgetting the window completely.*

LAURA *rests her head on* TIMP*'s shoulder whilst he rolls.*

LAURA *doesn't see* BENNY.

LAURA. It's nearly midnight.

TIMP. Hm.

LAURA. Why don't you ever tell the boys?

TIMP. They're usually away on holidays this time of year; never understood the fuss anyway.

LAURA. You want water?

TIMP. I'm alright.

LAURA *doesn't move.*

You not having any?

LAURA. Just wondered if you wanted it, that's all.

Pause.

You were talking in your sleep Monday; really badly; couldn't sleep at all.

TIMP. It's just dreams, eh.

LAURA. Shouting, kind of – like you were shouting at something. You grabbed me.

LAURA *shows* TIMP *the mark.*

TIMP *kisses the mark.*

TIMP. I'm sorry.

LAURA. You were asleep, eh.

TIMP. Yeah, but still.

Beat.

LAURA. It's horrible to watch, your face all screwed up, grinding your teeth. I can't take my eyes off you when you're like it – it's like a baby in pain or something.

TIMP. I can never remember a thing.

LAURA. Seems unfair.

TIMP. Why?

LAURA. Don't know – guess just, me having to watch you – just – you know, waking up after, fresh as a fucking daisy, not remembering.

TIMP. I can't help it.

LAURA. I'm not saying it's your fault – I'm just saying it doesn't seem fair, that's all.

TIMP. I'm asleep, aren't I?

LAURA. I know, I know. It's just – it's like there's an earthquake and you're right next to me but you're sleeping right through it and making me hold up the whole room on my own.

TIMP. I'm fucking asleep, Loz.

LAURA. I know – It's just weird, that's all – it doesn't matter.

TIMP *lights the spliff and starts smoking it.*

TIMP. I'm sticking to myself.

LAURA *goes to the sink and makes a towel wet, she lays it on* TIMP*'s forehead.*

LAURA. You ever think I should be a bit more…

TIMP. What?

LAURA. Sophie's sort of – sophisticated, isn't she?

TIMP. Is she?

LAURA. Yeah. I think so.

TIMP. She's from the south; southerners think their shit's sophisticated.

LAURA. I think you're sophisticated.

TIMP. That's because I am.

Beat.

LAURA. You ever think about what you'll be like when you're old?

TIMP. No.

LAURA. I sometimes look at the back of my hand and wonder what it will look like when it's all wrinkly. Like that same bit of skin right there, and either I die first or that will definitely happen – you ever think about that?

TIMP. It'll be different skin.

LAURA. Look at it though, imagine – isn't that weird?

TIMP. No.

LAURA. It's weird that there's no way round it.

TIMP. I'll buy you some hand cream.

LAURA. I remember being like ten and being naked on my bed and looking down at my flat little body and imagining what it would be when there were tits and pubes and things.

TIMP. Things?

LAURA. Tits and pubes. And thinking it was the weirdest thing that they would just be there. No other option; you know what I mean?

TIMP. I've yet to grow into my tits.

LAURA. Imagine all your tattoos; you'll look like a page of writing that's been rained on.

TIMP. Thanks.

LAURA. Timp?

TIMP. Yeah.

LAURA. I'll still love you; even when you're smudged.

TIMP smiles at LAURA, *gets up and goes and refills his glass.*

Them all graduating, makes you wonder, doesn't it?

TIMP. I hate this.

LAURA. What?

TIMP. When you get all, you know, thinky, in the middle of the fucking night. It does my nut in. Where is everyone – it's not even fucking midnight – why we given up so early?

LAURA. Shut up, I'm being clever.

TIMP. No you're not – you're being a pain in the arse.

LAURA. Doesn't it make you think about what you'll be – one day, when you're old?

TIMP. No. It makes me glad I've already got a job and didn't waste twenty K on a fucking useless degree.

LAURA. You know how I have a smoke every now and then – but, I wouldn't say I was a smoker though, would you?

TIMP. Laura? I love you very much.

LAURA. I know.

TIMP. But will you shut the fuck up?

LAURA. No listen, if you just smoke every now and then for ages well then you must actually become a smoker at some point and I wonder when that is. If it's an age or a time or – like I never intended to be a waitress, it was just something I was going to do for a bit until I stopped and did something proper and I just wonder when I stop being someone who was going to be a waitress for a bit and I just become a waitress. I don't want to be your wife and a waitress... for example.

TIMP. Stop thinking. It'll hurt your head.

LAURA. I think Cam might be really famous; my mum stuck his face on our fridge. I don't think I'd want that.

TIMP. Well, that's lucky cos you don't play the fucking violin.

LAURA. I know it's not very – I don't know – it's just, I only ever really think about being really good at being a mum. (*Beat.*) I know I shouldn't say that, but I don't know, somehow that seems like enough. Like it's really important, somehow. Don't know why. I'd like to make a home for us. Is that weird?

Beat.

TIMP. No.

LAURA. I sometimes wonder how Sophie feels, knowing that she wasn't enough to stop him. You know?

TIMP. Yeah.

LAURA. I'm going to make a cuppa; those pills have made me head hurt.

LAURA *goes over to the kettle.*

TIMP. Not sure a cuppa'll fix that.

LAURA. Give it a bash, eh? Timp?

TIMP. Yeah?

LAURA. Would you like to move in with me?

TIMP *looks up at* LAURA *in silent shock.*

Some time passes.

TIMP. Not yet eh? When we're a bit older... maybe.

LAURA. Just thought I'd ask. In case... doesn't matter though.

Unseen by TIMP *she gets a tiny cupcake and a candle out of the cupboard.*

LAURA *puts the candle into the cupcake.*

TIMP. I'd die without you, babe.

TIMP *exits.*

LAURA. I know, you big dildo.

LAURA *lights the candle and turns around to give* TIMP *the cake – but* TIMP *has gone.*

LAURA *stands – crestfallen – behind the candle light she sees* BENNY *on top of the fridge.*

LAURA *freezes a minute – unsure of what she's seen.*

BENNY. Hiya.

LAURA. Buggery wank fuck, Benny. You scared the life out of me – you shouldn't do that.

BENNY. Sorry.

LAURA. How long you been up there?

BENNY. I dozed off. Door woke me.

LAURA. I thought you'd gone to bed.

BENNY. Couldn't sleep.

LAURA. You want a cup of tea, babe?

BENNY. Yes please.

BENNY *climbs down.*

BENNY *sits and watches* LAURA *making tea – there is something calming about her.*

You looked out the window?

LAURA. No.

BENNY. Police van – exploded – burnt out. Twitter says they've arrested someone.

LAURA. Oh no. Where's your mug?

BENNY. Over there. Laura?

LAURA. Yep.

BENNY. You think it's more important to be honest or to be happy?

LAURA. Milk?

BENNY. Thanks.

LAURA. Sugar?

BENNY. No – thanks.

LAURA. I don't think I've ever made you a cup of tea before, isn't that funny?

Beat.

BENNY. But if –

LAURA *stops making tea for a moment and comes over and holds* BENNY'*s head in her hands, she kisses the top of his head and gives him a big cuddle.*

LAURA. I think we're quite similar you and me, Ben. Need things feeling safe before we can rest. Otherwise you get so anxious in your tummy, you know – so sort of scared, need things to feel, level.

BENNY. Yeah.

LAURA. Horrible innit, when it's all all over the shop?

BENNY. But?

LAURA. You know what I do. I – I have this picture in my mind of how things are going to look when they're all sorted; I sort of make a safe place in my head. Like me on a sofa with fluffy slippers, don't know why they're fluffy but they are – and Timp with his hand on my head, like he does, and us watching the TV and whenever things are looking a bit grim – I just focus really hard on that picture and I know that whatever happens now, doesn't really matter in the long run – just so long as I eventually get to that sofa – you know what I mean?

BENNY. But how do you know you're going to get there?

LAURA. Cos I can see it. I wouldn't be able to see it if it weren't real, would I?

BENNY. What if you lose your picture? If a bit of it breaks.

Beat.

LAURA. Can't see how I could lose it, it's in my head, int it? Who can steal it from in there – you plonker.

LAURA *passes* BENNY *his cup of tea and ruffles his hair.*

BENNY. But what if Timp /

LAURA. Stop thinking so much. It'll hurt your head.

BENNY. Laura?

LAURA. Don't, Ben.

Scene Two

SOPHIE *bursts through the door; she's got a bubble beard on and is looking for someone, she doesn't find them… she's laughing – excited.*

SOPHIE. Hi.

LAURA. Hey.

BENNY. I'm going to try and get some sleep.

SOPHIE. Oh no – come and play – look at my beard!

BENNY. It's brilliant. (*Beat.*) You seem so okay, Sophs.

SOPHIE. What?

BENNY. Everyone was so worried you'd… but actually you're fine.

Beat.

SOPHIE. I –

BENNY. I'm saying it's a good thing.

> BENNY *exits.*

> LAURA *still stands with her tea, relaxed.*

SOPHIE. You coming back through?

LAURA. In a minute.

> SOPHIE *turns to leave – just before she exits.*

> Sophs? Can you untwist my bra strap for me – it's digging right in and I can't reach it, keep trying and getting in a muddle.

SOPHIE. Sure.

> SOPHIE *approaches.*

> It's not twisted.

LAURA. Oh. It felt like it was.

SOPHIE. Nope – all fine.

LAURA. Who were you looking for?

SOPHIE. Hm?

LAURA. When you came in – you were looking for someone.

SOPHIE. Was I?

LAURA. It wasn't Benny or me.

SOPHIE. What?

LAURA. You looked like you hadn't found who you were looking for.

SOPHIE. Did I?

LAURA. Who were you looking for?

> SOPHIE *finishes doing the bra strap – pause – they stare at one another.*

SOPHIE. I was looking for my cardigan.

LAURA. Oh, it's here – I saw it earlier – one sec.

SOPHIE *stands, itching to get away* – LAURA *locates the cardigan and goes to hand it to* SOPHIE. SOPHIE *comes in to take the cardigan.*

SOPHIE. Thanks.

LAURA *doesn't let go of the cardigan.*

LAURA. You remember little Jenny that used to be round here all the time because she fancied Cam.

SOPHIE. Yeah.

LAURA. You remember how she'd play football with them in hot pants and sit and play computer games for hours.

SOPHIE. Yeah.

LAURA. The boys were like – 'so what if she likes computer games and tiny shorts – what's wrong with that.'

SOPHIE. Yeah.

LAURA. And we found it so mad that they were all totally blind to her high jinks, silly wee cow.

SOPHIE. What you getting at, Loz?

LAURA. Just she'd forgotten that boys might not speak girl – but she's forgotten we could spot it a mile off.

Beat.

LAURA *gives* SOPHIE *her cardigan.*

SOPHIE *takes the cardigan.*

SOPHIE. Thank you.

LAURA. I know we only really know each other because of the boys but – you're my friend. I consider you – my friend.

SOPHIE. You're my friend too.

LAURA. When our dog died my mum didn't shed a tear but went straight out and bought five goldfish and she fucking hates fish.

Beat.

SOPHIE. It's not a reaction.

LAURA. It probably doesn't feel like a /

SOPHIE. It's not. It's real.

LAURA. It probably feels like it's /

SOPHIE. I promise you. It's /

LAURA. It's just that… Benny, if he knew – saw – I don't know, what he'd do. It's not a small thing, Sophs.

SOPHIE. It's not a bad thing.

LAURA. Isn't it?

Beat.

SOPHIE. The first night I knew – um – the first – he – Mack – came to my flat – we spent nearly nine hours straight just talking. I'd never done that, with anyone – before. We sat on my roof, we had two big bottles of beer and two cigarettes and we shared them both. It was really warm – and we laughed, so much. You know the kind where tears and snot and everything is coming out of your face and your stomach and your cheeks hurt from it – and you barely breathe. We sat and watched the birds in the sky all night – it never got dark – the sky stayed the most amazing colour… completely clear and this purple blue, like a really light bruise – and the birds were so black against it and squawking and he does a great seagull impression. At about three – we walked through the meadows, just the two of us – the city was so quiet, like all the shadows were left from the night but the light was already there for morning, like the two shouldn't meet but they had and it created this other world, this amazing other place – which you can only see if you keep your eyes open for that long – a gap in the net – a slice of time that isn't day or night but some other… and he looked at me and I felt like it might eat me whole, and I knew – I knew right then, somehow I knew – that everything in the world would seem smaller from then on.

And then we started singing – (*Sings a line of 'Ain't got No/I Got Life' by Nina Simone.*) you know?'

LAURA *nods*.

We sang that and ran about until all the purple had bled out
of the sky and there were postmen – and then he had to go. I
went to kiss him and he said no – I had to make my choice
first.

LAURA. Choice?

SOPHIE. That night was the happiest I've ever been.

LAURA. It was before /

SOPHIE. We were singing and singing and running and –

LAURA. Sophie?

SOPHIE. What if it's bigger? What if it's bigger, more
important than /

LAURA. Are you out of your mind?

SOPHIE. Why can't it be?

LAURA. Because someone died.

SOPHIE. That night – how I feel is *so* /

LAURA. Mack fucks anything that moves. He fucked a
teenager last night, for God's sake.

SOPHIE. No he didn't.

LAURA. He did.

SOPHIE. He told me he didn't.

LAURA. Oh, well, in that case.

SOPHIE. Maybe I'm different – maybe what we have is /

LAURA. Sophs.

SOPHIE. Timp fucks people all the time and he still loves you.

Pause.

LAURA *takes a step away from* SOPHIE.

MACK *enters*.

MACK *goes straight over to the window, the girls remain silent.*

MACK. They've arrested that spacky pair of Goths from Princes Street Gardens for the police van.

SOPHIE. Really?

MACK. According to Timp according to Twitter.

LAURA. Bound to be bullshit.

MACK *turns back into the room.*

MACK. Anyone want a beer?

LAURA. No.

LAURA *exits.*

MACK. What's wrong with her?

Beat.

SOPHIE *stands and stares at* MACK – *she begins to sing 'Ain't Got No/I Got Life' by Nina Simone quietly into the silence of the room.*

In the distance we can hear drums beating – the muffled sound of loudspeakers. SOPHIE *continues to sing.*

Stop it.

SOPHIE *continues to sing.*

Stop it.

SOPHIE *continues to sing.*

Stop it!

Beat.

SOPHIE. Do you; have you ever actually felt any – guilt? Because it's come as a bit of a surprise that um, that – you, one, I don't, can't actually feel it. Like I can't get my body to do it, on its own, it's not something I can generate somehow, like, I – I find myself having to actually summon it, trying to encourage myself, to summon it and even then I can't do it, really, I can't feel it. I thought it might be shock at first and then – grief or but I think I might not feel it. I can't. I don't. All I can feel is total joy, total – peace. I look at you and I sometimes actually make myself think of him, I force him into my head and I don't feel guilty. What does that mean? What kind of person does that make me? (*Pause.*) Hm? Sometimes I think it's because – what we have is love, meant to be. (*Laughs.*) That we love each other, yes, Mack, that is what I sometimes think. Is that ridiculous? And sometimes I even think that that love is so important that it is bigger, or equal to – what he did. That they are just two feelings, one is love and the other is despair and both just have an action. And that those actions are different but that somehow they are equal – does that make me a monster? I sat at his funeral looking at his parents and Benny but all I could think of, all I could feel – was you.

But then I look at you and I wonder if it's actually there. I wonder if I added up the amount of minutes, hours, fucking days I have spent thinking about you, the amount of fucking longing I have done – if I added that up and weighed it against anything you have ever actually said... and – (*Pause.*)

But then you do the smallest thing you make me a cup of tea when I don't ask, or you touch my hand really lightly in a room full of people and I think no, Sophie, don't laugh – don't laugh because it's real and it's so much more real because it's unsaid and unspoken and un – un – un – it's so much more real because I can't touch it, because we can't say it and I can't see it, it's so much more real because I don't know if it's there.

Pause. MACK *doesn't say anything.*

Please say something. (*Pause.*) Please. Please tell me if...

She trails off unable to try any harder.

MACK *stands,* MACK *stares at her.*

MACK *does not,* MACK *cannot speak.*

A foghorn sounds loudly outside the window – the drum beats rise – the people are marching.

Scene Three

MACK *and* SOPHIE *stand, as before.*

The drum beat rises.

BENNY *charges in – excited, breathless.*

BENNY. They've fucking arrested that pink-haired fairy and the lanky fuck that sit by the bandstand.

No response.

For the van.

MACK *and* SOPHIE *look at him.*

There's no way it was them. No way – I've seen her spend fifteen minutes trying to get into a bag of crisps. There was no one but cops round those vans.

MACK. Alright, Poirot.

BENNY. It wasn't them.

MACK. So what if it wasn't?

BENNY. Two people just got arrested for something they didn't do.

SOPHIE *stands by the window looking out.*

MACK. Big deal.

BENNY. Something we know they didn't do.

MACK *gets himself a beer and ignores* BENNY.

It's wrong.

SOPHIE. There are lights coming down Lothian Road – torches.

BENNY. I'm going out there.

MACK (*lifting his beer above his head as if it's a sword*). By the power of Grayskull! (*Simulates fireworks and explosion akin to He-Man's transformation.*) I am the power!

BENNY *joins* SOPHIE *by the window.*

BENNY. Listen… you can hear drums.

TIMP *charges into the kitchen wielding a mop or something similar.*

TIMP. For the honour of Grayskull!

MACK (*in backing-track whispers*). She-ra, She-ra!

TIMP. I am She-Raaaaaa!

MACK. I am the power!

TIMP. What needs saving?

LAURA *wanders in after* TIMP. *She sits herself silently up on the side, almost unnoticed.*

BENNY. They arrested those Goths for the police van – they never did it.

TIMP. For the honour of Grayskull!

BENNY. I'm going out there.

TIMP. What? You can't.

BENNY. Why not?

TIMP. For the honour of Grayskull!

SOPHIE. There are drums – can you hear drums.

MACK. It's just the Kilted Celts down by the museum.

BENNY. It's nearly midnight – what they doing up at this time eh?

CAM *enters.*

CAM. What's going on?

SOPHIE. There's torches and drums.

CAM. No way – it's the Cavalcade? I fucking love the Cavalcade.

BENNY. It's the middle of the fucking night – no it's not the Cavalcade, you dumb fuck.

TIMP. We could have the Cavalcade in here!

BENNY. It's people – they're marching.

CAM. Can we?

TIMP. Course.

LAURA. Timp?

TIMP. Now – first things first – what's a fucking cavalcade?

CAM. Oh.

BENNY. They're marching with all their rubbish – look!
Fucking look! They're getting rid.

LAURA. Timp?

TIMP. Yeah, babe?

LAURA. Will you come home with me please.

TIMP. You poorly?

LAURA. No.

> *Beat.* TIMP *looks at* LAURA, *he knows something is wrong.*

BENNY. There's hundreds and hundreds look – they're all
carrying all their crap – they're carrying it, look, all those bin
bags – looks like a massive shiny black beetle – looks
beautiful.

TIMP. Sounds like it's all just about to kick off – why would we
leave?

LAURA. I want to go home, Timp.

TIMP. Come on, babe.

LAURA (*stares* TIMP *dead in the eyes*). I know.

> TIMP *freezes.*

BENNY. You coming? All of this – together, if we carry enough
each – we can get clear of it – get tidy. You all coming?

> *Pause.*

> BENNY *looks at the room, they don't move – they're fucked.*

Yeah?

TIMP. Mate – I would – I just – Laura's feeling poorly and –

LAURA. No I'm not.

TIMP. We're having a nice time, aren't we?

BENNY. Mack?

TIMP. By the power of Greyskull!

MACK. I am the power.

Beat.

BENNY. My dad talks about back in the eighties – spent fucking months on the picket lines and the things they did, the fucking bile they used to shoot at the scabs for not being with them. You know? Really fucking get at them, try and pull them apart – cos they reckoned by just letting it go on – you were as bad as joining the other side.

TIMP. You've done it again, haven't you?

BENNY. What?

TIMP. Benny, how many times – eh? We've talked about it – haven't we?

BENNY. What?

TIMP. You've been watching *Billy Elliot* again – haven't you?

BENNY. Fuck off.

TIMP. You know what it does to you.

Laughter.

BENNY. We should be out there.

TIMP. 'I don't want a childhood – I want to be ballet dancer!'

BENNY. Can't you hear the drums?

TIMP *starts drumming on the table.*

You'll let everyone out there risk their arses on your behalf and you're happy to just sit back and watch it happen? Cam? You a coward 'n' all?

CAM. No.

LAURA. Timp – I want to go home.

TIMP *picks up* LAURA *and starts to ballet-dance with her.*

Put me down.

TIMP. Cheer up.

MACK. Choosing in here is just as much of a choice as choosing out there. 'Choose life – choose a beer – choose a fucking knees-up.'

BENNY. Amazing how in here doesn't take any fucking balls though?

MACK. You reckon?

SOPHIE. Calm down.

BENNY. Why? Why? I don't want to calm – I don't want to sit, I don't want to fucking drink or snort or fucking – I want to move.

TIMP. 'I want to dance.'

BENNY. I don't want to live like this.

MACK. Go on then! Get out – go and do it! Go and join the fucking masses.

BENNY. Don't you think that looks amazing. All them people – moving – not shouting or screaming – just marching – look – with all those bags, that many people deciding one decision at one time and them all saying it – really quietly – doesn't that – make your fucking, doesn't that make your heart beat a bit faster? Sophs – make your heart beat faster?

BENNY *bends down close to* SOPHIE.

SOPHIE. My heart?

BENNY. Yeah.

Beat.

SOPHIE. He's right – we can – move it all. If you guys go downstairs and check the street and then – a few of you in the stairwell and then – a couple of us – stay up here and –

LAURA. Couple?

SOPHIE. Whoever. Look after the flat –

LAURA. Which couple?

SOPHIE. We can pass it down to you.

CAM. I'll go down.

TIMP. On who?

CAM. I'll help you, Benny.

LAURA. Which two, Sophs?

BENNY. We all have to go; together.

SOPHIE. I can stay here with /

BENNY. All of us.

SOPHIE. We're having a nice time, aren't we?

MACK. You should go if you want to go. Go with Benny.

SOPHIE. Fuck you.

> MACK *turns immediately on* BENNY *to disguise* SOPHIE*'s reaction.*

CAM. Whoa.

MACK. Why? Why together?

TIMP. Calm – down, Sophs – come here. Have a beer.

> TIMP *hands* SOPHIE *a beer.*

BENNY. Because I can't carry it all on me own.

> SOPHIE *puts some music on.*

> Sophs?

SOPHIE. I'm too high not to dance, I need to dance.

LAURA. Timp – I'm leaving.

TIMP. No you're fucking not.

MACK. Let's have some shots – eh? Line 'em up, Timp – let's get involved.

SOPHIE. Involved? All of a sudden you want to be involved?

LAURA. I'm leaving.

TIMP. No you're not.

BENNY. I got caught smoking weed in sixth form. It were just one joint but the headmaster wanted to make an example of me right? I was up for expulsion. I wouldn't have sat my A-levels I would have fucking flunked – but – but do you know what my brother did? Sophie?

SOPHIE *stops and looks at him a minute.*

TIMP. Tequila – it makes you happy! Loz? See. Cam – get away from that window.

CAM. It looks amazing.

MACK. Cam! Come here.

BENNY. He convinced the entire year group to confess to having also smoked a joint that day. There was a queue – fucking fifty people long outside the headmaster's office. What was he going to do – expel us all? We got an hour's detention each; that's all. Everyone – one hour's detention or I get expelled.

TIMP. Tequila?

BENNY. No.

TIMP. Sophs – get the lemons, hurry hurry.

SOPHIE *rushes to get lemons from the fridge.*

MACK. Lick 'em.

BENNY. Can't you see what I'm saying? It matters that there are numbers – it means we protect each other if we do it together – you see that?

Everyone licks the back of their hands.

MACK. Shake 'em.

MACK *pours salt all over the backs of people's hands.*

BENNY. Us sitting in here makes it more dangerous for them out there. Together we might get a little bruise – apart – we let one person fall completely.

Small beat.

MACK. Shoot 'em.

They all knock their shots back.

BENNY *grabs* SOPHIE.

BENNY. Don't you fucking care?

MACK *turns – savage and steps in the way.*

MACK. Let go.

BENNY. What does it matter to you? Every man for himself isn't it?

MACK. Let go of her.

BENNY. Why? She can take responsibility for herself, can't she?

Pause.

MACK *steps back – shrugs and walks away.*

SOPHIE *lunges at* BENNY *and goes to kiss him –* BENNY *flinches backwards and lets her go.*

What you doing?

SOPHIE *laughs,* BENNY *laughs nervously.*

MACK (*snaps*). Will you stop guilt-tripping everyone into helping you carrying your shit. You want to go and join your little gang out there – fucking go, Benny – but stop bleating. Because we're having a nice time – okay?

Beat.

CAM. I'll come with you – let's go. Let's do it.

TIMP. Oop – Bambi's got a hard-on.

MACK. He's making a fool of you, Cam.

BENNY. Come on – let's go.

MACK. Cam – there's no point.

SOPHIE. Let them go, right? If they've got the balls to fight for something they want – I say let them exercise their balls.

BENNY. Cam – go and check the stairwell, see how much we can get down and I'll start collecting it up.

LAURA. I'll come with you – let me get my bag.

TIMP. No one is fucking leaving! We're having a party – for God's sake it's not even midnight!

LAURA. Let me go.

TIMP. No!

CAM (*by the window*). The police – they're out the vans – they're stopping them, they've got fucking helmets and shields.

BENNY. They can't do that – not if it's peaceful – no one was doing anything.

CAM. They've stopped them; they're herding them like fucking cows.

BENNY. Come on, Cam.

TIMP. No one's fucking leaving – look, Sophs, turn the music up. Alright? (*Starts emptying it onto a plate.*) I was going to save it but – I've got fucking two hundred quid's worth of blow here. (*Starts desperately rolling a ten-pound note.*)

Who's in – eh? Fucking freebies. Let's go.

BENNY. Sophie? You with me?

SOPHIE *looks at* BENNY *a moment – turns to* TIMP *and does a line of coke.*

LAURA (*she's found her bag*). I'm coming with you – we'll go.

TIMP. I'm fucking three pills in – we're not ending this party! We're going till tomorrow!

BENNY. Cam?

CAM. One minute –

CAM *goes to do a line of coke.*

TIMP. You lot got any brains at all? You're about to walk out into a line of fucking coppers when you've each taken enough drugs to kill a small horse.

CAM *and* LAURA *stop.*

It's crawling with them out there. Curtains for your career, Cam; Loz, you've already had your hands smacked once.

BENNY. Who cares?

CAM. I don't want to get /

BENNY. You remember reading all that stuff in History or English about those lads going to war, Mack? Fucking sixteen seventeen some of them – I always sat and wondered if I would. I remember thinking, fuck – I'd like to know if I was the kind that would piss himself, or if I was the kind that would take on ten men and go out roaring – you ever wondered that? You ever wished you knew for sure – whether you're a coward?

CAM *looks at* BENNY *then up around the room.*

CAM. I'll go and check the stairwell.

CAM *exits.*

MACK (*comes in close to* BENNY). Well done, mate, just sent Cam to his fucking death – good pal you are.

BENNY *goes to hit* MACK *and* MACK *ducks it.*

Who you fighting, Benny-boy? Hm?

BENNY *tries shove* MACK *it doesn't do anything to him – he stands strong.*

TIMP. Strength of a bear, speed of a puma, eyes of a hawk.

MACK. I'm happy to roll up my sleeves but who are you fighting? The council? The landlord? The big bad government? The general fucking state of the nation?

BENNY. Fuck you.

MACK. Who do you think they're hurting – huh? You want to join those mindless little fuckers who haven't even begun to think it through – who?

BENNY (*pointing out the window*). At least they're doing something.

MACK. You are so much smarter than this, Benny.

BENNY. Am I?

LAURA *goes to leave.*

TIMP. Don't – Loz – please.

On the street outside there is an almighty explosion – we hear glass breaking, shouting – screaming – cheering.

MACK *starts to laugh.*

LAURA, SOPHIE *and* TIMP *are over by the window.*

LAURA. Fuck – they've just kicked in the window of the – fucking –

SOPHIE. They're throwing bricks. There's paint.

TIMP *yelps with joy – he starts screaming, running up and down.*

TIMP. That's the window of the bloody restaurant!

TIMP *picks* LAURA *up and starts spinning her round.*

That little firecracker down there just earned us a day off work, babe!

MACK (*to* BENNY). What you going to do? Go and kick the crap out of a shop window? Really feel like you're fighting 'the man' – when in fact, it's probably just a little old shopkeeper – that's worked his whole fucking life to build that shop up, and you'll kneecap him – in the name of what?

TIMP. We can wake up late and spend all fucking day in bed – I'll treat you like a princess, make you your eggy-bread you like – kiss your feet, use the old orgasmatron on your noggin, go to that posh coffee shop you like, I'll even read you a bit a *Harry Potter*!

MACK. Or are you going to go and wrestle with a cop? Except he's just doing his job; he's just a guy being paid to stand there. He doesn't give a shit about your problem, you think he's defending an 'idea' – a – a what? Why are you kicking him? Eh? Because I can guarantee you he's just thinking about his wife and kids and what he might have for breakfast. And he might put his fist in your face, but he's probably thinking about his brother or his dad – or the bloke his missus fucked whilst he was working late. It's just toddlers squabbling.

TIMP. Don't go home; babe – it'll all be alright in the morning, promise.

SOPHIE. They're throwing bricks, at the policemen.

MACK. You want to be part of that?

SOPHIE. They're coming into the street – they're trapping them in our /

LAURA. Cam's out there.

TIMP. Babe? Fucking day off – we're going have the best day ever.

LAURA *shakes her head.*

Don't make me come down on me own.

LAURA *puts her hand on* TIMP*'s face.*

MACK. Or are you going to fuck with a politician or a tutor – come on, tell me who am I hurting?

SOPHIE. Leave him, Mack. You've made your point.

MACK. Because this isn't anyone, do you see? This isn't a problem. The man that makes the decision to fuck you up doesn't know or care who you are and he probably doesn't have a choice.

SOPHIE. Leave him – Mack.

LAURA. Guys – Cam's out there.

MACK. He just has a boss and a wife and a wallet and he just pisses and wanks and cries like the rest of us, he's just cheap and scared and weak like the rest of us. So what is the point in fighting?

CAM *enters; he's carrying bags of rubbish, he's shaken, almost crying.*

CAM. The police are in the stairwell.

LAURA. It's okay.

CAM. They're afraid of fire. They told me to bring everything in off the landing. There's so much. I tried to tell him to go and fuck himself – to – say no but… I – I – didn't. He started asking me if I'd taken anything and I – I was scared.

Beat.

BENNY. But we can't take any more in here.

CAM. But he said /

MACK. We'll move it in.

BENNY *steps into MACK's way as he tries to leave they stand close.*

LAURA *grabs her cardi and runs with him.*

TIMP. Loz? Don't – it's dangerous.

Just before he gets to the door.

CAM. You can't.

BENNY. What?

CAM. We have to stay put – we can't leave the building until they say so.

LAURA. We're trapped?

BENNY. I'll talk to them.

CAM. They're not letting anyone out. We've just to bring the bags in off the landing.

BENNY. Well, say no!

CAM. I'm sorry, Ben. I'm really sorry.

TIMP. I declare that a fucking lock-in! On top of a day off! Hoo – yeah!

CAM, *downbeat, crushed – starts bringing the bags of rubbish in handful by handful.*

BENNY *stands and watches – the rubbish builds around him, higher and higher – it almost becomes a physical manifestation of* BENNY'*s interior state; we are overwhelmed, we are trapped – there is no way out – we are going to suffocate.*

BENNY (*calmly*). We have to try.

MACK. Why?

BENNY. We're students – we're the people who should /

MACK. Students, eh?

BENNY. What we have to say /

MACK. I was in a café few weeks ago – I see a professor marking exam essays – he flicks through three pages – doesn't even read 'em. Thinks for a minute chucks sixty-five per cent on the front; didn't even read it – Benny. People laugh at students – ethno scarves, drink too much – what you going to do – sew a little hammer and sickle on your army-surplus jacket? Eh? Fidel Castro T-shirt?

BENNY. We're the fucking future.

TIMP (*laughs*). I'm sorry, Ben – even I've got a have a little chuckle at that. You do sound silly.

MACK. What like him? (*Points to* CAM.) Good luck, mate. You know how old he is?

CAM. Shut up.

MACK. Anyone know how old he is?

LAURA. He's nineteen; it's in the paper –

MACK. Except he's not – he's twenty-one. Lied didn't you, Cam?

CAM. Shut up, Mack.

BENNY. That true?

MACK. Come on – no one cares. Tell 'em.

CAM (*really starting to get shaky*). Just leave me alone, okay.

MACK. Come on, pal, nobody minds – just tell 'em.

CAM. They put my age wrong in the paper – when I was ten – they said I was eight, my mum had written my brother's age by mistake and /

LAURA. You're not actually the youngest ever violinist in the Royal Scottish /

CAM. They said I was an eight-year-old prodigy so Mum said to just keep my mouth shut.

MACK. Ten years old and over the hill.

LAURA. / Oh my God.

TIMP. You're a twenty-one-year-old virgin?

CAM. Just fuck off!

MACK. The future's too busy making sure it's not past it to be doing very much else. Cam's investing in anti-wrinkle cream, not in fucking revolutions, mate.

BENNY. Why can't you try? What's so scary about it, Mack? Why does it – hurt you to try?

MACK. It's you that's going to hurt, Ben. Don't you see – we're fucked. How well you do doesn't have anything to do with how good you are – it's decided by some useless prick somewhere acting out of fear or jealousy or greed – even if you do alright, you're never going to earn what your parents did, you're never going to be able to afford the house that you grew up in – trying – all that nonsense out there – wouldn't bother.

BENNY. If you try hard and you've got passion and you've got fucking drive –

MACK. That what your mum said? What else is she going say – eh? 'It's largely to do with timing, image and nepotism – so always try and be in the right place at the right time, suck as much cock as you can and find a way to be better looking than God intended you'?

BENNY. I won't let you get in my head like you got in his.

MACK. I didn't get in anyone's head.

BENNY. You sure?

MACK. People make their own decisions.

Beat.

TIMP *picks up* LAURA *and spins her round.* TIMP *pours a shot and offers it to* LAURA – *he sprinkles it with coke – as if it's a magic potion.*

TIMP. It'll be magic.

LAURA. Yeah?

TIMP *nods.*

SOPHIE *corners* MACK *before he's able to leave to help* CAM *with the rubbish.*

SOPHIE. Looks like we're here until morning.

MACK. Looks like it.

BENNY. Cam – no – we can't have any more.

SOPHIE. Wonder how long you'll last?

MACK. Think you should have a sit down, Sophs.

SOPHIE. It would be brilliant, we would be /

MACK. Cool off, calm down.

SOPHIE. Do you remember the colour of the sky?

BENNY. Stop it – Cam, stop bringing it in.

MACK (*turning from* SOPHIE). Leave him.

TIMP. I love you.

LAURA. I know.

BENNY. Stop bringing it in.

CAM. We have to.

BENNY. I said stop.

CAM. They told us to.

TIMP. Shall we have some fun?

LAURA. Course.

> LAURA *knocks back her first shot and hands the shot glass back to* TIMP.

> More please.

SOPHIE (*getting louder*). Do you remember the colour of the sky?

> SOPHIE *gets up onto the table and starts dancing.*

> MACK *starts bringing the rubbish in with* CAM – BENNY *stands.*

BENNY. Stop. Stop.

> TIMP *refills the glass and goes to knock it back.* LAURA *stops him.*

LAURA. Na-uh. It's mine.

> LAURA *takes the shot glass from* TIMP *and sinks it herself.*

> And again – let's go.

TIMP. You sure.

LAURA. Barely started, babe.

TIMP. Good on ya.

LAURA. More please. More please, Timp.

TIMP. Everything alright, babe?

LAURA. I said more please.

TIMP. Your wish is my command.

> TIMP *fills another shot.*

> It's party time.

LAURA. Damn right it fucking is.

> LAURA *sinks another shot.*

> MACK *and* CAM *keep bringing in the bags.*

BENNY. Stop it – fucking stop it.

SOPHIE. Mack – I don't feel bad. Mack?

MACK *stops bringing the rubbish in and turns to her.*

BENNY. We didn't make this mess; this isn't our mess.

CAM. We have to /

BENNY. Stop bringing it in.

CAM. He said – we have to –

BENNY (*up close to* CAM). I said stop fucking bringing it in – you hear me?

LAURA. You got any pills left?

TIMP. How many you taken already?

LAURA. None.

TIMP. That's not true, babe.

CAM. But they're police, Benny – we have to /

BENNY. Stop being such a fucking coward.

CAM *stands opposite* BENNY *and juts his chin out.*

Now take these bags and put them back out there, because I've had enough – you hear? I've had enough of just bending over and taking it – I won't sink – I won't fucking sink – you hear? Pick 'em up.

CAM *stares at* BENNY.

SOPHIE. I don't feel bad.

MACK. Get down.

SOPHIE. I think it's worth it.

LAURA. Where are they? They in your pockets, babe? Are they?

LAURA *starts frisking* TIMP – TIMP *progressively uncomfortable tries to fend her off.*

TIMP. I think you've had enough.

BENNY. I said – Pick. Them. Up.

LAURA. Do you? I thought it was party time?

BENNY. Did you hear me?

MACK. Get down.

SOPHIE. Why won't you try, Mack?

LAURA *discovers* TIMP's *pills on him – she pulls the bag out of his pocket.*

LAURA. Ah-ha!

SOPHIE. Why won't you try?

CAM'*s bottom lip starts to go.*

BENNY. Don't start fucking blubbing.

SOPHIE. For me?

TIMP. Give it here.

MACK *stares at* SOPHIE, *unable to move – unable to answer.*

LAURA. What's the problem – worried you won't have any left?

BENNY. I said pick up the fucking bags – Cam I – said – pick them the fuck up!

TIMP. Give it to me.

CAM, *sniffling, starts scrabbling around trying to pick up all the bags –* CAM *stands and sees out the window past* BENNY.

CAM. There's fire – look – they've, they've set fire to it – the city's on fire.

LAURA. You reckon there's enough in here to kill me?

LAURA *pops one in her mouth.*

BENNY *goes to look out of the window – dumbstruck – distraught.*

BENNY. Whole fucking lot's going to burn.

SOPHIE (*to* MACK). Do you remember the colour of the sky?

TIMP. Give me the bag.

TIMP *lunges at* LAURA *and grabs the bag off her.*

BENNY. Whole fucking lot's going to burn.

SOPHIE. Do you remember the colour of the sky?

MACK. Get down, Sophs. Please.

SOPHIE. Do you?

LAURA *opens her palm and reveals three pills.*

BENNY. Whole fucking lot's going to burn!

SOPHIE *starts to sing 'Ain't Got No/I Got Life' – loud on the table staring directly at* MACK, *he can't seem to move – to speak.*

LAURA *laughs.*

TIMP. Don't – don't do that. Please – don't, you'll hurt yourself.

LAURA *sinks the three pills and laughs.*

BENNY (*snaps – something has broken in him, he can't contain it any longer, he roars*). We're going to fucking burn and you're still not looking! If this is a party, where are all the people? Used to be hundreds showed up!

LAURA. What do you care – as long as I keep laughing?

BENNY. You're just fucking swallowing it and it's going explode inside you.

LAURA *laughs hard and throws a bin bag at* TIMP. TIMP *stumbles backwards into the rubbish.* CAM *and* MACK *start throwing bags as well. A huge rubbish fight starts – bags being lobbed, as if to throw the bags at each other is all that they can do. The fight gets harder and harder – more and more painful – they are hurting each other, the pace builds and builds and builds until they are exhausted – they pant, and stare – as if they have been tickled so hard it hurts.*

They stand – all of them breathless, barely able to get air into their lungs. Red-faced – half-laughing, half-crying – an exhausted silence falls.

Long pause.

It's still here.

SOPHIE *stares at* MACK.

SOPHIE. Are you crying?

MACK *wipes his face and walks slowly over to* BENNY, *he's choked, he comes in close to* BENNY, *he's shaking.*

MACK. Please be quiet, Benny.

BENNY *grabs* MACK, *it's forceful – it's the strongest we've seen him, there's real power and control in it –* BENNY *drags* MACK *to the untouched chair and forces him to look at it – we see* MACK *stare.* MACK *turns to* BENNY *– and looks at him, it seems amazingly tender – as if everything in him wants to give him a hug but he can't.*

BENNY. Look at it.

MACK *can't.*

MACK (*almost sobbing, pleading*). Please don't make me cut your tongue out.

BENNY. Say his name.

The boys stand and stare at one another – an eternity seems to pass between them, neither can move.

LAURA *stumbles to her feet.*

LAURA. Boys don't have tongues. They go silent when you come in the room. They don't say anything. It feels like they don't like you – like you're not friends at all. (*Silence.*) How many people has he fucked since I've been with him?

Long pause.

TIMP. I'm so glad you're standing up, babe.

LAURA. How many?

Pause.

BENNY. Ten, approximately ten, Loz.

LAURA. Thank you.

BENNY (*turning on* MACK). Say his name.

TIMP. Please don't /

> TIMP *approaches* LAURA.

> LAURA *jerks away.*

LAURA. Don't.

BENNY (*calm, stronger now*). Say his name.

> MACK *stands – starts to shake, almost broken.*

> BENNY *picks up a sushi knife and holds it up at* MACK.

I said – say his name.

Beat.

MACK. You want to believe someone will catch you whatever happens, but they won't. We aren't made to be able to stomach the real weakness of each other.

BENNY. Say it happened – say we let it happen.

> BENNY *steps closer to* MACK.

MACK. Look at you – wide eyes and fucking needy and shrill and panicking – and asking, asking – fucking needing – it's repulsive. I find it – repulsive.

BENNY. Say his name.

MACK. I'm not your dad, Benny.

BENNY. Look me in the eye.

MACK. It's not my job to carry you.

BENNY. Fucking look at me – look at me, Mack.

> MACK *keeps his eyes on the floor.*

You're my best mate. You're my best mate in the whole world.

MACK. We're on our own.

BENNY. Say his fucking name.

MACK. It's not our fault!

BENNY. Try!

MACK. He didn't – did he? He didn't fucking try at all. He just bailed out and left the mess for the rest of us to try and fucking clear up, expected us to get up in the fucking morning!

BENNY *lunges at* MACK *with the knife.*

MACK *swerves it.*

BENNY *stumbles forward bringing the knife swooping down towards the table.*

CAM *lunges forward and puts his hand beneath the blade – the tip of two fingers on his right hand are sliced off.*

MACK *grabs* CAM*'s hand and manically tries to stem the flow.*

No – fucking no.

BENNY *stands and stares.*

CAM (*smiling*). It was an accident.

Scene Four

The kitchen is empty except for TIMP, *who makes himself a cup of tea.*

The soft twilight of the early hours swims across the kitchen.

It is the first time we have seen him quiet, calm, alone.

TIMP, *on his own, is somehow a different creature entirely.*

TIMP *finds the cupcake and candle that* LAURA *had previously tried to give him.*

TIMP *sits with his tea, putting the cupcake in front of him and he stares at it.*

LAURA *enters; she's got a bag of stuff with her.*

LAURA*'s still high – she's gurning and can't focus very easily.*

Pause.

TIMP. Twentieth birthday – my dad gave me a hip flask – and I had to work, at the restaurant – I was new, floor staff – that night, even though it was my birthday, so I filled up that flask and I went in to work with it. And it's really fucking funny, right – I'd had a bit to drink and I'd go and pick up the plates from the service hatch, and I'd stop in the corridor so I could see the faces of the fat rich fucks, all angry and waiting for their food and I'd just stand. I'd just stop and watch 'em waiting for me – getting angrier and angrier – and I thought I'll just stand here cos it's my birthday and they can fucking wait a bit longer; never waited more than a few seconds each time – but I felt like a fucking king. Isn't that funny?

Beat.

I was angry having to work – cos before that my birthday was always in the summer holidays. It's mad, I've been working full time for ten years and I still always – every year – expect there to be a summer holiday. Never is though. (*Beat.*) You still fucked?

LAURA. I've been sick. It's helped.

TIMP. Good.

TIMP *goes to touch* LAURA, *she steps away from him.*

Beat.

Sort of can't fucking believe I'll never get another summer holiday.

LAURA. I know.

LAURA *stands.*

TIMP. Thought we could go on a trip – just you and /

LAURA. Haven't got any leave left cos of helping Mum move house.

TIMP. Right. You want water or tea or – a – any /

LAURA. I'm going to go, Timp.

TIMP. You don't want to be alone in that state.

LAURA *takes a step towards the door.*

You coming back?

Beat.

I never thought I'd be lucky enough to land you.

LAURA *turns to go.*

It's not because I don't l[ove] – it's – it's not even the – it's just – just the window to put the party in – it's so small, you got to make the party really big.

LAURA. Doesn't feel like a party.

Beat.

TIMP. No.

TIMP *moves towards* LAURA *to hold her.*

LAURA. Can't though – undo things. (*Beat.*) Funny you being thirty.

Pause.

TIMP. Not that funny.

LAURA. No.

LAURA *goes to leave.*

TIMP. Loz?

LAURA. Yeah

Long pause – TIMP *thinks – he's got nothing.*

Where you going to live when the boys leave?

Beat.

TIMP. Couple of the freshers from the party the other night said they might move in – fill the spots. I might stay on.

Beat.

LAURA. Right.

Beat.

LAURA *leaves*

TIMP *sits back down in front of the candle and lights it – he watches it burn.*

BENNY *enters.*

TIMP *stares at him.*

BENNY *goes over to the window and looks out.*

BENNY. They've put most of it out.

TIMP. Yeah?

BENNY. Is Laura still /

TIMP. No – she's gone.

BENNY. She'll be fucking dancing till tomorrow night.

BENNY *tries to laugh a little,* TIMP *won't go with him.*

TIMP. She was sick.

BENNY. Right. (*Beat.*) I'm sorry, Timp – I'm really sorry – I shouldn't have, I didn't have a right to.

TIMP. Course you did; you're her mate.

Pause.

BENNY. Is it your birthday?

TIMP. Yeah; fucking thirty.

BENNY. No?

TIMP. Yeah.

Beat.

BENNY. Timp – what's your name?

TIMP. What?

BENNY. On the contract this morning it said C. Timpson and I realised I don't know your first name.

Pause.

TIMP. It's Colin.

Beat.

They both laugh – it is a relief.

BENNY. Oh.

TIMP. Yeah – alright.

BENNY. I'd stick with Timp, mate.

TIMP. Thanks.

Silence falls.

You seen any more pills about?

Beat.

BENNY *nods, picks one up off the table.*

Alright if I have it?

BENNY. Course.

BENNY *hands the pill to* TIMP.

TIMP *takes it.*

TIMP. Ta.

BENNY *nods.*

Benny?

BENNY. Yeah.

TIMP. Will you come and watch some Disney with me – for a bit? Just till I'm –

BENNY. Course... Colin.

The boys go to leave – before they do, SOPHIE *enters, she's carrying a bag.*

Sophs.

SOPHIE. Hi.

TIMP. We're going to watch a Disney movie, you game?

SOPHIE. Plane leaves in a few hours. I'll see ya.

TIMP. See ya.

TIMP exits.

BENNY. Bye, Sophs.

SOPHIE hugs BENNY goodbye.

SOPHIE. Benny, I /

BENNY. I'm going to go watch some Disney.

BENNY leaves.

SOPHIE stands, surveys the room.

SOPHIE stands on Peter's chair.

SOPHIE. I'm sorry, Peter.

MACK enters.

MACK sees her standing on the chair and stops in his tracks.

MACK. What you doing?

SOPHIE. Wondered what it looked like from up here.

MACK. And?

SOPHIE. Smaller.

MACK nods.

MACK helps her down – it's gallant.

MACK. You want /

SOPHIE (*laughing softly*). Tea? No.

Pause.

SOPHIE stares at MACK.

MACK. What?

SOPHIE. Nothing.

MACK. What you looking at?

SOPHIE *shrugs*.

It's like I'm a fucking hero. Like you're expecting me to fucking levitate or something.

SOPHIE *looks away, hurt*.

No one ever looks at me like that.

SOPHIE. Like it?

MACK. Feels like you're asking for something, for something I don't have. (*Pause*.) You got so much – of this… even when you're being a fucking mentalist – you got like… grace – somehow.

SOPHIE. No I /

MACK. I'm just a person. Pretty shit one at that.

SOPHIE. No you're not.

MACK. It can't be fucking dawn for ever, Sophs.

SOPHIE. I know. But it could be /

MACK. What?

SOPHIE. We could go away.

MACK. There's not a fucking country we can fly to where he's still alive – where we can talk him through it, where it hasn't happened how it has.

SOPHIE. I know.

MACK. Do you? Do you really?

SOPHIE. Yes.

MACK. We can't fly back to that fucking evening and just /

MACK *stops himself – he looks at her in the twilight*.

You are the most beautiful thing I think I've ever fucking seen.

Beat.

SOPHIE. Will you do your seagull impression?

MACK. What?

SOPHIE. Will you? Please.

MACK. No.

SOPHIE. Please.

MACK. Fuck off.

SOPHIE. Quietly.

> MACK *does his seagull impression.*
>
> *He stops and looks at her.*
>
> *She smiles.*
>
> I don't think you're a god. You're not even a very good seagull.

MACK. Thanks.

> *Beat – they smile.*

SOPHIE. Come with me. Just see.

MACK. Then what?

SOPHIE. Don't know.

MACK. Come back, tell Benny – make even more fucking mess.

SOPHIE. Maybe it will be worth it.

MACK. I can't... when I, when I – look at you – it's like, in my head, you're always crying.

SOPHIE. I'll stop. Eventually.

MACK. Ever since – it's amazing how something like that – um – how it, sorry. It – it starts ripping the walls down – you know? It's like that morning – since then everything just emptied – like words are lies before they've even got out your mouth.

> SOPHIE *kisses* MACK *tenderly. She holds his face.*

SOPHIE *steps back.*

SOPHIE. My plane leaves in two hours.

MACK. Where you going?

SOPHIE. Italy.

MACK. Oh, *bonjour.*

SOPHIE. That's France.

MACK. Oh yeah.

   Pause.

   I can't.

SOPHIE. Please.

MACK. No.

SOPHIE. I don't want it to start hurting, yet.

MACK. I'm sorry.

SOPHIE. Okay.

   SOPHIE *grits her teeth and leaves.*

   MACK *watches her go.*

   MACK *hears the door slam – stands a moment and exits.*

ACT THREE

Scene One

The sun is up – it is a bright morning, sunlight streaks in through the windows.

BENNY *enters in his dressing gown.*

BENNY *goes to his brother's cupboard and takes out a packet of Coco Pops. He pours himself a bowl of Coco Pops and fills it with milk.*

BENNY *stands wondering where the hell he is going to find a spoon in the mess.*

TIMP *enters, he's in his pants – Mohican organised, chipper and bubbly.*

TIMP. Alright, Benny-boy – you seen my whites? I'm late as fuck and I can't find 'em anywhere.

BENNY. You going to work?

TIMP. Yeah. Only gone and fixed that fucking window the fuckers.

BENNY. Bloody hell.

TIMP. I'd take it off but two black marks already – can't risk it.

BENNY. Aren't you fucked?

TIMP. You got any fucking idea how boring that job is if you're not? You couldn't have a look out there for me – whilst I scout in here, could ya?

BENNY. Will you look for a spoon?

TIMP. What?

BENNY. I can't find a spoon for me Coco Pops.

TIMP. Right. Hey, Benny?

BENNY. Yeah?

TIMP. I was thinking – I could do with a fucking party tonight –
you know – few beers?

Pause. BENNY *looks at* TIMP.

BENNY. Alright if I have a little think about that?

TIMP. Course.

BENNY *exits.*

TIMP *searches through the rubbish, trying to find his
clothes.*

TIMP *pulls out a hugely long novelty spoon from the
rubbish.*

Hey, Ben! Look at this – it's that massive spoon from
Frankenstein's! Ha!

TIMP *drops the spoon at the middle.*

Benny, come and have a look! Ew it's all sticky.

TIMP *sniffs it – winces.*

Euch – it's fucking sambuca – I think I'm going to /

LAURA *enters, she's dressed for work.*

TIMP *hears her enter but doesn't turn around.*

TIMP *turns, retching and holding the massive spoon.*

Oh, hello.

LAURA. Hello.

TIMP. Laura, I –

LAURA. That's a big spoon.

TIMP. Yes.

LAURA. Don't tell me you're looking for your whites?

TIMP. Laura.

LAURA. You're late you do know that – they'll cut your
bollocks off, that's every day this week.

TIMP *looks at her.*

What?

Beat.

We need to go, come on.

TIMP. Course.

LAURA. Fucking state in here.

TIMP. Laura?

LAURA (*sees his whites underneath a chair*). They're here, you plonker. Hurry up, you dumb fuck.

TIMP *stalls – he's genuinely moved.*

What? Why you staring? Will you hurry the fuck up?

LAURA *leaves.*

TIMP *jumps into his whites.*

BENNY *enters.*

BENNY. I couldn't find them – Laura's in the –

TIMP *kisses* BENNY *full on the mouth.*

TIMP *spanks* BENNY *on the bum with the spoon.*

TIMP *exits.*

BENNY *picks up the spoon and also discovers it's sticky in the middle.*

BENNY *goes to wash the spoon but the sink is full.*

BENNY *gives up and holds the spoon at the far end.*

BENNY *tries to eat the Coco Pops with the spoon but it is slightly longer than he can maneuver into his mouth.*

BENNY *tries again and the Coco Pops spill.*

MACK *enters – he has a large bag slung across his body, he's dressed to leave.*

BENNY *looks at him.*

Beat.

MACK. What's that?

BENNY. Coco Pops.

MACK. Why you eating it like a retard?

BENNY. Can't find any fucking cutlery.

MACK. What's that?

BENNY. Monster spoon, from Frankenstein's. Remember?
Meant to be like Frankenstein's spoon.

MACK. Hold it lower down.

BENNY. It's sticky in the middle with Sambuca.

MACK. Wash it.

BENNY. Sink's full.

Pause.

MACK. Come here.

MACK goes to feed BENNY his Coco Pops.

BENNY. No you're alright – no – come on –

MACK. Open your mouth.

BENNY. Fuck off.

MACK. Open your fucking mouth.

*It looks like MACK is going to feed BENNY from the spoon
– when he picks up the bowl instead.*

BENNY (*with his mouth open*). Don't fucking throw it at me.

MACK. Just drink it from the bowl. You dumb ass.

BENNY. Right.

MACK. Don't need a spoon.

BENNY. Yeah. Long night, eh?

MACK. Not long enough to be that retarded.

Beat.

BENNY. What's the bag for?

MACK. I'm going.

BENNY. Right.

MACK. I've left enough cash for…

Beat.

You heard from Cam?

BENNY. No.

MACK. Will you tell him – I'd stick about but / (*Checks his watch.*)

BENNY. Yeah.

MACK. Thanks.

Beat.

BENNY. He was selfish. You're right. Cop-out – left us to clear it up – eh? Just us. Not very good at it.

MACK. No.

BENNY. I – I – miss you. I'm sorry if that sounds /

MACK. I've really got to go.

BENNY. Alright.

MACK. Ben – ?

BENNY. Yeah.

MACK. I think it will – get better – eventually.

Pause.

MACK *turns to go.*

Beat.

BENNY. Better have me Coco Pops back then.

MACK. Sorry.

MACK *goes to hand* BENNY *the bowl of Coco Pops.*

Oh hello.

MACK *spots something, a little toy soldier floating in the bowl.*

You got the prize. Little soldier. Bang. There you go.

BENNY. You have it.

Beat.

MACK. Thanks.

BENNY. Fingers crossed.

BENNY *goes to hug* MACK.

MACK *offers him his hand.*

BENNY *nods and shakes it.*

MACK *exits.*

BENNY *cries.*

Scene Two

The door opens – BENNY *thinks it's* MACK.

BENNY. Thank fuck for /

CAM *enters.*

Oh – Cam.

BENNY *recovers himself.*

Mate, you're back. What happened?

CAM. Where's Mack off to?

BENNY. Holiday.

CAM. What?

BENNY. I think. How's the hand?

CAM. Bit sore.

BENNY. What were the nurses like?

CAM. Wouldn't stop rolling her eyes and saying it was amazing how little pain I was feeling considering the injury.

BENNY. What's it like out there?

CAM. Mad. Trees all look like little burnt matchsticks – shite everywhere. Funny though – once you're out at the Western General, out the city – you can see the hills in the distance all clean and green and – it's like nothing ever went wrong, feel silly for thinking... then you drive back in and it's like it'll never get clean. You sort of can't work out how much to – how worried to /

BENNY. Yeah.

BENNY *smiles at him.*

BENNY *goes to the window to look out.*

You want tea?

CAM. Yes please. Can you put a bit of sugar in it?

BENNY. Course. Funny how the first bit of morning always looks a bit like a sunset. You reckon you could tell – if someone just woke you up and said – dawn or dusk – you reckon you could tell?

CAM. Rises in the east, sets in the west.

BENNY. Not this far north. Up and down in almost the same spot.

Beat.

CAM. It's fucked – right through Cowgate – all the old town; fire started down at the Parliament and just went right on up.

BENNY. That's all the library stores; burnt their own fucking books, the idiots.

CAM. Didn't even fucking touch the Parliament Building – you know what I mean? What is that – all that old stuff, all cobbles and history and fucking thousands of years of – and it burns in just one night because of some fucking... and that

fucking ugly son of a bitch Parliament Building is still
standing. Blows your mind.

BENNY *hands* CAM *his tea – he goes to take it with his
right hand – but realises it's bandaged and has to take it with
his left.*

BENNY. You sad about it?

CAM. The fire?

BENNY. Your hand.

CAM. I –

BENNY. I can't even say how sorry I – I mean for ever I'll –
did they say there were ways of fixing it, of /

CAM. Shut up, man. I'm glad.

BENNY. What do you mean you're glad?

CAM. It was the weirdest thing, she's sitting there telling me
I'll never play again, not like I had before and I felt so much
– better. I'm not sure I even really wanted to do it, I never
chose to – I was just good at it and so that was it – and it
seemed stupid not doing something that you were good at
but – I never wanted to.

BENNY. You don't mean that.

CAM. It's fucking great – I feel fucking great. I can do what I
want now and I didn't even have to make the decision.

BENNY. What do you want to do?

CAM. Don't know yet.

BENNY. Right.

CAM. Think I might apply to university.

BENNY *laughs.*

It'll be four years before I'm out – so maybe – things will
have… you know…

BENNY. Good idea, pal. You want a biscuit?

CAM. Yes please.

BENNY *finds one and gives it to him.*

BENNY. Last summer – me and Pete – we ended up in this cathedral together – it was a family holiday, Mum and Dad were having an argument outside so he and I decided to go in. It was all dark, except these little red candles; you know those racks of candles, in lines, where you're meant to pay and you light it and it's for someone in heaven? They had one of them, but it was modern – so the candles were little LED thingies, you know electric. And this woman comes up, Spanish, big fat one, red lips, black hair – and she puts the euro in the slot and one of the candles flickers a bit, but it goes out. It doesn't work, right? So she waddles over to complain. This electrician comes over and he's really sweating and he unlocks the back of this thing and you can see all the wires. She sees all the wires, right? The electrician fiddles with it finishes and locks the thing back down and gives her back her euro. The old woman puts her money in the slot... and one candle lights up... and she prays, she prays like she really fucking means it.

Beat.

CAM. This another God squad thing, Ben?

BENNY. Even though she'd seen the wiring.

CAM. So?

BENNY. I said it was fucking idiotic. Made me angry. Turned to Peter – he were crying. It was the last time I saw him cry – he said it was fucking amazing, being able to do what she did.

Beat.

CAM. Don't get it.

BENNY. Never mind.

The pair of them look at the room.

We should get his lot tidied up.

CAM. In a bit.

BENNY. You want to give me a hand?

CAM. What you going to do with it.

BENNY. Don't know, yet.

The buzzer goes.

Who's that?

CAM. I'll get it.

CAM *exits.*

BENNY *looks at the rubbish.*

BENNY *finds a bin bag – heads over to his brother's cupboard and starts to empty it into the bin bag. Job complete, he turns back to the kitchen and looks at the mess – he's overwhelmed.*

CAM *enters – he's carrying a jumper.*

BENNY. And?

CAM. It was the Renault Mégane.

BENNY. What did she want?

CAM. Said to give this back to Mack – said to thank him – for stopping her.

BENNY *goes over and takes the jumper from* CAM.

BENNY. I gave him this.

The jumper has He-Man on it.

CAM. Will we put some music on – help us tidy?

BENNY. iPod got fucked. Stereo still works though.

CAM *turns it on and the tuner fuzzes.*

CAM *looks out at the room.*

CAM. You reckon we'll get this tidied up?

BENNY. Yeah.

CAM. You think or you know?

BENNY. I think.

> CAM *switches it to CD and presses play.*
>
> BENNY *looks at the jumper and puts it on.*
>
> *A violin solo plays – beautiful, haunting.*
>
> What's this?
>
> *Beat.*

CAM. It's me.

> *Beat.*
>
> BENNY *tries to tidy again but gives up quickly.*
>
> CAM *stares out into the morning… listening – realising.*
>
> BENNY *picks up his Coco Pops bowl and drinks from the bowl – chocolate milk spills down the front of the He-Man jumper – he tries to clean it off.*
>
> *Pause.*
>
> *Lights down.*
>
> *End of play.*